17, 19 (loop), 13 loop, 18, 22
14 (Yr day)

Hike 7 (pg 60)

Hiking
South Carolina

John F. Clark
John Dantzler

FALCONGUIDES ®

GUILFORD, CONNECTICUT
HELENA, MONTANA
AN IMPRINT OF THE GLOBE PEQUOT PRESS

FALCONGUIDES®

Copyright ©1998 Morris Book Publishing, LLC
Previously published by Falcon Publishing, Inc.

Cover photo by Tony Arruza.

Library of Congress Cataloging-in-Publication data is available.

ISBN 978-1-56044-602-6

Manufactured in the United States of America
First Edition/Eleventh Printing.

♻ Text pages printed on recycled paper.

To buy books in quantity for corporate use
or incentives, call **(800) 962–0973**
or e-mail **premiums@GlobePequot.com**.

This book is dedicated, with much love, to our mothers,
Ellen Bryant Clark and Anne Salmonsen Dantzler.

Contents

Acknowledgments

This book would not have been possible without the assistance of numerous people. Two individuals in particular worked tirelessly to provide a tremendous amount of indispensable help: Yvonne Michel and Jim Schmid. They will forever have our deepest gratitude.

We are also deeply appreciative of the hard work, patience, and skills of our current editor, David Lee. Randall Green was our original editor, and we are indebted to him for his encouragement in providing us the opportunity to create this work.

But preparation of this stew was aided by many other seasoners. We give our thanks to Grant Bridgwood, Leann Brown, Jameen Chester, Jay Clark, Kathy Clark, Woody Clark, Susan Colvin, Michele de Carlo, Tom Dawson, John Mark Dean, Doug Dobson, Amy Dodds, Robert Earle, Evans Elliott, Phil Gaines, Al Graves, Jean and Sonny Graves, Michel Hammes, Virginia Hawkins, Teresa Hurley, Dell Isham, David Justice, Melody Lamm, Bonnie Lawson, Bill Marrell, Gary McCombs, Patricia Metz, Carole Mullis, Susan Nelle, Rowena Nylund, Walt Oliver, Nancy Phillips, Irvin Pitts, George Polk, John Powell, Robin Roecker, Marisa Santamaria, Jon and Sharon Sattler, Bud Shields, Ben Sill, Gene Singleton, John and Helen Stonestreet, Arnold Taylor, Lenair Thrower, Charlee Tisdale, Bill Turner, Tom Vose, Charles Wiggins, Ron Wilder, and Shin Yun. We also extend our appreciation to the Columbia Chapter of the South Carolina Writers' Workshop; the Tuesday Night Writers' Group; the South Carolina Chapter of the Sierra Club; Palmetto Trails; Foothills Trail Conference; the South Carolina Department of Parks, Recreation, and Tourism; the South Carolina Department of Natural Resources; the Clark and Dantzler extended families; the South Carolina State Library; the Richland County Public Library; and the many trail managers who provided information and comments on our draft texts and maps.

John Dantzler extends special gratitude to his father, Dr. Malcolm U. Dantzler, for his material and moral support.

LEGEND

Interstate	(26)	Campground	
US Highway	(17)	Bridge	
State or Other Principal Road	(66) (690)	Cabins/Buildings	▪
Forest Service Road	708	Elevation	3,294 ft. x
Interstate Highway	⟹	Gate	•—•
Paved Road	⟹	Mine Site	⚒
Gravel Road	⟹	Overlook/Point of Interest	▣
Unimproved Road	= = = ⟹		
Trailhead/Parking	○ (P)	State Park, W.M.A. Boundary	
One Way Road	One Way →	Map Orientation	N
Railroad	▭▭▭▭▭	Scale	0 0.5 1 Miles
Described trail	⌁⌁		
Secondary Trail	– – ⌁	Hike Locator	
River/Creek/Falls			
Lake/Pond		State Boundary	N . C. / S . C.
Marsh/Swamp			
Boardwalk	▦▦▦▦▦		

viii

STATE LOCATOR

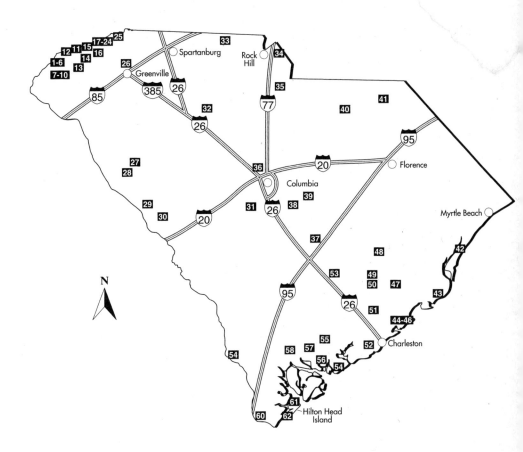

x

Foreword

by Judge Alex Sanders
President, College of Charleston

I once had a week-long outdoor adventure in Idaho's ultra-pristine Frank Church Wilderness Area. The ranger told me that whatever I brought in, I would have to carry out—including my own feces. For the next week, I didn't have any. That was the all-time worst outdoor advice I ever received. This book contains the best.

This book is a complete guide to various South Carolina hikes, which the authors describe in exquisite detail, but it is much more than a travelogue. Abiding love and deep respect for our natural treasures shines through on every page. The reader experiences the fields and forests, the woods and waters, the earth and sky of the Palmetto State in all its splendor.

And what splendor! Although South Carolina is a small southern state known for its graciousness and refinement, it hosts some of the eastern United States' most spectacular mountain waterfalls, ancient old-growth forests, wild and scenic rivers, luxurious blackwater swamp sanctuaries, sandy barrier island beaches, and beautiful coastal marshlands. Those who know this fair state's diversity love her. Those who hike the mountain gorges, the foothills forests, the plantation rice fields, and the gently sloping beaches come to treasure her.

The rewards of experiencing South Carolina's wildlands are multiplied by the year-round temperate climate of these latitudes. Although some snow occasionally falls in the extreme northwest mountains, winters are mild across the state, and the coast is virtually frost-free. Summers are warm with sparse rains and mostly clear skies, inviting you to spend the long days deep in the woods, along a river's edge, atop a mountain, or amid gentle salty sea breezes.

Wildlife abounds, from the pileated woodpeckers and wild turkeys of the lowland pine forests to the bald eagles, beavers, and otters along the rivers to the ubiquitous white-tailed deer roaming throughout the state's fields and woodlands. Wildflowers compete with the wildlife for your attention, especially when mountain laurel and rhododendron are in full bloom or wild lilies carpet the forest floor at Easter, or dogwoods and wild azaleas dazzle the forest understory.

To borrow a phrase, "A journey of a thousand miles begins with a single step." Similarly, a hike of more than 60 pleasing trails begins with a single book, and this is that book.

The Whitewater River. John Clark photo

Introduction

HIKING SOUTH CAROLINA

South Carolina is made for hiking. The hikes in this volume are numbered from the northwest to the southeast, from the mountains to the sea. The mountainous region provides challenges and dramatic scenery in a very compact area, while the central part of the state offers fascinating variety and the coastal area presents serene beauty.

If you're not in the best of shape, but are hoping to improve your fitness by taking up hiking, you may choose to work your way from the sea to the mountains instead, reversing the order of this guide's hikes. Start in late winter on the Coastal Plain trails to get your feet and heart habituated to exercise. When spring arrives, move up to the attractive and diverse terrain of the upper Midlands. The rolling hills of the Midlands also provide valuable training for the Mountains. When summertime rolls around, the cool, wet Mountains offer exciting hiking and the most comfortable weather in the state.

However you choose to use this book, we are confident that a sampling of the hikes described in the following pages will heighten your appreciation of South Carolina's bountiful natural heritage.

South Carolina packs a delightful diversity of terrain into a relatively small area. The sliver of mountains at the northwest corner of the state features a dazzling array of gorges and waterfalls, as well as the wild and scenic Chattooga River, famous as the setting for James Dickey's *Deliverance*. The rolling foothills that stretch from the mountains to the center of the state are ideal for hiking. The Sandhills, the remnant of a belt of ancient sand dunes, separate the foothills from the low, flat coastal plain, which covers the southeastern third of the state.

South Carolina's population centers are Greenville-Spartanburg, the hub of the state's booming industrial sector; Columbia, the governmental and commercial center; and Charleston, one of the busiest seaports on the East Coast and a thriving tourist mecca. However, in spite of the growth of industrial prosperity and the three mid-sized metropolitan areas, South Carolina remains primarily a state of small towns and rural communities where the people revere their natural, agricultural heritage.

The state's tourism industry is huge, hosting more than 30 million visitors annually. Most tourists come for the superb beaches, golf, tennis, entertainment, restaurants, shopping, and fine weather at the coastal areas of Myrtle Beach, Charleston, and Hilton Head Island. These destinations offer tremendous attractions, but the rest of the state of South Carolina offers the same seductive weather and much more. The Palmetto State presents charming small towns, quaint bed and breakfast accommodations, numerous historic sites (the state's recorded history dates back to 1526), beautiful rural countryside, a variety of recreational opportunities, and—best of all—outstanding hiking.

How to Use This Guide

Hiking South Carolina describes outstanding hikes throughout the state. The suggested hiking routes range in length from 1 mile to 42 miles, and vary in elevation from beaches and rice fields at sea level to the top of Sassafras Mountain at more than 3,500 feet. The terrain varies from the boardwalks of coastal swamps to the rocky cliffs of the Mountain Bridge Wilderness Area.

INFORMATION ON EACH HIKE

The individual hike descriptions are the heart of this book. The 62 hike descriptions are numbered and are organized into three regional subsets—Mountains, Midlands, and Coastal Plain. A summary overview of each region is provided prior to the first hike description in each region. You can find additional information on the regions of the state in the "Regional Overview" section of the Introduction.

Each hike description contains a standard set of information:

General description: A brief description of the hike and its highlights.

General location: A short description of the hike's location. This description complements the locator map inset on each trail map.

Distance: The distance and hiking time of the trail or trails described. It is a good idea to prefix any mention of trail distances with the term "about." Because the mileages given by reliable sources sometimes differ, all mileage information should be considered a best estimate. Also remember that an estimate of the time needed to complete a trail must combine length data with terrain and other considerations pertaining to difficulty.

Difficulty: Each hike is classified as "easy," "moderate," "strenuous," or some combination thereof (for example, "moderately strenuous"). The classifications assume the hiker is an adult in average physical condition walking at a normal pace, and length has not been taken into account. Thus, some short hikes are rated strenuous because they require steep climbing, while some very long hikes are rated easy because they involve only walking on level ground. Individuals can decide a trail's overall degree of difficulty for themselves by combining the guide's assessment of terrain difficulty with personal assessment of their own abilities to hike the described distance within the estimated time. (School-age children, for example, should be able to walk short distances on any trail designated easy.) Be sure to factor the weather into your calculations as well; hot and humid weather can make a long but otherwise easy hike quite difficult indeed.

Trail conditions: Provides information on trail surfaces, ease of discerning and moving along the trailway, and on the level of use the trail receives.

Maps: This heading provides information on where to find additonal maps, usually available from the organizations listed in Appendix A: For More Information. The names of the U.S. Geological Survey (USGS) maps for the area are also provided. The USGS maps typically used by hikers are 7.5-minute latitude and longitude quadrangles. In South Carolina, these "quads"

4

measure roughly 8 miles on each side; each hike may trek across one or more quads. The USGS maps are essential if you plan to hike away from designated trails, and they're helpful to anyone wanting a detailed understanding of the terrain surrounding each trail. Quad maps are available at the South Carolina State Library in Columbia, some academic and public libraries, and at the South Carolina Division of Land Resources (see "Finding Maps," Appendix A), where the maps are available for purchase.

Fees: Most areas do not assess fees, but some do. We have provided the fee information available as of the spring of 1998, but fees are subject to frequent change. In 1998, the Forest Service began preparations to charge nominal fees for use of some areas previously open at no charge, but exact plans were not final at press time. Fee schedules at some state park facilities were also being considered for modification in 1998 and 1999.

Finding the trailhead: How to drive to the beginning of the trail, and, in some cases, how to reach both the beginning and end of a suggested non-loop hike.

The hike: A narrative description of the trail, to be used in conjunction with the hike map.

Facilities: Covers availability of rest rooms and drinking water, along with other amenities, such as picnic areas and refreshment stands.

Lodging and amenities: Camping opportunities and lodging, eating, and other services in the vicinity of the trailhead(s).

For more information: Provides the name of the organization(s) to contact for more information about hiking and camping at the site; usually this is the organization responsible for trail management and maintenance. The full mailing address and telephone number of the organization is given in Appendix A: For More Information, along with e-mail and website addresses, when available.

The maps provided with each hike description show routes for described trails, connecting and secondary trails, trailheads, overlooks, campgrounds, and many other items. Please refer to the Map Legend on page vii for an explanation of the symbols you'll encounter.

For hikes of at least 4 miles that have an elevation change of at least 500 feet, an elevation profile has also been provided.

In using this book, please take note of the distinction between "loop" and "one-way" trails. A loop trail begins and ends at the same trailhead, meaning you'll need only one vehicle to visit the site. A linear, one-way trail, on the other hand, leads from one trailhead to another, so that two vehicles are required to hike the trail as described. If you have only one vehicle, you can still take a one-way hike: Simply turn around and return to your starting point.

Highway and road designations are important and can sometimes be a little confusing. In this guide, we distinguish between five types of highways and secondary roads:

1) Interstate highways are designated "Interstate 26" on first reference and abbreviated "I-26" thereafter. The state is crisscrossed by five

interstate highways: 20, 26, 77, 85, and 95. They are shown on our maps using the familiar interstate highway shield symbol. All hikes are located within a convenient distance of one or more of these five thoroughfares.

2) Roads in the older U.S. highway system are indicated on maps by the familiar badge-shaped symbol in use on road signs across the country. In each chapter, these roads are written first as "U.S. Highway 17," and thereafter as "US 17."

3) South Carolina Highways are state-maintained primary highways marked on roadways by signs displaying the highway number against a miniature outline of the state. We indicate these roads by placing the road number inside a circle. These highways are written "South Carolina Highway 11" on their first mention in a chapter, and "SC 11" thereafter.

4) Secondary roads are nonfederal roads other than the primary highways listed above. They usually have no roadside markers other than the black signs commonly found at intersections. These black signs, usually mounted above stop signs, are emblazoned with a combination of white letters and numbers. For example, if you are traveling to Lower Whitewater Falls (Hike 12), you might find yourself on a road designated S-37-413. The "S" indicates this is a secondary road, the "37" marks the county (in this case, Oconee), and the "413" is the road number. In the text, this road would be called "Secondary Road 413" in the first reference and "SR 413" thereafter. As a result of the statewide 911 addressing effort, these roads now have written names as well, sometimes indicated on the maps and usually provided in the text. Secondary roads are indicated on our maps by numbers inside circles in the same way as primary state highways. Secondary roads are usually, but not always, paved.

Keep in mind that secondary road designations often change from county to county. For example, Key Bridge Road, the route that leads to the Turkey Creek Trail (Hike 29), changes from SR 227 to SR 68 at Key Bridge, where the road leaves Edgefield County and enters McCormick County. Do not be surprised at occasional sudden changes in secondary road numbering.

5) Forest Service roads are designated "Forest Service Road 708" on first reference, and "FS 708" thereafter. Forest Service roads are typically improved gravel roads, but may also be unimproved dirt tracks or even paved roads. They are extremely valuable for the access they allow to remote country. On our maps, we show Forest Service roads using a white rectangle.

We have done our best to provide accurate and detailed information for these 62 hikes. We personally hiked each of the described trails between 1996 and 1998, and we have also consulted numerous individuals and written sources. In the spring of 1998, in order to ensure maximum accuracy, we sent draft write-ups and maps to the managers of all trails described in the book, and we incorporated the updates and modifications provided to us at that time. We also sought and received input from a variety of other professionals involved with the trails, including the state trails coordinator of the South Carolina Department of Parks, Recreation, and Tourism.

The material in this book is accurate at the time of publication. Nevertheless, hiking information in South Carolina is dynamic. Trail construction and expansion is booming, and both the written and map information is subject to change over time. Data on hours and dates of operation, fees, and camping are particularly subject to change. The most up-to-date information available can be obtained by contacting the organizations listed in the "For more information" line at the end of each write-up. Another good source for current information is the state trails website, published by the South Carolina Trails Program at www.sctrails.net.

SEASONS AND WEATHER

The climate of South Carolina is ideal for hiking; almost all the trails here can be hiked year-round. Winters (December through February) are mild. Both spring (March through May) and autumn (September through November) are glorious. Some summer (June through August) days can be uncomfortably warm, but the shade and the proximity of bodies of water along or near most trails, along with the use of appropriate clothing usually shield hikers against most hot weather problems.

Admittedly, many summer days in South Carolina are quite hot. Visitors often say, "It's not the heat, it's the humidity." Actually, it is *both* the heat *and* the humidity. However, frequent rains (often in the form of spectacular afternoon thunderstorms) cool the air and make summer recreation pleasant. Summer daytime temperatures in the mountains range from average highs of 84 degrees F to average lows of 62 degrees F. In the Midlands, average summer temperatures range from 91 degrees F to 70 degrees F. Because of its sea breezes, the coast has somewhat milder summers, with temperatures ranging from 88 degrees F to 70 degrees F. Summer is a good time to hike everywhere in the state except in some of the low-lying coastal areas, where insects can be a problem.

Apart from midsummer (mid-June to mid-August), South Carolina's weather is very temperate. The long, delightful spring and autumn seasons make these times excellent for hiking throughout the state. These are our prime hiking seasons.

Daytime temperatures during the short winter (December through February) range from 51 degrees F to 28 degrees F in the mountains and from 61 degrees F to 49 degrees F along the coast, where many of the best winter hiking opportunities can be found. In the mountains and other deciduous forest zones, denuded trees in winter make for better scenic vistas, and winter hiking along the coast generally means no insect problems, no heat problems, low trail undergrowth, and good opportunities to view birds and other forms of wildlife. Winter, along with late fall and early spring, is the best time to hike the Coastal Plain.

The state's moderate rainfall (about 49 inches annually) is distributed fairly evenly seasonally and geographically. However, the state's rainfall does tend to be somewhat greater in summer in the Midlands and along the coast, where its cooling effects are most appreciated.

BE PREPARED: BACKCOUNTRY SAFETY AND HAZARDS

Most hiking in South Carolina requires little in the way of special equipment or elaborate preparation. A short nature trail may require no more than shorts, a T-shirt, and soft-soled walking shoes. Longer hikes can require a full set of backpacking gear. A full equipment checklist is provided in Appendix C.

Nearly all of the hikes in this book can be approached as day hikes. With the sole exception of the Jocassee Gorges Segment of the Foothills Trail, longer hikes can be broken into a series of day hikes by use of the many road access points along the way. Day hikers usually need only carry a small day pack (equivalent in size to a book bag) or fanny pack. Don't take along a large framed backpack unless you intend to camp overnight along the trail.

Always dress comfortably and carry sufficient water for every member of your party. Do not go out for a long day hike without ample food and water. Your body needs to replace lost fluids, and it needs nourishment to restore the energy you burn on the trail. Starvation dieting and hiking do not mix.

In South Carolina, the main threats to hiker comfort are heat and bugs in the summer, cold in the winter, and wet weather and sore feet in all seasons. Precautions against these threats are easy to take.

Adequate footwear can help you avoid much discomfort. Choose sturdy hiking boots and cushioned hiking socks, preferably ones that will keep your feet warm in winter and dry when passing through low-lying wet areas. In warm weather, lighter boots and lightweight hiking socks make for more comfortable hiking. Whatever footwear you choose, make sure it provides adequate ankle support and nonslide soles if you plan to hike in the mountains or along trails that require the fording of slippery, rocky streams. For many of the easier hikes on dry, flat terrain, ordinary athletic shoes with soft soles are perfectly adequate, provided they are appropriate for weather conditions. Consider carrying extra socks and shoes in case the ones you are wearing become either wet or uncomfortable. Soft-soled sandals or aqua shoes, which make fording streams safer, are good choices, especially on trails where stream fording is expected.

Hiking outfitters offer a wide selection of **rain gear** that will keep you dry under the wettest of conditions. Some of the breathable synthetics on the market can keep you both comfortable and dry in mild weather. Even when rain is unlikely, it is a good idea to carry at least a compact, inexpensive plastic rain cape.

Hiking in South Carolina in summer is generally fun if you come prepared for warm weather. A majority of the hikes in South Carolina are along

8

well-shaded trails, and a light, wide-brimmed **hat** provides easy protection from the sun in all seasons. We have also found that wide-brimmed hats give flies a higher target to shoot for, above eyes and noses.

Bring plenty of **water** and get in the habit of eating and drinking frequently when hiking. On long hikes where it is impossible to carry sufficient water, do not drink directly from streams. Water must be boiled for at least five minutes, chemically treated, or passed through a water filter, available in outdoors stores. Assume that all waters in the state carry the microorganism *Giardia lamblia*, source of giardiasis, an unpleasant intestinal disorder. Other pathogens resident in untreated water can even be deadly. Be safe and drink only treated water.

Mosquitoes, gnats, deer flies, and other **flying pests** can be a nuisance in warmer months, especially in the Coastal Plain. Apply adequate insect repellent, preferably anything containing DEET (although some hikers swear by the method of dropping powdered sulfur into a sock and patting themselves down with it). Also bring an ointment to treat bug bites.

Tick protection is important, especially in spring and summer in the Coastal Plain. Keep arms and legs covered, tuck pant legs into socks, and spray legs and feet with repellent. Wearing light-colored clothing will make searching yourself for ticks easier. Most ticks in South Carolina are more an annoyance than a serious health threat, and, compared with other areas of the country, relatively few cases of Lyme Disease or Rocky Mountain Spotted Fever (both carried by ticks) have occurred in the state. Nevertheless, the adage, "An ounce of prevention is worth a pound of cure," has never been truer than in application to these diseases, which are difficult to diagnose and frequently mistaken for other conditions.

South Carolina's winters are generally mild, but some days can be quite cold. In **cold weather**, it is advisable to dress in layers, being sure that the inner layer is chosen for its ability to wick moisture away from the body. Synthetic fabrics designed specifically for this purpose are best.

We also recommend that you take along a compass, this book, detailed maps of the area, a whistle, sunscreen, lip balm, a first aid kit, a pocket knife, and an emergency flashlight. Many hikers like to carry walking sticks, which are especially helpful in negotiating the ascents and descents of mountain trails and in thwarting spider webs that block trails. Some can also be used as monopod camera stands.

It is always advisable to **stay on marked trails**, not only to avoid possible hazards but also to prevent damage to the delicate ecosystems through which the trails pass. The most basic rule of trail safety is simply to stay on the trail.

If you get caught in a **lightning** storm, avoid summits, exposed places, lone trees, streams, and rocks. Find shelter in a densely forested area at the lowest possible elevation. Remove metal-frame backpacks and stay away from lakeshores and other areas of open water.

Hypothermia, the sudden and catastrophic loss of body heat, can be experienced even in warm weather; in fact, it is prevalent in temperate places like South Carolina, where a sudden rainstorm can soak and chill lightly dressed hikers. Symptoms of hypothermia include shivering and disorientation. If a member of your party appears to be suffering from hypothermia, you must get the person into warm clothes and do everything possible to raise his or her core body temperature. Make sure the afflicted person is wearing a hat; the majority of body heat is lost by way of the head. Feed him or her hot, sweet liquids—never alcohol. Most importantly, get the victim moving again as soon as possible, because movement is the most effective way to improve internal body heat.

Poisonous snakes in South Carolina include the eastern diamondback rattler, the timber (or canebrake) rattler, the copperhead, the cottonmouth (also known as the water moccasin), and the coral snake. Although you may occasionally encounter snakes, the probability you will have a problem with them is extremely low, especially if you stick to designated trails. Snakes normally stay out of sight and out of the way. If you leave snakes alone, they are more than happy to do the same for you.

Alligators can be surprisingly fast-moving over short distances. They are seldom a threat to humans, but pets occasionally become meals when they wander too close to the edge of alligator habitat. For this reason, pets are prohibited on some coastal trails. Even humans would be wise to pay alligators the highest respect by keeping their distance.

Biting or stinging insects can be encountered on any trail, but are seldom anything worse than a nuisance unless you are allergic to bee or wasp stings. Be aware that wasps, yellow jackets, and hornets often get surly as autumn turns to winter and their colonies break up. This is another good reason to stay on the trail.

Poison ivy, poison oak, and poison sumac can be encountered alongside almost any trail. Since you may not be allergic to one species of these plants and yet highly allergic to another, it is best to avoid all of them by staying on the trail. Learn to recognize these plants, which consist of vines with three leaves per cluster. If in doubt, avoid.

A final note of caution pertains to **horses**. On trails that are open to equestrians, such as Long Cane Trail (Hike 27) and Buncombe Trail (Hike 32), be careful not to scare the horses you meet along the way. Step to the downhill side of the trail and let horses pass. Move easily and naturally and talk to horses and their riders in a calm, level voice. The horses need to recognize you as a friendly human, not something to fear.

The great majority of trails in this book are appropriate for **hiking with children.** The exceptions are found mostly in the mountains. Trails which bring you close to precipices or in close proximity to rocks adjacent to flowing streams are not appropriate for small children. (See Appendix D for a list of trails appropriate for children.) Approach trails in the Coastal Plain, where snakes and alligators make wandering off-trail especially inadvisable, with caution.

If you bring children on the trail, treat everything we have said about preparations and hiking essentials as doubly important. Carry enough water and food for your children and encourage them to drink and eat, especially during hot weather. In cold weather, carry hot drinks or soup in a thermos; nothing is better if a child becomes chilled.

Dress your children appropriately for the hike you have chosen, and for the season. Cool-weather hiking with children poses special challenges. Be aware that just bundling a child in urban-style outerwear may not keep him or her warm. There is no substitute for effectively layered, high-quality socks and other clothing. Substantial mittens should also be a basic requirement.

Focus on comfort and safety. Items such as sunscreen, hats, insect repellent, and topical anesthetic for bug bites and sunburn are the ingredients for a successful family hike.

Hunting is allowed during certain periods in many hiking areas around the state. In general, hunting is not allowed in state and national parks, but it is allowed at limited times in national and state forests, national wildlife refuges, state wildlife management areas, and state heritage preserves, as well as on the Jocassee Gorges property presently owned by Duke Power.

For the most part, hiking and hunting coexist well. Hunting seasons are constrained to distinct periods, and even when hunting activities are going on, hikers should be safe if they wear international orange vests and headgear while on the trail. Hunting is generally not allowed on Sundays, regardless of the season.

Hunting seasons vary from region to region and site to site, and according to such factors as use of dogs, gender of prey, choice of weapons, type of game hunted, and a number of other factors. Information on the hunting rules and seasons in South Carolina is available in the Department of Natural Resources's *Rules and Regulations,* published each fiscal year (see Appendix A: For More Information).

Deer are the most commonly hunted game in the hiking areas described in this book, although game species in South Carolina also include turkeys, ducks, geese, doves, quail, feral hogs, squirrels, rabbits, raccoons, opossums, foxes, bears, beavers, bobcats, minks, muskrats, otters, skunks, grouse, and weasels.

Generally, deer hunting seasons begin in the fall and continue until January 1, beginning earlier the nearer the site is to the coast. On private lands along the outer Coastal Plain, deer hunting seasons can begin as early as August 15. The seasons typically begin sometime in September for private areas in the inner Coastal Plain and lower Midlands areas in the vicinity of the Sandhills. In the upper Midlands and the Mountains, deer hunting seasons on private lands are likely to begin in October. On public lands in all areas, however, the specified dates on which hunting is allowed are typically much more limited and vary greatly from site to site. The simplest way to learn about hunting in an area you intend to hike is to contact the organization listed in the "For more information" notation in each hike description.

ZERO IMPACT

It is important to minimize your impact on the land by following certain practices, particularly when backpacking and camping.

Respect the needs of wildlife. Hike on existing trails and try to camp at previously used sites. Wear waterproof boots so you can cross muddy and boggy areas. Circling around these spots creates additional paths, increasing your impact on the land. Do not make shortcuts by creating switchbacks; this creates erosion.

Pack it in, pack it out. This is the key rule. Please consider "packing it out plus one"—in other words, carry out your own trash, plus one piece of litter left by some earlier, less considerate visitor. Garbage, even an apple core or an orange peel, does not biodegrade swiftly, but does quickly degrade the appearance of the trail. If you smoke, put out cigarettes with great care. Pack out butts rather than scattering them trailside. Please, take only photographs; leave only footprints.

Properly dispose of what you cannot pack out. Bury human waste at least 6 inches deep and at least 100 feet from water sources.

Leave what you find. Leave rocks, plants, archaeological artifacts, and other objects of interest, such as fossils or antlers, as you find them so that others can enjoy them, too. Do not construct lean-tos, tables, chairs, or other structures. Avoid damaging live trees and plants. Sketch flowers or take photographs instead of picking them.

Use fire responsibly.

Do without campfires whenever you can. Should you wish to cook as part of your outing, consider carrying a small portable gas stove instead of building a fire. Gas stoves save trees and they also obviate the need for unsightly fire rings. If you must build a fire, use only dead, fallen wood. Douse the fire repeatedly until it is completely out, then bury all traces.

In summary, please make it your personal challenge to see that the trails you hike are at least as free (preferably freer) from human impact when you leave as they were when you arrived. To learn more about no-trace principles, contact Leave No Trace (see Appendix A: For More Information).

TRAIL MANAGEMENT AND REGULATIONS

South Carolina's hiking trails traverse lands controlled by a variety of public and private groups, all of which have different rules for public access and use. The greatest number of hikes in this book are on state park and national forest properties, but there are many other owners and managers of appealing hiking trails.

State parks are under the management of the South Carolina Department of Parks, Recreation, and Tourism. Many parks offer access at no charge, but there are small entrance fees for a few of the most popular, especially during summer at those that offer swimming. Annual passes are available which provide unlimited admittance to all parks. Hunting is not permitted in any state park.

In 1997, the South Carolina State Park Service began a series of mission and name changes for the parks in its system. Some parks which preserve important historic features are being renamed State Historic Sites (e.g., Oconee Station and Landsford Canal). Parks having outstanding natural features will be called State Natural Areas (e.g., Keowee-Toxaway). Most of the parks in the State Park Service fall into the remaining categories, which include Traditional parks, Regional parks, and Outdoor Recreation parks. The names of these parks will not change, although management practices will be altered to a greater or lesser degree.

Wildlife management areas and **heritage preserves** are under the jurisdiction of the South Carolina Department of Natural Resources. Wildlife management areas are managed for hunting, and hikers are well advised to learn the hunting seasons, especially the periods for deer hunting in autumn (see **Hunting,** above). Each wildlife management area has its own particular parameters and limitations for hunting. Heritage preserves are managed to preserve unique habitats, often protecting endangered plant or nongame animal species. However, hunting for game animals is allowed in some preserve areas. Both wildlife management areas and heritage preserves are sometimes closed to public access in order to protect wildlife during sensitive seasons. There are no fees for admission to these properties.

South Carolina owns three **state forests**, managed for a variety of uses. Although only Harbison State Forest is featured in this book (as Hike 36), Manchester State Forest (next to Poinsett State Park) and Sandhills State Forest (adjacent to Carolina Sandhills National Wildlife Refuge) also offer miles of pleasant hiking, mountain biking, and equestrian trails.

National forests are administered by the U.S. Forest Service, a division of the U.S. Department of Agriculture, for multipurpose use, including timber harvest and recreation of various types. Hunting is generally allowed,

A live oak tree. YVONNE MICHEL PHOTO

but both hunting and timber harvest are prohibited along the Chattooga River Wild and Scenic River corridor. South Carolina has two national forests, Francis Marion and Sumter. Sumter, located in the upper portion of the state, is composed of three diverse and geographically distinct units: Long Cane Ranger District and Enoree/Tyger Ranger District in the Midlands and Andrew Pickens Ranger District in the Mountains. Presently there are no admission fees for use of national forest trails, but this situation is likely to change.

Although there are no large national parks in South Carolina, the state has six smaller units of the national park system called **National Monuments.** This book describes hikes in two national monuments, Congaree Swamp National Monument (Hike 38) and Kings Mountain National Military Park (Hike 33), neither of which charges an admission fee. These are managed by the National Park Service, a unit of the U.S. Department of the Interior, and no hunting is allowed.

National wildlife refuges, operated by the U.S. Fish and Wildlife Service of the Department of the Interior, are primarily managed as wildlife habitat, particularly for migratory birds. Hunting is permitted on a limited basis. There are six national wildlife refuges in South Carolina, including five—Carolina Sandhills, Cape Romain, ACE Basin, Pinckney Island, and Savannah—which have trails described in this book. These refuges do not charge admission, but access is sometimes restricted because of wildlife breeding seasons.

Local governments operate facilities with trails, a few of which are described in this book. Stumphouse Tunnel Park, operated by the Pendleton District Commission, serves as the trailhead for the Blue Ridge Railroad Historical Trail (Hike 8). Cypress Gardens (Hike 50) is owned by Berkeley County. Rules at locally managed government facilities vary greatly.

Moreover, there are a number of publicly accessible trails at facilities owned and managed by **private groups,** some of which charge fees. Privately controlled trails in this book include Rainbow Falls (Hike 21), the Anne Springs Close Greenway (Hike 34), and Magnolia Gardens (Hike 52). A large portion of the Blue Ridge Railroad Historical Trail (Hike 8) passes through private property.

Until recently, Duke Power Company owned almost all of the property above Lake Jocassee known as the Jocassee Gorges, as well as property extending substantially eastward and westward of Lake Jocassee and the rivers feeding into it. However, the state and the Forest Service have purchased most of these lands, and management of 32,000 acres in South Carolina is now under the auspices of the state's Department of Natural Resources. Much of the land around the North Carolina portion of the Foothills Trail above Lake Jocassee has been transferred to the management of the Nantahala National Forest unit of the Forest Service. However, Duke Power has maintained ownership of some of the property along the Jocassee Gorges section of the Foothills Trail (Hike 11), in the area of Lower Whitewater Falls and the Bad Creek Hydroelectric Station.

14

NATURAL HISTORY OF SOUTH CAROLINA

The trees and plants of South Carolina are as diverse as its geography. The Mountains are dominated by oak-hickory forest, a habitat known for its huge diversity of plant species, including numerous varieties of oaks. Wetter areas are dominated by lovely mountain laurel and rhododendron, a special pleasure in the late spring when they bloom riotously.

The rest of the state is mostly covered by oak-pine forest, but exceptions are the rule along our hiking routes. We chose many of the hikes in the Midlands and Coastal Plain regions especially for the distinctive habitats through which they pass; several of them pass through coastal forests, which are characterized by vegetation resistant to the effects of salt spray and wind. Trees in these forests include live oak, laurel oak, Carolina palmetto, and slash and loblolly pines. Other common plants include hollies, red bay, dwarf palmetto, wax myrtle, and redcedar.

The wetlands of the Coastal Plain are particularly attractive for hiking. The swamps feature tea-black water, Spanish moss, and baldcypress and tupelo trees. Marshland reclaimed from the coastal rice plantations of centuries past can also be quite enticing. These areas, often managed as habitat for migratory birds, are achingly beautiful, especially when wildflowers such as irises and spider lilies are blooming.

The wildlife of the state is also quite diverse. The mountains harbor species usually found much farther north, such as the raven and the endangered peregrine falcon. Species common in Florida or other subtropical

A butterfly along the Swamp Fox Trail. Yvonne Michel photo

areas can be found at the southern end of the state. In between are large populations of white-tailed deer and wild turkey. Black bears live secretively in the mountains and, surprisingly, on secluded Carolina bays (see below) within a few miles of the highly developed Grand Strand coastal resort area. Other mammals in the state include beavers, foxes, raccoons, bobcats, feral hogs, and river otters. Opossums, the only marsupials native to North America, are also quite common.

South Carolina is under-appreciated as a birding region, although sites such as Huntington Beach State Park and Savannah National Wildlife Refuge are becoming better known to birding enthusiasts the world over. More than 350 species have been identified in the state. Generally, the wetlands along the coast are popular year-round as host sites for wading birds such as herons and egrets. Ducks winter along the coast, and numerous species pass through all regions of the state during the spring and autumn migration periods. Songbirds and woodpeckers fill the forests during all seasons, while various birds of prey prowl the skies.

The Carolina bay, a type of wetland found in the Coastal Plain, is under serious threat. Most of these unusual elliptical depressions (often, but not always, filled with water) have been filled or drained to make room for farming, roads, or other development. (The word bay refers not to water, but to the bay trees which are usually the dominant vegetation in the vicinity of Carolina bays.) Efforts to protect the remaining Carolina bays continue, particularly through the work of the Heritage Trust program of the South Carolina Department of Natural Resources (see Appendix A: For More Information).

Wild easter lilies near the Edisto River. Yvonne Michel PHOTO

All environmental damage is not caused by humans. Nature, too, can be capricious. South Carolina periodically suffers population explosions of the southern pine beetle. In 1995, the worst outbreak in the state's history affected nearly half of South Carolina's counties, concentrating in the northwestern and southern parts of the state. Enough timber to build 26,000 houses was destroyed by the beetle.

Hurricane Hugo was another disaster for South Carolina and its ecosystems. On September 21, 1989, this killer storm slammed into the South Carolina coast just above Charleston, dramatically transforming the landscape in its path. The tidal surge washed completely over many barrier islands, including Bull Island and the Isle of Palms. The fishing village of McClellanville, just north of the spot where the eye of the hurricane made landfall, was almost leveled. Furthermore, Hugo tracked rapidly inland, its extremely high winds causing severe damage far from the coast, through Camden all the way past Charlotte, North Carolina. The devastated woodlands of Cape Romain National Wildlife Refuge and Francis Marion National Forest will continue to display the scars of Hugo for decades to come.

South Carolina harbors many endangered and threatened species. The most prominent of these is our national symbol, the bald eagle, which is making a strong comeback in South Carolina. The same is true for alligators, which are now numerous in the swamps and marshlands of the coastal plain. The red-cockaded woodpecker is badly threatened due to habitat loss, but South Carolina has some of the nation's largest remaining populations of this species.

South Carolina preservationists also work hard to protect nesting areas for loggerhead sea turtles along the coast and habitat for gopher tortoises in the sandy areas of the lower Savannah River Valley.

REGIONAL OVERVIEW

Geologists divide the state into three (sometimes four) physiographic provinces, all of which extend into the neighboring states of Georgia and North Carolina. The Blue Ridge province, strictly defined, covers only the extreme northwestern mountainous edge of the state. The Piedmont (foothills) province runs from the Blue Ridge approximately to the center of the state. The Sandhills, the remains of the ancient seacoast, stretch across the state's midriff in a belt from Cheraw through Camden, Columbia, Lexington, and on to North Augusta. Some scientists consider the Sandhills to be part of the Piedmont or Coastal Plain physiographic provinces, while others identify them as a separate province. South and east of the Sandhills, the Coastal Plain province covers the rest of the state. It is characterized by very flat terrain and a plethora of wetlands. A subregion of the Coastal Plain is the Coastal Zone, the narrow strip bordering the Atlantic Ocean.

Other observers identify geographic regions in South Carolina in a variety of ways. Frequently used regional terms include Foothills, Upcountry, Upstate, Midlands, Savannah River Valley, Lowcountry, Pee Dee, Grand Strand, and the Coast.

For the purposes of this book, the state is divided into three regions: the Mountains, the Midlands, and the Coastal Plain. The Mountains region is separated from the Midlands region by Interstate 85, while the border between the Midlands and the Coastal Plain is Interstate 95. (An exception to this division is Hike 59, Webb Wildlife Center, located slightly north of Interstate 95 in the southern part of the state, but described in the Coastal Plain section.)

PALMETTO TRAIL

The Palmetto Trail is a series of connected recreational trail segments, still under development, that will eventually extend more than 400 miles from South Carolina's mountains to its seacoast. Spur trails will connect other trails in the state to the Palmetto Trail's central spine.

Palmetto Trails, a private nonprofit organization created in 1994 by the Palmetto Conservation Foundation, coordinates the development of the Palmetto Trail system. In this visionary effort, Palmetto Trails works closely with the South Carolina Department of Parks, Recreation, and Tourism, though the Palmetto Trail partnership also consists of many other public and private partners.

Hikers are welcome on all segments of the Palmetto Trail, and most portions are also open to mountain bikers and, in some cases, equestrians.

The complete route of the Palmetto Trail is not yet set. At present, the trail begins northeast of Charleston, in the community of Awendaw, and heads 68 miles north to Lake Moultrie. The planned route will cross the Midlands and traverse the Mountains, either on new trails or on less trafficked trails already in existence. It is expected that the exact route will be

Palmetto Trail

fully set by the year 2000. The trail will be completed in the early years of the new millennium.

Segments of the Palmetto Trail already in existence include the Lake Moultrie Passage (Hike 48) and the Swamp Fox Passage (Hike 47) in the Coastal Plain; and the High Hills of Santee Passage (connecting with Poinsett State Park, Hike 37) and Sumter Passage (connecting with the Buncombe Trail, Hike 32) in the Midlands.

Mountains

In the Mountains region, you can enjoy numerous handsome waterfalls. Waterfalls exist here for two reasons: rain and terrain. South Carolina's mountains lie at the southern end of the Blue Ridge mountain range, on a long precipice called the Blue Ridge Escarpment, or Blue Wall. The drop-off along the escarpment ranges from 1,000 to 2,000 feet. The mountains are also by far the rainiest part of the state, and among the rainiest places in North America.

Another attraction is the Wild and Scenic Chattooga River. Since it is closed to boats and rafts above South Carolina Highway 28, practically the only way to experience this famous whitewater river along its upper stretch is to hike the Chattooga Trail (Hike 2). Also in this area are the magnificent river gorges that funnel stunningly beautiful rivers into Lake Jocassee, as well as the Mountain Bridge Wilderness Area, the crown jewel of South Carolina hiking.

The Mountains contain twenty-six of this book's featured hikes, most of which are scattered across, above, and just below the Blue Ridge Escarpment. A large portion of the hikes are in the Mountain Bridge Wilderness Area (managed by the State Park Service), the Andrew Pickens District of Sumter National Forest, and Duke Power Company's former holdings in the area commonly known as Jocassee Gorges, which has been sold to South Carolina and is being managed by the state's Department of Natural Resources. Please note: The Mountain Bridge Wilderness Area is *not* a federally designated wilderness; it is simply a designation of the state park system.

Although historically the Mountains and Piedmont together are often referred to as the Upcountry, this book's Mountains region closely resembles the Upcountry tourism district, a much smaller four-county area. The towns of Greenville, Pickens, Walhalla, and Clemson are major points of departure for the hikes in this area.

Interstate 85 provides easy access to the mountains, but the best route to reach points in this region is South Carolina Highway 11, the Cherokee Foothills Scenic Highway. Providing easy driving and great views of South Carolina's Blue Ridge Mountains, the Cherokee Foothills Scenic Highway takes travelers eastward from I-85 at the Georgia state line past Lake Hartwell State Park, Walhalla, Oconee Station State Historic Site, Devil's Fork State Park, Lake Keowee, Keowee-Toxaway State Park, Table Rock State Park, and Jones Gap State Park, then continues on through rolling countryside and peach orchards to Cowpens and Gaffney.

Greenville, Easley, Pickens, Clemson, Seneca, and Walhalla all offer accommodations and other services, as do the I-85 exits in the area. Pendleton, Salem, and Walhalla offer attractive bed-and-breakfast accommodations in laid-back settings. The Laurel Valley Restaurant and Lodge, on the Foothills Trail beside the trout-laden Eastatoe Creek, is a unique treat.

FOOTHILLS TRAIL

The Foothills Trail is the mother of South Carolina's long trails. Conceived by the Sierra Club and built by Duke Power; the National Forest Service; the South Carolina Department of Parks, Recreation, and Tourism; and other public and private groups, the trail stretches along the state's mountainous northwestern border.

Efforts to build a continuous trail in this area began in the 1960s, and when the first section was built in 1968 in the Andrew Pickens District of Sumter National Forest (adjacent to Oconee State Park), it plunged down grades of as much as 30 percent. Subsequent relocations have smoothed the path considerably.

The nonprofit Foothills Trail Conference, governed by an 18-member board, was organized in 1974, and since that time it has served as the chief coordinator, facilitator, and administrator of matters pertaining to the trail. One of its most important functions is the publication of *Guide to the Foothills Trail*, an excellent volume of detailed maps and descriptions of the Foothills Trail.

The original Foothills Trail runs from Oconee State Park in the west to Table Rock State Park in the east, a distance of about 85 miles. In the mid-1980s, a connector to the Caesars Head area was established through Gum Gap. Some now consider the eastern terminus of the Foothills Trail to be Jones Gap State Park, which connects to the main stem of the Foothills Trail via the Jones Gap and Gum Gap trails, traveling from there all the way to Oconee State Park, a distance of almost 100 miles. In our guide, we describe the elements of the Foothills Trail in five segments, described in the following paragraphs.

The Chattooga Valley Segment of the Foothills Trail (Hike 1) extends from Oconee State Park to the Bad Creek Hydroelectric Station near Lower Whitewater Falls. The Jocassee Gorges Segment (Hike 11) runs between the Bad Creek facility and Laurel Valley. The Sassafras Mountain Segment (Hike 15) covers the area from Laurel Valley to Table Rock State Park, with Sassafras Mountain being an intermediate point along the route. These three segments make up the original Foothills Trail, and many observers still recognize these three segments as the official Foothills Trail.

Our book describes two more trail portions recognized by some observers as the bona fide Foothills Trail, though regarded by others as simply a spur. The Gum Gap Segment of the Foothills Trail (Hike 17) takes hikers from the top of Sassafras Mountain to U.S. Highway 278 in the Caesars Head State Park area, and the Jones Gap Trail (Hike 22) connects with the Gum Gap Trail to take hikers on to Jones Gap State Park along the valley of the Middle Saluda River.

There is much difference of opinion among Foothills Trails aficionados regarding whether east to west or west to east is the better direction to hike the trail. The short answer to the east versus west debate is this: there is no easy way to hike the Foothills Trail. East to west is about as difficult as west to east. This book in no way resolves the issue, as it describes different segments in different directions. We generally tried to follow the easiest direction for each segment, but did not necessarily succeed. We suggest that

FOOTHILLS TRAIL

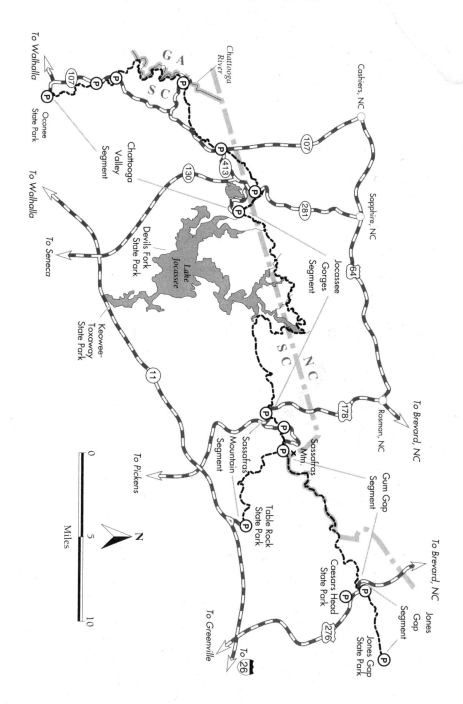

you read the descriptions, examine the elevation graphs, and make your own choices for your selected segment.

The Foothills Trail and its connecting trails provide almost 200 miles of hiking options, including several stretches in North Carolina and 45 miles of trails in the Mountain Bridge Wilderness Area.

MOUNTAIN BRIDGE WILDERNESS AREA

The Mountain Bridge Wilderness Area is a spectacular 40,000-acre natural wonderland located along the Blue Ridge Escarpment north of Greenville. It is called the Mountain Bridge because it serves as a bridge of permanently protected land spanning the gap between the Poinsett and Table Rock watersheds. These watersheds are fiercely protected from encroachment because they provide the city of Greenville's water supply. The Mountain Bridge Wilderness Area was set aside by a series of acquisitions and conservation easements negotiated by the Naturaland Trust, a private nonprofit organization founded in 1972 through the vision and dedication of Greenville attorney and photographer Tommy Wyche. Most of the area is now under the management and protection of the South Carolina Department of Parks, Recreation, and Tourism, the South Carolina Department of Natural Resources, the Naturaland Trust, and the Greenville YMCA.

Comprehensive information on the Mountain Bridge Wilderness Area trail system is provided in *Mountain Bridge Trails*, an excellent guidebook published in 1994 by Naturaland Trust.

The passion flower. YVONNE MICHEL PHOTO

MOUNTAIN BRIDGE STATE NATURAL AREA

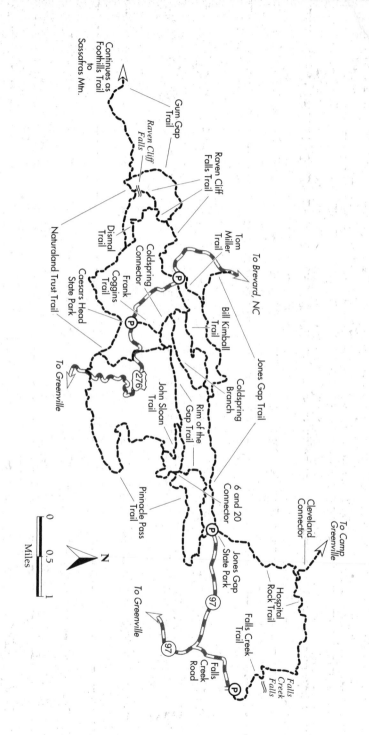

Central to the Mountain Bridge are Caesars Head and Jones Gap state parks. These parks offer little in the way of traditional state park amenities. On the other hand, they are both among the best places to picnic in the state. They also offer solid environmental education and excellent trail information. Hikers wanting to camp trailside must register and pay in advance at either park.

All hikers in Mountain Bridge Wilderness Area must register before setting out. Convenient boxes are provided at all trailheads for this purpose. The precaution of registering is absolutely necessary. This wilderness is not a wilderness only in name; this is real backcountry land, far from any help. Should you become lost or injured, the head start you provide rangers by alerting them of your hiking plans may save considerable discomfort and difficulty.

This guide describes seven hikes composed of portions of the Mountain Bridge Wilderness Area trail system. The Mountain Bridge trail network is composed of 17 numbered trails totaling 45 miles in length. They connect to the older Foothills Trail system through Gum Gap Trail.

Signage in Mountain Bridge Wilderness Area is simple. Wooden posts are stuck in the ground with a trail number etched into them, along with mileage information such as the distance back to the trailhead. The odd symbol surrounding the trail number represents a mountain and a bridge. Trails are blazed in different colors; black metal markers in the distinctive Mountain Bridge shape have been placed in trees at just above eye level to tell you which pathway you are on.

See the table below for help in matching Mountain Bridge signage and blazes to the seven Mountain Bridge hikes described in this book.

Mountain Bridge Trail Name	Mountain Bridge Trail Number	Hike Number in this book	Color of blaze
Jones Gap Trail	1	22	Blue
Tom Miller Trail	2	22	Blue
Coldspring Branch Trail	3	19	Orange
Bill Kimball Trail	5	19	Pink
Rim of the Gap Trail	6	23	Yellow
Coldspring Connector	7	19	Blue
Raven Cliff Falls Trail	11	18, 20	Red
Dismal Trail	12	20	Purple
Gum Gap Trail	13	17, 20	Blue
Naturaland Trust Trail	14	20	Pink
Frank Coggins Trail	15	20	Purple
Pinnacle Pass Trail	20	24	Orange
John Sloan Trail	21	23, 24	Pink
6 and 20 Trail	22	23, 24	Purple
Hospital Rock Trail	30	25	Orange
Falls Creek Trail	31	25	Orange
Cleveland Connector	32	25	Pink

1 Foothills Trail, Chattooga Valley Segment

General description:	A long 3-day backpacking trip, offering waterfalls and the majestic beauty of the Whitewater and Chattooga rivers.
General location:	North of Walhalla, in the northwest corner of the state.
Distance:	33 miles one way.
Difficulty:	Moderate. Bad Creek Hydroelectric Station to Upper Whitewater Falls portion strenuous when traveled east to west.
Trail conditions:	Conditions are good. Traffic is light to moderate.
Best time to go:	Year-round.
Maps:	*Guide to the Foothills Trail*, Foothills Trail Conference; Trail Guide, Andrew Pickens Ranger District, Sumter National Forest, Forest Service; Tamassee, Satolah, and Cashiers USGS quads. See Appendix A: For More Information.
Fees:	$2 per vehicle at Oconee State Park trailhead. No fees at other access points.

Finding the trailhead: To reach the northeastern trailhead from the intersection of South Carolina Highway 28 and SC 11, just south of Walhalla, follow SC 11 (also known as the Cherokee Foothills Scenic Highway) northeast 12 miles, then turn left (northwest) on SC 130 and travel 10 miles to the entrance to Duke Power's Bad Creek Hydroelectric Station on the right (east), just before the North Carolina state line. Turn right onto Bad Creek Road, register at the guard gate, then enter the Bad Creek property and follow the signs about 2 miles to the parking lot for Whitewater Falls and Foothills Trail on the left (northeast).

To reach the southern trailhead from the intersection of SC 28 and SC 11 south of Walhalla, head north on SC 28 for 9.5 miles. At the fork, go right (northeast) on SC 107; the Oconee State Park entrance is another 2.4 miles, on the right (east). The Foothills Trail's western terminus is toward the southeastern end of the park. Turn right (south) at the first opportunity after passing the guard gate and head east, passing the campground; bear right (east) at the fork. The Foothills Trailhead, identified by a sign, is a few yards farther on the left (north). Park in the small parking lot 10 yards past the trailhead, on the right (south).

The hike: This segment of the Foothills Trail is described east to west, beginning at the northeastern Bad Creek Trailhead. There are advantages and disadvantages to going in either direction. The east-to-west route involves an 1,100-foot ascent to the top of Upper Whitewater Falls in the first 2.5 miles of the hike. Much of the rest of the hike, however, is a long, gradual,

Foothills Trail, Chattooga Valley Segment Overview

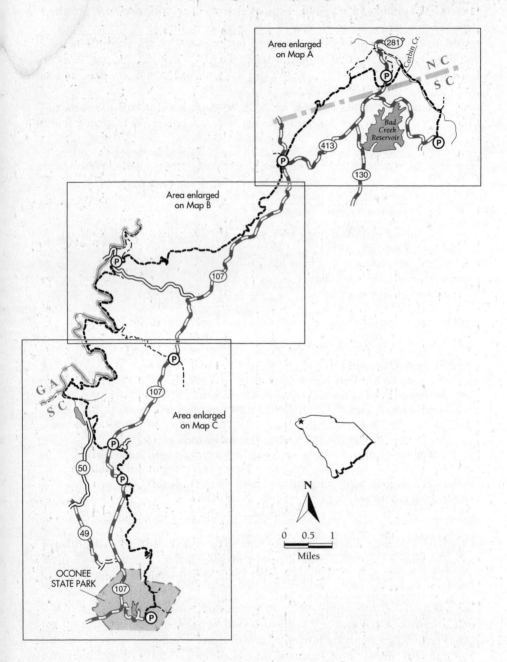

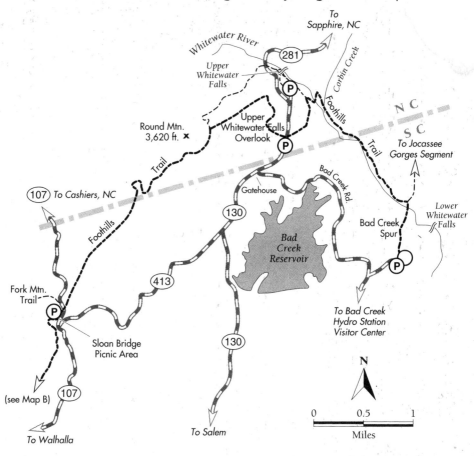

1,400-foot descent, with numerous ups and downs along the way. The east-to-west route can be eased by beginning at the parking lot for Upper Whitewater Falls, but there is great beauty in the section along the Whitewater River that would be bypassed. The west-to-east route involves a long ascent, followed by a short, steep descent.

From the Bad Creek parking lot, follow the 0.6-mile blue-blazed spur trail over a ridge to its connection with the Foothills Trail (just past the crossing over the Whitewater River). Turn left (northwest) and follow the white-blazed Foothills Trail along the east side of the Whitewater River. (A right turn takes you to the Lower Whitewater Falls overlook spur and along the Jocassee Gorges Segment of the Foothills Trail toward Laurel Valley.)

The trail crosses a bridge over a small tributary, afterward offering intermittent stairs and boardwalks as it rises and falls. After another bridge, the trail enters a mixed forest with many beautiful riverside hemlocks, sometimes proceeding along the river bank and sometimes on bluffs 100 feet

Foothills Trail, Chattooga Valley Segment Map B

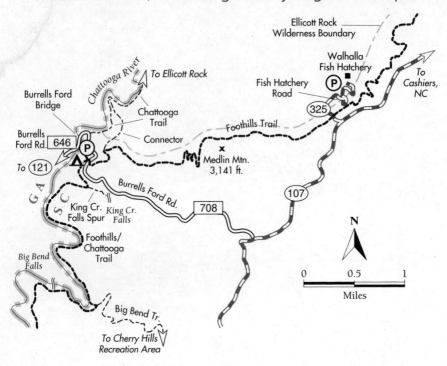

above the rushing water, to enter North Carolina and the Nantahala National Forest after about 1 mile.

About 0.5 mile past the state line, you cross roaring Corbin Creek. If you are lucky, a foot bridge is in place. If you are unlucky, the bridge has again been torn asunder by the ravages of winter storms, and you must ford the creek by means of fallen trees, boulders, and a guide rope.

After another 0.1 mile, you cross the Whitewater River on a long, sturdy bridge with great views downstream as well as up, where Upper Whitewater Falls is visible in the distance. Enjoy these views restfully, because the next

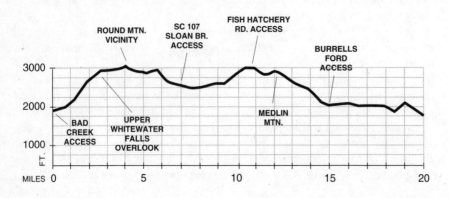

0.5 mile takes you 600 feet up the western bluff on stairs and switchbacks. The way crisscrosses a brook and weaves among boulders, old-growth hemlocks, rhododendrons, and mountain laurel.

About 300 feet from the crest of the bluff, the Foothills Trail turns sharply left (southwest), away from the river.

If you have the stamina, however, continue upward to the fenced overlook at the crest. The climb offers truly breathtaking views of the 400-foot drop of Upper Whitewater Falls.

More scenic vistas await you at the crest of the bluff, as does a 0.2-mile paved walkway to a national forest parking area just off North Carolina Highway 281, which continues SC 130. The parking area offers rest rooms and drinking water.

Return down the stairway to the point where the Foothills Trail turns south, away from the river, and proceed by turning right.

You now move through an area of boulders left over from the construction of the nearby highway and parking area and pass a short spur leading east to the parking area and rest room. About 0.75 mile from the turn away from the river, you pass another small parking area on the east side of NC 281, just above the North Carolina–South Carolina border. Cross the highway and enter the woods on the west side of the road at the end of the guardrail.

Over the next mile, you cross a small, steep stream by stepping over rocks and enjoy impressive views at switchbacks as you approach the Grassy Knob Escarpment. As you move along the escarpment, you are treated with great views of Lake Jocassee and the foothills to the south.

The trail moves away from the escarpment and, at a gap below Round Mountain, 3 miles from the river, turns left (west) at a junction. (A right turn to the right, or east, heads downhill across a number of streams and past several good campsites before reaching NC 281, 1.4 miles away.)

The next stretch is filled with the beauty of hemlock, rhododendron, mountain laurel, galax, ferns, and a variety of trilliums as the trail crosses a small, split stream, then moves southwest along the north side of the Chattooga Ridge. The trail then crosses the ridge and moves along its south side, offering more southern vistas before crossing back to the north side of the ridge and heading downhill, at 4.4 miles from the river.

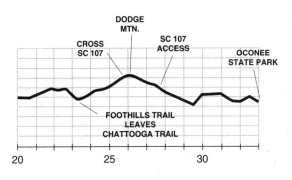

At 4.6 miles from the river, the trail crosses the South Carolina–North Carolina state line, which is also the boundary between North Carolina's Nantahala National Forest and South Carolina's Sumter National Forest to the south. The crossing is

marked by survey markers and a sign. From here, the trail rises to the top of a ridge with more southern vistas and then descends moderately to SC 107 and Sloan Bridge Picnic Area.

(Sloan Bridge Picnic Area, 25 miles north of Walhalla and 8 miles south of Cashiers, North Carolina, provides convenient vehicle access to the Foothills Trail. Just north of the picnic area is the trailhead for Fork Mountain Trail.)

From Sloan Bridge Picnic Area the Foothills Trail proceeds southwest on the east side and within earshot of the East Fork of the Chattooga River. The trail crosses a small cascade and numerous streams, and is decorated with mountain laurels, rhododendrons, hemlocks, white pines, oaks, hollies, cucumber trees, tulip poplars, rattlesnake plantains, ferns, galax, Jack-in-the-pulpits, and velvety mosses. Fork Mountain looms to the west, beyond the East Fork. Good views to the west can be had on clear winter days.

After 3.3 miles, the trail crosses paved Fish Hatchery Road. The Walhalla Fish Hatchery and the trailhead for the East Fork Trail are 1.7 miles downhill to the right (west). SC 107 is 0.3 mile uphill to the left (east).

From Fish Hatchery Road, the trail ascends about 1 mile along the southern boundary of the Ellicott Rock Wilderness to the crest of Medlin Mountain. After following a ridgeline, the trail begins a 3-mile, 900-foot southwesterly descent toward Burrells Ford Road. There are excellent winter vistas and a mixed forest, including giant oaks, sassafras, hemlocks, mountain laurels, and rhododendrons.

At 3.3 miles past Fish Hatchery Road, you reach a fork in the trail. The signage indicates that the red-blazed right fork leads to the Chattooga Trail, 1.1 miles west. The Foothills Trail continues to the left (south), passing the top of a small cascade and crossing unpaved Burrells Ford Road 0.6 mile past the fork.

(The Burrells Ford parking lot, a few yards west of the road crossing, is another vehicle access point for the Foothills Trail. The trail can be found at the northeast corner of the parking lot, behind a large brown sign board.)

A sign just past the Burrells Ford Road crossing informs you that you are 17 miles from Oconee State Park and that the next 8.1 miles of the Foothills Trail run concurrently with the Chattooga Trail. On the left (east), less than 1 mile past the road crossing, a red-blazed, 0.5-mile-long spur departs for 70-foot Kings Creek Falls, a delightful cascade, well worth the detour.

Beyond the spur, the trail arrives at the banks of the Chattooga River and continues downstream, alternately traveling at the water's edge and ascending bluffs some distance above the river. This stretch is an extremely pleasant walk, offering frequent fishing and swimming spots and great views of granite boulders, mountain laurel, and rhododendron on the Georgia side of the river. There are many attractive potential camping sites along this stretch.

At 2.9 miles beyond Burrells Ford, on the left (east), you come to the turnoff for the Big Bend Trail. The Big Bend Trail takes hikers to Cherry Hill Recreation Area and the beginning of Winding Stairs Trail, 2.7 miles away. For 0.5 mile past the trail intersection, you follow the horseshoe-shaped Big Bend of the Chattooga River, followed by Big Bend Falls, a powerful 30-foot plunge, the Chattooga's largest single drop.

Foothills Trail, Chattooga Valley Segment Map C

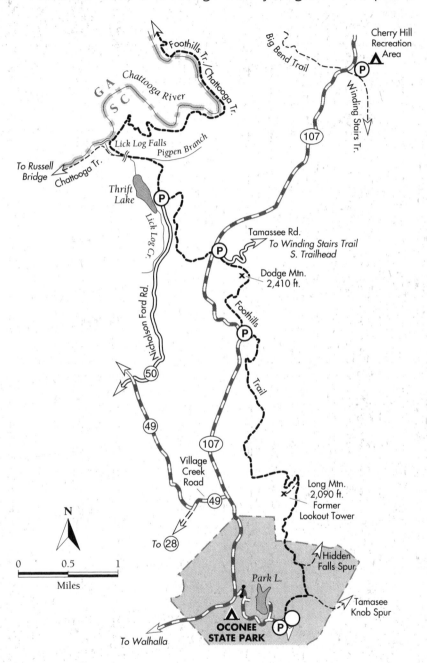

Foothills Tr./Chattooga Tr.

Big Bend Trail

Cherry Hill Recreation Area

Chattooga River

GA
SC

107

Winding Stairs Tr.

Lick Log Falls

Pigpen Branch

To Russell Bridge

Chattooga Tr.

Thrift Lake

P

Lick Log Cr.

Tamassee Rd.
To Winding Stairs Trail
S. Trailhead

P

× Dodge Mtn.
2,410 ft.

Nicholson Ford Rd.

Foothills

P

50

Trail

49

107

Village Creek Road

49

× Long Mtn.
2,090 ft.
Former Lookout Tower

N

0   0.5   1
Miles

To 28

Hidden Falls Spur

Park L.

Tamasee Knob Spur

OCONEE STATE PARK

P

To Walhalla

33

Upper Whitewater Falls. JOHN CLARK PHOTO

The trail next turns away from the river slightly and follows ridges along the side of Round Top Mountain, then returns to ascending and descending along the banks of the river. Mountain laurel, rhododendron, white pines, oaks, maples, tulip poplars, morning glories, and blackberries grow in profusion, and the presence of beavers is occasionally in evidence.

At 5.2 miles past the Big Bend Trail turnoff, the Foothills Trail turns east, away from the river, while the Chattooga Trail continues southeast toward Russell Bridge, 3.7 miles away. Before taking the Foothills Trail fork, you should detour 0.25 mile farther along the Chattooga Trail to enjoy the upper and lower falls of Lick Log Creek.

Proceeding on the Foothills Trail from the Chattooga Trail intersection, you cross Pigpen Branch and Lick Log Creek and pass the parking area at the end of unpaved Nicholson Ford Road (Secondary Road 50). Approaching Dodge Mountain, the Foothills Trail climbs 500 feet from the banks of the Chattooga to the SC 107 crossing, 2.4 miles from the Chattooga Trail intersection.

The Foothills Trail crosses SC 107 at its intersection with unpaved Tamassee Road (Forest Service Road 710) and briefly follows Tamassee Road before heading south. There is a small parking lot on the left (north), about 30 feet along a gravel road, and a larger parking lot about 100 feet from the paved highway. These vehicle access points are 3.6 highway miles north of the entrance to Oconee State Park.

The next couple of miles trek through mixed forest along a ridge on the east side of Dodge Mountain. The path is well shaded, with clear understory and excellent vistas to the east. Although this area was burned severely in 1978, it has recovered nicely. At 1.5 miles from Tamassee Road, the trail emerges briefly at the edge of SC 107 before plunging back into the forest. There is a small parking area here, marked by a mound of gravel.

The trail moves through hardwoods and offers more scenic vistas, including glimpses of Lake Jocassee in the distance. As the trail begins a moderate descent, it passes through mixed oak and hickory stands and plunges into a lush emerald ravine, crossing back and forth over Tamassee Creek and its tributaries. Three of these crossings are over footbridges. Here are breathtaking views of lush mountain laurel and rhododendron.

After 1 mile in the ravine, the trail climbs and follows a ridge on the side of Long Mountain, heading through a mixed forest and reaching a short spur to the 2,080-foot summit, about 4 miles from Tamassee Road. The fire tower at the top of the mountain was removed years ago, but several communications towers have replaced it.

The next stretch descends gradually through mixed hardwoods and pines. When the trail crosses the Oconee State Park boundary and reaches an old logging road, bear left (east) on the road as you emerge from the forest. The trail continues via a set of steps a few yards to the right (south). A sign indicates that Hidden Falls may be reached by continuing east on the logging road. These falls are 1 rugged mile away.

The trail soon passes through a small, galax-filled ravine, then follows level terrain through mixed forest to an intersection with the Tamassee Knob Trail. Tamassee Knob is 1.6 miles away on the left (eastern) fork. The Foothills Trail continues on the right fork for 0.4 mile of level terrain to a paved park road and a large sign marking the western terminus of the Foothills Trail.

Facilities: Water, rest rooms, drink machine at western (Oconee State Park) trailhead; portable toilets and pay phone at eastern trailhead (Bad Creek Hydroelectric Station parking lot).

Lodging and amenities: Campsites are available at Devil's Fork and Oconee state parks and at Cherry Hill Recreation Area and Keowee-Toxaway State Park; primitive camping is allowed at Burrells Ford and various places along the trail. Full services are available at Walhalla, Clemson, and Seneca, South Carolina, and at Cashiers, North Carolina.

For more information: Foothills Trail Conference; Andrew Pickens Ranger District of Sumter National Forest; Duke Power Company; Oconee State Park. See Appendix A: For More Information.

---

2   Chattooga Trail

General description:	A two-day backpack on an undulating trail along the Chattooga River, a pristine National Wild and Scenic River.
General location:	In the northwest corner of the state.
Distance:	15 miles, one way. (11.8 miles south of Burrells Ford Road and 3.2 miles north of Burrells Ford Road)
Difficulty:	Moderate.
Trail conditions:	Conditions are average. Traffic is light to moderate.
Best time to go:	Year-round, though heavy rains can submerge portions of the trail and winter ice makes for precarious footing.
Maps:	Trail Guide, Andrew Pickens Ranger District, Sumter National Forest, Forest Service; Chattooga National Wild and Scenic River, Forest Service; Tamassee, Satolah, and Cashiers USGS quads. See Appendix A: For More Information.
Fees:	None.

Finding the trailhead: If you are following the trail from north to south, drive to the intersection of South Carolina Highway 28 and SC 11 just south of Walhalla. From there, travel north 9.5 miles on SC 28, then take SC 107,

Chattooga Trail

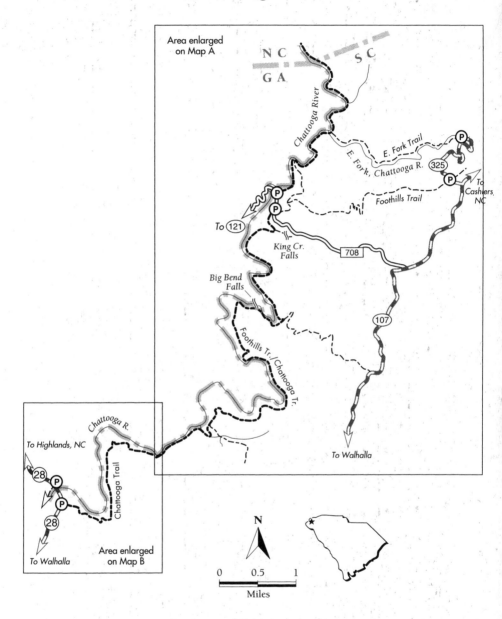

Area enlarged on Map A

NC
GA

SC

Chattooga River

E. Fork Trail

E. Fork, Chattooga R.

P

325

P

To Cashiers, NC

To 121

P

P

Foothills Trail

King Cr. Falls

708

Big Bend Falls

107

Foothills Tr. / Chattooga Tr.

To Walhalla

Chattooga R.

To Highlands, NC

Chattooga Trail

28

P

P

28

To Walhalla

Area enlarged on Map B

N

0   0.5   1

Miles

The Ellicott Rock Area. John Clark photo

Chattooga Trail Map A

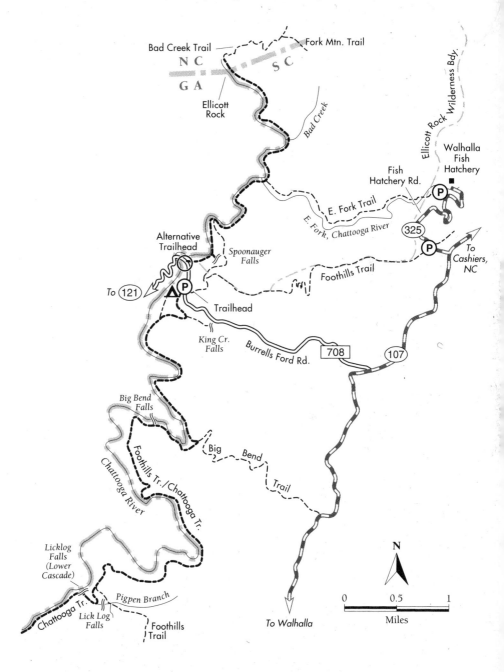

Chattooga Trail Map B

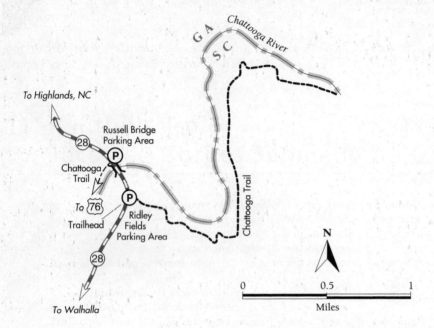

the right fork, and go 10.3 miles. Turn left and follow unpaved Burrells Ford Road (Forest Service Road 708) 3 miles to the Burrells Ford parking lot, on the left. The trailhead for the Chattooga and Foothills trails is at the northeast corner of the parking lot, behind a large brown sign board.

To follow the trail from south to north, go to the Russell Bridge access point on SC 28, at a parking lot just south of Russell Bridge, about 5 miles northwest of the intersection of SC 28 and SC 107.

The best place to reach the upper (northern) portion of the Chattooga Trail is 0.4 mile west from the Burrells Ford parking lot along Burrells Ford Road, at a spot marked by three boulders and a sign pointing to the Ellicott Rock Wilderness Area. Park on the shoulder of the road near the boulders. If you reach the Burrells Ford Bridge, you have gone a few yards too far and missed the trailhead. From here, Ellicott Rock is 3.2 miles.

The hike: The Chattooga is a wild, rushing river with crashing waterfalls, coves lush with mountain laurel, and banks covered in brilliant wildflowers. The Chattooga Trail is a favorite of hikers, who, because boating and rafting is banned along this stretch, share their delight only with other hikers and the occasional fly caster near Burrells Ford. Fans of the movie *Deliverance* may recognize the terrain south of the Russell Bridge, where much of the film's whitewater footage was shot. Despite the large number of rapids on the Chattooga, locations for taking a cool dip abound.

Spoonauger Falls. YVONNE MICHEL PHOTO

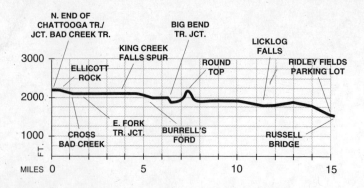

Elevation profile showing, from left to right:
N. END OF CHATTOOGA TR./ JCT. BAD CREEK TR. • BIG BEND TR. JCT. • LICKLOG FALLS • KING CREEK FALLS SPUR • ROUND TOP • RIDLEY FIELDS PARKING LOT • ELLICOTT ROCK • CROSS BAD CREEK • E. FORK TR. JCT. • BURRELL'S FORD • RUSSELL BRIDGE

Vertical axis: 3000, 2000, 1000 FT. Horizontal axis: MILES 0, 5, 10, 15

SOUTHBOUND FROM BURRELLS FORD ROAD:

The trail travels along the Chattooga River for much of the hike, often along the river's banks and sometimes high up on the bluffs. The mountains and cliffs on the Georgia side of the river form a scenic backdrop. You ascend and descend frequently as you cross numerous small streams and wind your way around and through a seemingly endless series of coves and ravines.

Before heading directly to the river you should begin with a detour east along a red-blazed 0.25-mile spur to roaring King Creek Falls, which makes a spectacular 70-foot tumble down a steep granite face into a gorge smothered in mountain laurel and rhododendron.

For the first 8.1 miles south from the Burrells Ford parking lot, the Chattooga Trail runs concurrently with the Foothills Trail. You encounter a camping area about 0.5 mile from the trailhead. After another 2.5 miles, you'll come to the Big Bend Falls, which, with its 15-foot cascade followed by a 15-foot vertical plunge, is the Chattooga River's single largest drop. The trail closely parallels the river, but rambles up and down, moving from water's edge to bluffs and back down again. At some points the trail follows the riverbank so closely that it winds up literally in the river after heavy rain. A number of small bridges cross singing brooks, and sandy beaches entice you to cool your feet.

Immediately past the fork where the Foothills Trail peels off to the left (east) toward Dodge Mountain and Oconee State Park, you reach picturesque Lick Log Falls, two sets of falls on the Lick Log Creek tributary. At the base of the upper falls is a clear, sandy-bottomed, deep-water swimming hole, while at the lower falls the creek hurtles 25 feet over a granite outcrop and into the roaring Chattooga. The area between the two falls offers excellent campsites.

Russell Bridge is 3.7 miles past the Foothills Trail intersection. The Chattooga Trail continues beside the river for another mile, then climbs away as it follows ridges and crosses gullies along the side of Reed Mountain before descending to Ridley Fields parking area, on SC 28 just south of the Russell Bridge. From the parking lot, an old roadbed leads down to a stretch of the river especially favored by fly anglers. One mile south along SC 28 is Russell Homestead, a historic site open to the public.

NORTHBOUND FROM BURRELLS FORD ROAD:

North from the three boulders at Burrells Ford Road, the Chattooga Trail follows the river. After 0.2 mile, a 200-yard spur departs to the right (east) for beautiful Spoonauger Falls. The Chattooga Trail continues north and, 1.5 miles from Burrells Ford Road, crosses a substantial footbridge over the East Fork of the Chattooga River into the Ellicott Rock Wilderness Area. The south side of the footbridge makes a good camping area. North of the footbridge, the Chattooga Trail heads upstream another 1.7 miles to Ellicott Rock, while the East Fork Trail heads right from the footbridge 2.5 miles to the Walhalla Fish Hatchery.

About 0.5 mile farther upriver on the Chattooga Trail, you must choose among several dodgy options in fording Bad Creek. After your crossing, continue along the increasingly rocky pathway toward the end of the Chattooga Trail at Ellicott Rock, near the three-way border separating South Carolina, North Carolina, and Georgia. Ellicott Rock is not a particularly scenic point, but a historic surveying point obscurely marked and easy to miss.

From here, you have several options: You can return to Burrells Ford Road; return to the East Fork Trail and hike to the Walhalla Fish Hatchery; or head east 7.5 miles along the Fork Mountain Trail, to the Sloan Bridge Picnic Area.

Facilities: No rest rooms or drinking water.

Lodging and amenities: Camping is allowed at Burrells Ford Campground and along the trail, except within 50 feet of the river and in the Ellicott Rock Wilderness. Cherry Hill Recreation Area and Oconee State Park have campgrounds with facilities. Most services are available at Walhalla, Seneca, and Clemson, South Carolina, and at Cashiers, North Carolina.

For more information: Andrew Pickens Ranger District of Sumter National Forest. See Appendix A: For More Information.

3   Fork Mountain Trail

General description:	A long day hike in the Ellicott Rock Wilderness Area, along the ridges and through the coves of Fork Mountain, finishing along the Chattooga River.
General location:	North of Walhalla, in the northwest corner of the state.
Distance:	10.9 miles one way.
Difficulty:	Moderate.
Trail conditions:	Conditions are good to average. Traffic is light to moderate.
Best time to go:	Year-round, although the portion along the Chattooga River can be difficult in icy conditions.
Maps:	Trail Guide, Andrew Pickens Ranger District, Sumter National Forest, Forest Service; Ellicott Rock Wilderness, Forest Service; Cashiers and Tamassee, USGS quads. See Appendix A: For More Information.
Fees:	None.

Finding the trailhead: From the intersection of South Carolina Highway 28 and SC 11 south of Walhalla, travel north 9.5 miles on SC 28, then take SC 107, the right (northeast) fork, and go 13.3 miles to Sloan Bridge Picnic Area, on the left (west) just past the right turn onto SC 413. From the picnic area's parking lot, walk north across the highway culvert over the East Fork of the Chattooga River. The sign for the trailhead is at the line of trees on the left (west), immediately past the culvert.

John Clark along the Chattooga River. Yvonne Michel photo

Fork Mountain Trail

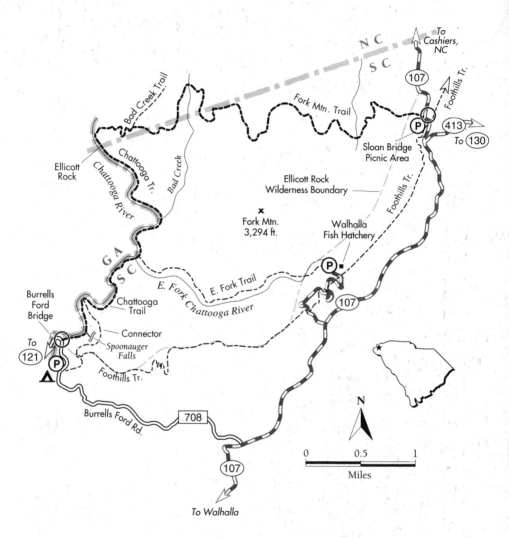

The hike: This hike through the Ellicott Rock Wilderness Area circles the north side of Fork Mountain along the Fork Mountain Trail, then departs from the mountainside via a short stretch of the Bad Creek Trail. The trail finishes along the Chattooga Trail, heading along the Chattooga River past Ellicott Rock and all the way to the bridge at Burrells Ford. The suggested hike provides direct connections to a number of other routes, including the East Fork and Foothills trails in South Carolina and the Bad Creek trail in North Carolina.

Ellicott Rock and the Ellicott Rock Wilderness Area are named for Andrew Ellicott. In 1811, Ellicott surveyed the 35th parallel, which forms the boundary between North Carolina and Georgia. He determined that the

The Chattooga River. John Clark photo

Chattooga River (the boundary between Georgia and South Carolina) crosses the 35th parallel at a certain rock in the river. This rock—now called Ellicott Rock—thus marks the point where the boundaries of South Carolina, North Carolina, and Georgia come together. He inscribed the rock, on the east side of the Chattooga, with an "NC"

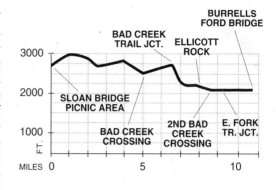

which is now barely perceptible. However, he was a little off in his calculations, and the true tri-state boundary was marked two years later on Commissioners Rock, a few feet to the south (and marked only slightly more legibly, "NC SC LAT 35 AD 1813").

Established in 1975, the Ellicott Rock Wilderness Area contains 9,012 acres in three national forests and three states: Sumter National Forest in South Carolina, Nantahala National Forest in North Carolina, and Chattahoochee National Forest in Georgia. The federal government prohibits logging, motorized vehicles, and other activities which would disturb the natural, pristine character of the area. The truly adventurous who are both experienced in survival and equipped with compasses and topographical maps will find the Ellicott Rock Wilderness a good place to hike cross-country, away from designated trails, and explore the crest and hidden coves of Fork Mountain.

From Sloan Bridge Picnic Area, the Fork Mountain Trail plunges immediately into a sea of mountain laurels, rhododendrons, Fraser magnolias and green ferns, with the canopy being almost tunnel-like in places. Less than 0.5 mile from the trailhead, a superb campsite sits in a rhododendron thicket beside Slatten Branch Creek.

The trail weaves along the flank of Fork Mountain, ascending and descending while darting around and through numerous coves and ravines. Trail maintenance is minimal, and you must negotiate a number of fallen trees. The rust-colored blazes that supposedly mark the trail are few and far between. For the most part, the understory is fairly open, but there are a few segments along sparsely forested high ground where the heavy undergrowth impedes progress. Such difficulties are the tradeoff we make for the solitude of a little-used trail.

White-tailed deer, raccoons, and squirrels inhabit the region, as do reclusive, seldom-seen black bears. Birds include red-breasted nuthatches, red crossbills, ravens, golden-crowned kinglets, robins, and varieties of woodpeckers, warblers, and hawks.

At 6.3 miles, Fork Mountain Trail forks and the hike goes left (west) along a short stretch of the Bad Creek Trail, moving downward 1.2 miles along a steep series of switchbacks to emerge at 2,100 feet of elevation on the

Chattooga Trail, just above the South Carolina–North Carolina–Georgia boundary. (The right fork, also the Bad Creek Trail, carries hikers north 2.3 miles to Bull Pen Road in North Carolina.)

The Chattooga Trail goes south along the Chattooga River past Ellicott Rock, frequently along an uneven, rocky path that crosses small tributaries as it continually ascends on bluffs and descends to the riverbank. At Bad Creek, about 1 mile along, you must choose between following a path a short distance inland and wading the creek or crossing the creek on a large, fallen tree trunk several feet above the Bad Creek rapids as they begin their descent to the Chattooga.

The area between Bad Creek and the East Fork of the Chattooga offers good camping, swimming, and fishing sites, as well as several sandy beaches and great views of the Chattooga River and the bluffs along the Georgia side of the river.

The bridge over the East Fork is 1.9 miles from the intersection of the Bad Creek and Chattooga trails (1.7 miles from Ellicott Rock). Here, you may choose to turn left (east) and hike 2.5 miles up East Fork Trail to the Walhalla Fish Hatchery. You can continue up Fish Hatchery Road 1.7 miles, then north on the Foothills Trail 3.3 miles to return to the Sloan Bridge Picnic Area.

From the East Fork bridge, the hike finishes out in an easy 1.5-mile walk along the Chattooga River to the trailhead just above Burrells Ford Bridge. At a fork 1 mile past the East Fork bridge, you should bear right (southwest) toward the Burrells Ford Bridge, rather than left (east) toward Medlin Mountain, the Foothills Trail, and the Burrells Ford parking area. (If you do bear left, you can walk 1.1 miles to the intersection with the Foothills Trail, then turn northeast and walk 6.6 miles to the Sloan Bridge Picnic Area.) Between this last fork and the trailhead, a 200-yard spur leads east to Spoonauger Falls, a gorgeous cascade that is well worth the short detour.

Facilities: None.

Lodging and amenities: Campsites with facilities are available at Cherry Hill Recreation Area, on SC 107 south of Sloan Bridge, and at Oconee State Park. There are primitive campsites at Burrells Ford Campground, and camping is also allowed along the trail. Most services are available at Walhalla, Seneca, and Clemson, South Carolina, and at Cashiers, North Carolina.

For more information: Andrew Pickens Ranger District of Sumter National Forest. See Appendix A: For More Information.

4   East Fork Trail

General description:	Half a day's hike along the East Fork of the Chattooga River and the Chattooga River itself. Walhalla Fish Hatchery, the enchanting East Fork gorge, and beautiful Spoonauger Falls make this hike a delight.
General location:	North of Walhalla, in the northwest corner of the state.
Distance:	4 miles one way.
Difficulty:	Easy.
Trail conditions:	Conditions are good. Traffic is light to moderate.
Best time to go:	Year-round, though footing can be hazardous in icy conditions.
Maps:	Trail Guide, Andrew Pickens Ranger District, Sumter National Forest, Forest Service; Ellicott Rock Wilderness, Forest Service; Tamassee USGS quad. See Appendix A: For More Information.
Fees:	None.

Finding the trailhead: From the intersection of South Carolina Highway 28 and SC 11 just south of Walhalla, travel north 9.5 miles on SC 28, then take SC 107, right (northeast) 12 miles to Fish Hatchery Road (Secondary Road 325), on the left (west). Follow Fish Hatchery Road 2 miles to its terminus at the Walhalla Fish Hatchery parking lot. The East Fork Trail begins at the bridge over the East Fork of the Chattooga, just past the Fish Hatchery and the picnic area.

The Chattooga River. YVONNE MICHEL PHOTO

East Fork Trail

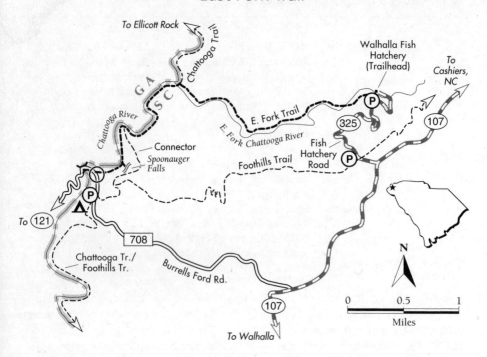

To reach the trailhead at Burrells Ford, return to SC 107 and drive south 1.2 miles. Turn right (west) and follow unpaved Burrells Ford Road (Forest Service Road 708) 3.4 miles to the small sign on the right indicating the way to Ellicott Rock Wilderness Area. This spot, marked by three large boulders, is 0.4 mile past a large parking area on the left. Park on the shoulder of the road near the boulders. If you reach the Burrells Ford Bridge, you have missed the trailhead and gone a few yards too far.

The hike: The East Fork Trail leads through a lush, fertile gorge filled with hemlocks, mountain laurels, winterberries, sweet pepper-bushes, and unusually large white pines. Except for short distances at the two ends of the trail, the entire length of the East Fork Trail lies within the southernmost reaches of the Ellicott Rock Wilderness Area, a pristine 9,012-acre preserve on national forest lands closed to logging, vehicles, and activities which would disturb the area's natural state. This hike provides an easy walk along the playful, scenic East Fork of the Chattooga River, then down the majestic Chattooga itself, with a short side trip to Spoonauger Falls. Alternatives include a round-trip hike along the East Fork, from the Walhalla Fish Hatchery to the Chattooga River and back, and a long loop utilizing a portion of the Foothills Trail. Ellicott Rock, on the Chattooga Trail 1.7 miles north of the intersection of the East Fork and Chattooga trails, can be added as a side trip to any hike along the East Fork Trail.

A bridge over the East Fork of Chattooga River. YVONNE MICHEL PHOTO

The Walhalla Fish Hatchery at the East Fork Trailhead is worth a visit. Operated by the South Carolina Department of Natural Resources, it is open to the public from 8 A.M. to 4 P.M. daily, including weekends. In addition to the large outdoor tanks where the growing fish can be easily seen, visitors can view an interpretive display.

The East Fork is a large, swift, rocky stream that dances over rocks and around boulders along the south side of the East Fork Trail, which gradually descends about 500 feet over its length, fording a tumbling tributary at the foot of low, picturesque falls about 1 mile from the trailhead, and joining the Chattooga Trail a few feet from the banks of the Chattooga River, at 2.5 miles.

At the junction with the Chattooga Trail, you may choose to turn right (north) and hike 1.7 miles to Ellicott Rock at the South Carolina–North Carolina–Georgia border.

We suggest you turn left (south) here and cross the long and substantial foot bridge over the East Fork to continue toward Burrells Ford Road, 1.5 miles away. The drooping hemlocks in the vicinity of the foot bridge shelter a number of spacious campsites.

This section of the Chattooga Trail alternates between bluffs high above the river and walks beside sandy riverside beaches. Spectacular views to forests of mountain laurel across the river in Georgia sometimes reveal themselves.

After 1 mile, the main fork of the Chattooga Trail heads to the left (east) toward a junction with the Foothills Trail 1.1 miles away. (Fish Hatchery Road is another 3.3 miles northeast from the Foothills junction; Burrells Ford parking area is 0.6 mile southwest of the Foothills junction.) Our suggested route continues on an alternate Chattooga Trail route, down the right (southwest) fork toward Burrells Ford Bridge, 0.5 mile south. In addition to being the shorter option, this route provides an even greater benefit: Spoonauger Falls.

About 0.3 mile along the right fork a sign indicates that Spoonauger Falls is on a spur 200 yards to the left (east). Take this spur, which follows switchbacks along a cascading series of small falls on Spoonauger Creek before climbing to the base of Spoonauger Falls, a spectacular crashing cascade also known, for reasons that are self-evident, as Rock Cliff Falls.

Return to the Chattooga Trail, cross Spoonauger Creek, and continue 0.2 mile south to the trailhead at Burrells Ford Road, just east of Burrells Ford Bridge.

Two pleasant options are available for hikers with only one vehicle: a 5-mile round-trip hike on the East Fork Trail from the Walhalla Fish Hatchery to the Chattooga River and back; or a 9.6-mile loop following the East Fork Trail for 2.5 miles, the Chattooga Trail for 2.1 miles, the Foothills Trail for 3.3 miles, and Fish Hatchery Road for 1.7 miles. A 3.4-mile round-trip detour to Ellicott Rock can be added to any of these hikes.

Facilities: There are rest rooms and drinking water at the Walhalla Fish Hatchery. The entire facility has good barrier-free access and even offers a barrier-free pier for fishing on the East Fork. There are no facilities at Burrells Ford.

Lodging and amenities: Campsites with facilities are available at Cherry Hill Recreation Area and at Oconee State Park. There are primitive campsites at Burrells Ford Campground, and camping is allowed along the trail. Most services are available at Walhalla, Seneca, and Clemson, South Carolina, and at Cashiers, North Carolina.

For more information: Andrew Pickens Ranger District of Sumter National Forest. See Appendix A: For More Information.

5   Big Bend Trail

General description:	An easy day hike through beautiful rhododendron and mountain laurel glens to the Chattooga River and powerful Big Bend Falls.
General location:	Northeast of Walhalla, in the northwest corner of the state.
Distance:	6.8 miles one way.
Difficulty:	Easy to moderate.
Trail conditions:	Conditions are fair to good. Traffic is light to moderate.
Best time to go:	Year-round, though footing can be hazardous in icy conditions.
Maps:	Trail Guide, Andrew Pickens Ranger District, Sumter National Forest, Forest Service; Tamassee USGS quad. See Appendix A: For More Information.
Fees:	None.

Finding the trailhead: From the intersection of South Carolina Highway 28 and SC 11 just south of Walhalla, travel north 9.5 miles on SC 28, then take SC 107 right (northeast) 8.8 miles to Cherry Hill Recreation Area, on the right (east). Just south of the entrance to the recreation area, look for the trailhead on the left (west) side of SC 107. It is marked by a small sign across the highway from the Winding Stairs Trailhead.

To reach the Burrells Ford parking lot trailhead from Cherry Hill Recreation Area, take SC 107 north for 1.5 miles. Turn left (west) and follow unpaved Burrells Ford Road (Forest Service Road 708) 3 miles to the parking area on the left (south). The trailhead for the Chattooga and Foothills trails is at the northeast corner of the parking lot, behind a large brown sign board.

The hike: This trail connects the Winding Stairs Trail and Cherry Hill Recreation Area with the Chattooga and Foothills trails, which run concurrently along this section of the Chattooga River. Big Bend Trail can be hiked in a number of ways: a 6.4-mile round-trip visit to Big Bend Falls, a 6.3-mile hike to the Burrells Ford area, a 10.3-mile partial loop to the intersection of SC

Big Bend Trail

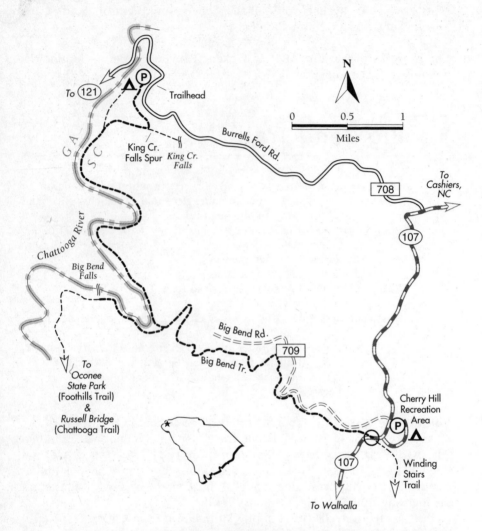

107 and Tamassee Road via the Foothills Trail, and several other variations through connections on the Chattooga and Foothills trails. For more than half its length, Big Bend Trail runs fairly close to, and occasionally within sight of, unpaved Big Bend Road (Forest Service Road 709).

Marked by red blazes, Big Bend Trail plunges immediately into a cool, inviting forest of hemlocks, white pines, oaks, rhododendrons, mountain laurels, galax, and thick, green ferns.

Passing a gurgling spring, crossing Crane Creek on a sturdy footbridge, and circling the headwaters of Pigpen Branch, the trail traverses numerous brooks and ridges and dodges around a succession of ravines. The trail

Big Bend Falls. JOHN CLARK PHOTO

descends gently along a well-marked, well-shaded path crowded with mountain laurel. Footing is easy, and you begin to catch glimpses of Georgia's mountains in the distance, on the other side of the Chattooga. Eventually, the trail drops into a lush stream basin, following the stream past a small camping area to the intersection with the Chattooga/Foothills Trail.

A short distance to the left (south) of this intersection, a path leads from the trail down to the U-shaped turn in the Chattooga River known as Big Bend. The river flows swiftly here, and the spot is an ideal place for picnicking or fly fishing from the smooth boulders. The mountain laurel on the Georgia side of the river provides a beautiful backdrop.

Back on the trail, 0.5 mile south of the path down to the Big Bend, a ridge 100 feet above the river provides scenic vistas of roaring Big Bend Falls. The water cascades 15 feet on a 30-degree slope, then plummets over a 15-foot vertical drop. This is the largest drop on the Chattooga River. The hydraulic created by the plunge of the huge volume of water exhibits tremendous power.

The 3.1-mile hike north from the falls to the Burrells Ford parking area is delightful, the trail alternating gently between ridge and river bank as it heads upstream. The bounty of mountain laurel and rhododendron continues, and blackberries and partridgeberries decorate the way. There are many smooth boulders and sandy beaches to entice waders and swimmers. Anglers are seen more frequently as the trail nears the Burrells Ford Campground.

At a fork alongside the river, 0.25 mile from the campground, you can choose to bear left (northwest) through the camping area and on to the parking area, a distance of about 1 mile. Alternatively, you can bear right (northeast) and head to King Creek Falls, a detour well worth the time and effort of the additional 0.5-mile ascent.

The Chattooga River. JOHN CLARK PHOTO

Glorious King Creek Falls cascades 70 feet into a laurel-blanketed gorge. A sandy beach allows easy wading, and a fallen tree trunk provides a bridge and bench where you can enjoy the spectacle while luxuriating in the misty spray. Burrells Ford parking area is slightly less than 1 mile farther along the Foothills/Chattooga Trail.

Facilities: Cherry Hill Recreation Area has rest rooms and drinking water.

Lodging and amenities: Campsites with facilities are available at Cherry Hill Recreation Area and at Oconee State Park. There are primitive campsites at Burrells Ford Campground and along the Chattooga River. Most services are available at Walhalla, Seneca, and Clemson, South Carolina, and at Cashiers, North Carolina.

For more information: Andrew Pickens Ranger District of Sumter National Forest. See Appendix A: For More Information.

6   Winding Stairs Trail

General description:	A pleasant, easy walk through a forest filled with rhododendron and mountain laurel. The trail passes Miuka Falls, one of the state's most impressive cascades.
General location:	Northeast of Walhalla, in the northwest corner of the state.
Distance:	3.5 miles one way.
Difficulty:	Easy when hiked north to south; moderate from south to north.
Trail conditions:	Conditions are good. Traffic is light.
Best time to go:	Year-round.
Maps:	Trail Guide, Andrew Pickens Ranger District, Sumter National Forest, Forest Service; Tamassee USGS quad. See Appendix A: For more information.
Fees:	None.

Finding the trailhead: To reach the northern trailhead from the intersection of South Carolina Highway 28 and SC 11 just south of Walhalla, travel north 9.5 miles on SC 28, then take SC 107, the right fork, and go 8.8 miles to Cherry Hill Recreation Area, on the right. The trailhead is on the right (east) side of the highway, just south of the entrance to the recreation area.

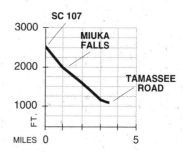

Winding Stairs Trail

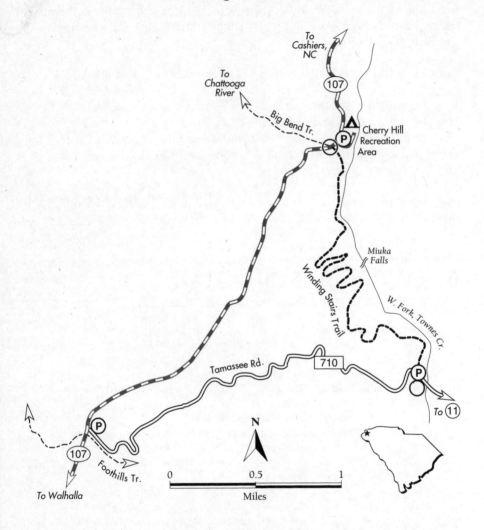

To reach the southern trailhead from the entrance to Cherry Hill Recreation Area, drive south on SC 107 for 3 miles and turn left (east) on unpaved Tamassee Road (Forest Service Road 710). The trailhead is a small parking area 2.5 miles on the left (north), across the road from a clearing surrounded by large rocks, just west of Townes Creek.

The hike: This is a great mountain hike for beginners, a pleasant morning or afternoon outing, or a good warm-up for more demanding trails. Offering views of one of the state's prettiest waterfalls, Winding Stairs Trail connects with the 2.7-mile Big Bend Trail to form an interesting 6.2-mile eastward spur of the Chattooga and Foothills trails.

Author John Clark on the Winding Stairs Trail. KATHY CLARK PHOTO

The trail moves through a mostly hardwood forest of red oaks, post oaks, hickories, tulip poplars, white pines, and white cedars; the relatively open understory is decorated with a multitude of wildflowers and shrubs. The forest is alive with ravens, warblers, indigo buntings, common yellowthroats, yellow-breasted chats, vireos, and thrushes, as well as white-tailed deer, squirrels, and feral hogs.

From the northern trailhead off SC 107, the trail heads south as a path through the woods, but for the most part it follows old logging roads that offer gentle grades and easy footing. Just south of the trailhead, on the right, is an old cemetery clearing where Native American artifacts have been found.

The trail soon comes to parallel the rushing cascades and sounds of the West Fork of Townes Creek, which flows swiftly on the left. After 1.2 miles on the trail, you arrive at Miuka Falls (also known as Cheohee Falls), a 70-foot cascade followed by a smaller cascade 50 feet downstream. You'll need to leave the trail to get the best view of the falls.

The trail zigzags its way down the hillside, requiring you to cross a number of musical brooks and trek through cool, magical coves filled with mountain laurel. In winter, you can look southeast for views of Lake Cherokee, fed by Townes Creek. After 3 miles, the trail levels out and ends 0.5 mile farther along at the southern trailhead, a small parking area on the north shoulder of Tamassee Road.

Facilities: Cherry Hill Recreation Area has rest rooms and drinking water.

Lodging and amenities: Campsites with facilities are available at Cherry Hill Recreation Area and at Oconee State Park. There are primitive campsites at Burrells Ford Campground and along the Chattooga River. Most services are available at Walhalla, Seneca, and Clemson, South Carolina, and at Cashiers, North Carolina.

For more information: Andrew Pickens Ranger District of Sumter National Forest. See Appendix A: For More Information.

7   Oconee State Park

General description:	A day's worth of excellent mountain hiking opportunities in a very popular state park. Oconee offers brilliant fall colors, spectacular views from Tamassee Knob, the remains of a historic waterwheel, pretty mountain lakes, wildlife, wildflowers, and appealing terrain.
General location:	Northeast of Walhalla, in the northwest corner of the state.
Distance:	Recommended Oconee Trail/Old Waterwheel Trail loop is 4.5 miles (about 3 to 4 hours); Oconee Trail is 2.5 miles; Old Waterwheel Trail is 2.5 miles; Tamassee Knob Trail is 4.2 miles round-trip (3–4 hours); Hidden Falls Trail is 4 miles round-trip (3–4 hours).
Difficulty:	Moderate.
Trail conditions:	Conditions are good. Traffic is light to moderate.
Best time to go:	Year-round.
Maps:	Oconee State Park brochure; Tamassee and Walhalla USGS quads. See Appendix A: For more information.
Fees:	$2 per vehicle parking fee.

Finding the trailhead: From the intersection of South Carolina Highway 28 and SC 11 south of Walhalla, head north on SC 28 for 9.5 miles. At the fork, go right (northeast) on SC 107; the park entrance is another 2.4 miles, on the right (east) side.

Upon passing the park's entrance gate, bear right (south). The trailhead for the Oconee and Old Waterwheel trails is at the park's campground. The trailhead for the Foothills Trail, toward the southeastern end of the park, provides access to the Hidden Falls and Tamassee Knob trails. To reach this trailhead from the campground, head east (away from the park office), and bear right (southeast) at the fork. The Foothills Trailhead, identified by a sign, is a few yards farther on the left (north). Park in the small parking lot

Oconee State Park

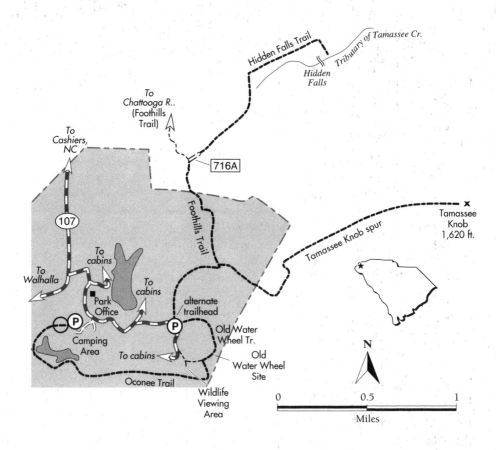

10 yards past the trailhead, on the right (south). The Hidden Falls and Tamassee Knob trails are spurs of the Foothills Trail.

The hikes: Oconee State Park was created in the 1930s, and its rustic facilities bear the stamp of the efforts of the Civilian Conservation Corps (CCC). The park offers four major trails, each with its own special attractions. The Oconee and Old Waterwheel trails are entirely within the park's boundaries, and are treated as one long trail. The Tamassee Knob and Hidden Falls trails are spurs of the Foothills Trail, each leading to its own namesake natural feature.

At 1,165 acres, Oconee State Park encloses two mountain lakes. Although the landscape is not conspicuously mountainous, the lovely rolling terrain makes for surprisingly challenging hiking. The park is open from November to March, 7 A.M. to 7 P.M., and from April to October, 7 A.M. to 9 P.M.

The Oconee Trail starts at the amphitheater in the park's campground. The trail is very distinct, being frequently marked with both green blazes and small white signs inscribed with "OT" in the style of a skeleton key. The trail passes the second of the park's two lakes and crosses the dam. If you come in the morning, you may see fairy mists dancing on the surface of the lake. On the other side of the lake, turn right.

This trail was constructed by Boy Scouts. It dives into every hollow, then climbs out again. This is very fun, but it's also a workout. The trail crosses a path which leads back to the campground.

The next trail crossing provides another opportunity to circle back to the park. Go left (west) to return to the park road. The trail to the right (east) is unmarked and follows a ridge. Along this way, there is a fabulous view of the surrounding countryside about 100 feet from the junction, well worth a short detour.

Continuing along the Oconee Trail, you descend from the ridge on a series of switchbacks. The trail makes a T junction at a sign that points left (west) or right (east) to the orange-blazed Old Waterwheel Trail. To complete the Oconee Trail, go left; you'll come out on the park road next to cabin 7. From this point, you have to hike back to the trailhead on the park road—continuing on the Old Waterwheel Trail is much more fun.

The Old Waterwheel Trail descends on stairs made from railroad ties. Quickly, you reach the bottom, where a sign for the old water wheel site points to the right. This is an enjoyable setting, effectively shaded by rhododendrons. The water wheel is gone (relocated to park's swimming lake), but most of the rest of the structure still stands. The water wheel was used to pump drinking water a distance of 1 mile to the CCC crews building the park.

The trail continues from the turnoff for the water wheel. The stream that turned the water wheel runs through, and frequently under, interesting rock formations. The trail crosses the stream on a bridge constructed from railroad ties and goes straight up again. At the first fork, turn left (west). (To the right is a dirt road, across which is one of the largest, most twisted white oaks you will ever see.)

The trail continues descending and rising with steady frequency. Eventually, while still barreling over hill and dale, the difficulty eases off a little. For a brief span near its end, the trail is blazed both orange and green. It comes out adjacent to the Oconee State Park terminus of the Foothills Trail. Scarlet oaks are particularly plentiful in the park and are prime contributors to the spectacular fall colors seen here.

Begin on the Foothills Trail to hike either the Tamassee Knob Trail or the Hidden Falls Trail. The Foothills Trail originates in mixed, new-growth forest. After 0.4 mile, a sign indicates that the white-blazed Foothills Trail continues on the left (north) fork. Bear right (east) and follow the rust-colored blazes of the Tamassee Trail toward Tamassee Knob.

The well-maintained Tamassee Knob Trail moves gradually into a more mature hardwood forest, with a number of large, old-growth trees in the cove on the left (north) as the trail leads out of Oconee State Park and onto a ridge in the adjacent national forest.

Mountain laurel at the park entrance. YVONNE MICHEL PHOTO

The earth slopes dramatically away from both sides of this ridge. The trees are widely spaced, with no obscuring canopy or understory, and the vistas on both sides are outstanding. The right (south) side of the trail presents attractive views of the South Carolina foothills as they descend into the plains and valleys beyond.

Past the ridge, the trail moves along the very steep southeast side of Tamassee Knob. The trail rises as it approaches the peak of the granite outcropping that is the "knob," reached after 2.1 miles of gentle ascent and descent. From the knob, a spectacular view opens out across the Tamassee Creek valley, stretching far north to the Blue Ridge Mountains of North Carolina.

Access to the Hidden Falls Trail also begins along the Foothills Trail. After 1 mile of hiking, the Foothills Trail crosses Forest Service Road 716A (closed), while Hidden Falls Trail turns right. After about 0.1 mile on the Hidden Falls Trail, a sign points to the left (north). The trail is quite distinct and easily identifiable without the sign.

The Hidden Falls Trail's yellow blazes are not numerous but since there are no turnoffs this is not much of a problem. This trail, carved into the hillsides, winds along ridges and in and out of ravines. Northern red oaks, chestnut oaks, and tulip poplars dominate. There are very good winter views, although footing is difficult in icy conditions. Hidden Falls is about 1 mile northeast of the Foothills Trail turnoff, but this mile is rugged. The falls are in a delightful glen and as secluded as their name implies.

Facilities: Water, drink machine, rest rooms.

Lodging and amenities: Oconee State Park offers a 150-site campground (including 10 walk-in campsites), 19 cabins (reservations usually needed far in advance), a park store, and swimming. Lodging and most services are available at Walhalla, Seneca, and Clemson.

For more information: Oconee State Park. See Appendix A: For More Information.

8   Blue Ridge Railroad Historical Trail

General description:	A shady day hike from Stumphouse Mountain to the outskirts of Walhalla along an uncompleted nineteenth-century railbed. The hike features the remains of tunnels, a dramatic gorge, beautiful mountain laurel, wildflowers and berries in season, and good winter views.
General location:	North of Walhalla, in the northwest corner of the state.
Distance:	6.5 miles one way.
Difficulty:	Moderate to strenuous.
Trail conditions:	Conditions are fair to poor. Traffic is light.
Best time to go:	Year-round.
Maps:	Walhalla USGS quad. See Appendix A: For More Information.
Fees:	None.

Finding the trailhead: To reach the northwestern trailhead, follow South Carolina Highway 28 north from Walhalla. After 5.5 miles, immediately beyond Yellow Branch Picnic Area (on the left), is Stumphouse Tunnel Park, on the right (east). Turn into the park and go 0.4 mile; turn right (south) for the Issaqueena Falls parking area, the northwestern trailhead.

To reach the southeastern trailhead, take SC 28 north from Walhalla and turn right (east) on Pickett Post Road (SC 181). Follow Pickett Post Road east until you reach the convenience store at the intersection of Pickett Post Road and White Cut Road (Secondary Road 174). This is probably the best place to park. Walk 0.2 mile west, back on Pickett Post Road, then turn right (north) onto Frog Pond Lane, where the trail begins.

The hike: The Blue Ridge Railroad was the grand dream of South Carolina statesman John C. Calhoun, who was a member of the original surveying team. The idea was to link the port of Charleston with the farms and burgeoning cities of the Midwest. The Civil War intervened, and the railroad was never completed. Today, its greatest monument, Stumphouse Mountain Tunnel (which wasn't completed either), has been permanently sealed due to danger to visitors from falling rock. Although the railroad was never built, the trail along the railroad bed endures, and offers fine hiking year-round. The trail, developed in 1976, has fallen into disrepair, and though the Blue Ridge Council of the Boy Scouts of America, which now maintains the trail, has made great strides in rebuilding and re-marking it, there are still some confusing spots. Except for the short portion in Stumphouse Tunnel Park, the entire trail is on private property.

The Blue Ridge Railroad Historical Trail starts just above Issaqueena Falls, in Stumphouse Tunnel Park (maintained by the Pendleton District Commission).

Blue Ridge Railroad Historical Trail

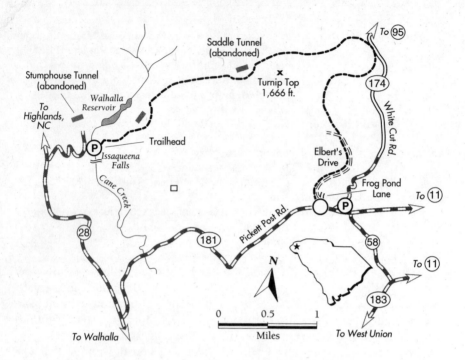

If time permits, by all means explore the beautiful 100-foot cascade of Issaqueena Falls. Legend says that Issaqueena, an Indian woman married to an Englishman who was captured by the Cherokees, escaped from her captors and, in her flight, leapt over the precipice. She fell only a short distance, and eluded capture by hiding under the highest overhang, a spot reached in less dramatic fashion these days via a short trail. This trail runs 0.2 mile from the parking area down to the bottom of Issaqueena Falls.

From the northwestern trailhead at Stumphouse Tunnel Park, take the footbridge across Cane Creek. Before the waterfall overlook turn left (northeast) and hike steeply uphill on a clay track through rhododendrons. At the top, the trail turns sharply right (east), but levels off for a good distance. A gorge to the right of the trail offers good views.

The trail is marked with yellow blazes, red ribbons, and badges that resemble red-on-white rail-crossing signs. For its first 2 miles, this is a very easy trail, but do not be deceived. The railway was intended to follow a ridgeline, and gaps and gorges in the ridgeline were to be filled in with boulders and bridges. However, the Blue Ridge Railroad was never completed, and the gaps were never filled in. Thus, you are afforded the opportunity to scramble up and down a good number of these gaps as the hike continues.

Trees include oak (mainly chesnut and chinkapin), maple, pignut hickory, tulip poplar, sassafras, pine, black walnut, locust, rhododendron, mountain laurel, dogwood, and sourwood. One of the more valuable timber trees in the world, princess-tree (royal paulownia), overhangs the trail; it's known for its elephant-ear leaves. Flora underneath the trees include trailing arbutus, elderberries, asters, wild hydrangea, Indian pink, honeysuckle, nettles, and snakeroot. Some compensation for the difficulty of the trail comes in the form of blackberries and blueberries, in season.

Birds you may encounter include red-eyed vireos, downy and pileated woodpeckers, rufous-sided towhees, quail, and chickadees. Box turtles wander onto the trail, and white-tailed deer are plentiful.

About 0.5 mile from the trailhead, you can see the Middle Tunnel, filled with water and almost out of sight, off to the left (north) of the trail. About 2.1 miles from the trailhead, Saddle Tunnel, also filled with water, begins. The trail skirts the tunnel on the left (south) to climb Saddle Mountain, reaching the north end of Saddle Tunnel at 2.6 miles. The trail follows a rolling railbed along the flank of Turnip Top Mountain, on the right (south), emerging at unpaved White Cut Road (SR 174) at 3.6 miles. Turn right (south) on White Cut Road and walk about 0.1 mile. At the yellow-blazed tree stump on the right, turn southwest and leave the road.

The path quickly veers west (right). (Going straight ahead deadends you in a field). The next 2 miles are the most arduous of the hike, as the trail climbs up and down through numerous deep gaps in the railbed. The trail crosses many property lines, indicated by barbed wire, and, in one case, a marker resembling a tombstone.

The trail gradually rises until the 5-mile mark, where it skirts the flanks of an 80-foot gorge. This is a glorious place, but don't even think of coming here at dusk or after dark, because the trail runs literally at the brink of a steep cliff. The trail turns right from the gorge and continues up and down for the next 1 mile or so. Finally it levels off and becomes a defined road.

At a private residence at 6.1 miles, the trail becomes Elbert's Drive, a red dirt road. Follow this road 0.4 mile south until it comes out on Frog Pond Lane, less than 0.1 mile from Pickett Post Road.

The Blue Ridge Railroad Trail originally ran all the way into Walhalla, but suburban development has swallowed up the last leg of the trail.

Facilities: No rest rooms, but there are picnic facilities at Stumphouse Tunnel Park.

Lodging and amenities: Oconee State Park and Cherry Hill Recreation Area have campsites with facilities. Walhalla has motels, bed-and-breakfasts, and restaurants. Other services can be found at Clemson and Seneca.

For more information: Pendleton District Commission. See Appendix A: For More Information.

9 Oconee Station State Historic Site

General description:	A short, easy hike from the historic Oconee Station through woods and wildflowers to a lovely waterfall.
General location:	Near Walhalla, in the northwest corner of the state.
Distance:	3 miles round trip.
Difficulty:	Easy.
Trail conditions:	Conditions are good. Traffic is light to moderate.
Best time to go:	Year-round.
Maps:	Walhalla USGS quad. See Appendix A: For More Information.
Fees:	None.

Finding the trailhead: From the intersection of South Carolina Highway 28 and SC 11 just south of Walhalla, take SC 11 (also known as the Cherokee Foothills Scenic Highway) northeast 6.3 miles. Turn left (northwest) onto Secondary Road 95 (Oconee Station Road). Oconee Station State Historic Site is 4 miles ahead, on the right (east). The recommended trailhead is at the site of Oconee Station, 200 feet back up the driveway from the parking area. It is well marked. To shorten the hike (or when the park is closed), proceed on SR 95 for 0.2 mile past the Oconee Station site and you will see a small parking area on the left (west).

The hike: Oconee Station Historic Site is open from 9 A.M. to 6 P.M. from Thursday to Sunday, March through December. It is closed January and February. The hike begins at the old structures that comprise Oconee Station. Built around the turn of the 19th century, Oconee Station features the oldest building by European settlers in Oconee County. There are in fact two historic structures here: a blockhouse (built in 1792) and a trading post (built in 1805). The garrison during its brief lifetime was entrusted with the dual task of protecting the settlers from the Indians and protecting the Indians from the settlers.

The trail sports an array of wildflowers not easily equaled, particularly in the springtime. Excellent populations of pink lady's slipper orchids are found near the trail. Relatively rare plants in the area include yellow lady's slipper and horse balm.

From Oconee Station, follow the trail toward Station Cove Falls. Shortly after the trail begins, you'll see the foundation of an old building to the left. State Park Service historians have yet to determine what the building was; it may have been the fort's powder magazine. The trail descends to a manmade pond where wild azaleas, deer moss, and spike moss thrive. Park personnel built a new trail around the pond in 1998. You can take either fork and you will wind up at Station Cove Falls; just follow the signs. If you decide to cross the dam (i.e., take the right fork), you will see many beaver slides.

Oconee Station State Historic Site

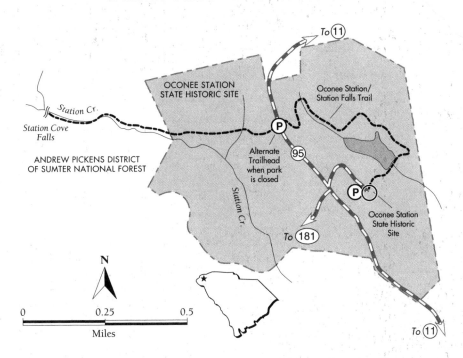

All the trees near Oconee Station are new growth, having begun life around the time of World War II. The felled pines represent an attempt to contain the Southern pine beetle; there was a very bad outbreak of this pest in 1995. The trail makes a big loop to avoid the worst devastation. A pile of bricks the trail passes was once the chimney of a tenant farmer's house.

After roughly 1 mile, the trail crosses SR 95, passing the small parking area noted above. On the west side of the road, the wildflowers become more numerous. To the left (south) of the trail is a beaver-made swamp, dominated by alders.

The trail follows a stream, then crosses it over rocks. Station Cove Falls is just ahead. The trail runs right up beside the waterfall, a scenic cascade that tumbles 60 feet over a rock ledge. Return the way you came.

Facilities: Rest rooms, drinking water.

Lodging and amenities: Camp sites with facilities are available at Oconee State Park, Devil's Fork State Park, and Keowee-Toxaway State Natural Area. Other services, including bed-and-breakfast and budget accommodations, can be found at the pleasant town of Walhalla, as well as at Seneca and Clemson.

For more information: Oconee State Station Historic Site, Andrew Pickens Ranger District of Sumter National Forest. See Appendix A: For More Information.

10 Lee Falls

General description:	Half a day's hike to one of South Carolina's most beautiful and seldom-visited waterfalls.
General location:	North of Walhalla, at the northwest corner of the state.
Distance:	3 miles round trip.
Difficulty:	Moderate, with some very difficult stretches.
Trail conditions:	Conditions are average to poor. Traffic is light.
Best time to go:	Year-round.
Maps:	*Trail Guide, Andrew Pickens Ranger District*, Sumter National Forest, National Forest Service; Tamassee USGS quad. See Appendix A: For More Information.
Fees:	None.

Finding the trailhead: From West Union, just east of Walhalla, take South Carolina Highway 11 northeast 7.2 miles. Turn left (north) onto Secondary Road 172. After 1.4 miles, turn left (northwest) onto SR 375. Turn left (west) after 1.1 miles onto SR 95. After 0.5 mile, turn right (northwest) onto Jumping Branch Road (County Highway 9). Look for unpaved Forest Service Road 715A on the left (west) about 1.3 miles later. Proceed along FS 715A for 1.5 miles, until you reach a culvert over Tamassee Creek. The trail departs from a small parking area on the right, just before the culvert.

The hike: From the trailhead, follow the path alongside rocky, playful Tamassee Creek. The trail leaves and rejoins the creek several times, passing four Forest Service experimental fields. At the last field, the trail can become overgrown in late summer. Bear right (northwest) and stick near the forest edge, and you will have no trouble holding to the trail.

Much of the trail follows an old roadbed. Where the road first crosses the creek, you must ford. In most conditions, you should be able to get across with dry feet, especially if you cross over a fallen tree that bridges the creek.

Fallen trees occasionally necessitate short detours from the otherwise clear trail. Unfortunately, the last 0.25 mile or so is rather indistinct. At this point, simply continue upstream (and uphill) until you reach the viewing spots for the uppermost portion of the waterfall. Exercise due caution, however, because the footing can be treacherous. In the final portion of the ascent you must clamber over moss-covered boulders, around tangles of forest debris, and through slippery mud.

Tamassee Creek drops 100 feet in four tiers to form Lee Falls. A modest set of lower falls serves as a prelude to the splendid main cascade, which falls 50 feet from a mighty granite cliff. Contributing to the ambiance is the rhododendron- and mountain laurel–dominated mountain cove into which the falls are tucked. Sunlight does not penetrate all the way into the falls, and there is a darkness about the rocks.

Lee Falls

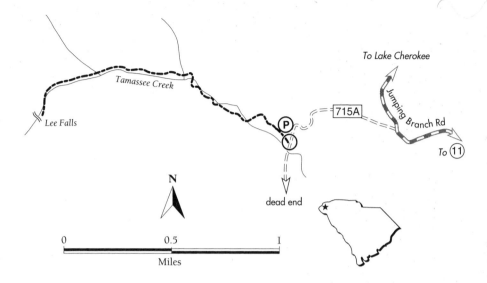

The Lee Falls area, especially the area of the cove within the waterfall's spray, is noted for wildflowers and a variety of sedges and mosses. Plant life includes wild geraniums, halberd-leaf violets, silver bells, phlox, yellow mandarins, perfoliate bellworts, May apples, rue anemones, showy orchis, Canada violets, and fringed phacelia. Many of these are usually found considerably farther north.

This is an excellent area for migratory songbirds, including numerous wood warblers, tanagers, and thrushes. You are also likely to see a large number of migratory raptors, especially broad-winged hawks. If you are lucky, you might also see peregrine falcons and bald eagles.

Lee Falls has long been considered one of the most beautiful waterfalls in this area of the state. Robert Mills, South Carolina architect and designer of the Washington Monument, remarked favorably upon the falls in 1826, but also complained about the difficulty of getting to them. Lee Falls are still a challenge to reach, but more than worth the effort.

Just below the waterfall, on the other side of the stream from the trail, is the remains of what legend says was a gold-smelting operation. Historians say it was more likely a lime kiln.

To finish the hike, retrace your path back to the trailhead.

Facilities: None.

Lodging and amenities: Camp sites are available at Oconee State Park and Cherry Hill Recreation Area. Primitive camping is allowed along the trail;

you must first obtain a permit from the Andrew Pickens Ranger District. Other services, including bed-and-breakfast and budget accommodations, can be found at the pleasant town of Walhalla, as well as at Seneca and Clemson.

For more information: Andrew Pickens Ranger District of Sumter National Forest. See Appendix A: For More Information.

11 Foothills Trail, Jocassee Gorges Segment

General description:	A challenging three-day journey around the north end of Lake Jocassee. Scenic waterfalls, steep-sided river gorges, lush vegetation, and solitude are among the attractions of the Jocassee Gorges.
General location:	Northeast of Walhalla in the northwest corner of the state.
Distance:	31 miles one way.
Difficulty:	Moderate to strenuous.
Trail conditions:	Conditions are generally good. Traffic is generally light.
Best time to go:	Year-round.
Maps:	Guide to the Foothills Trail, Foothills Trail Conference; Cashiers, Reid, and Eastatoe Gap USGS quads. See Appendix A: For More Information.
Fees:	None.

A view of Lake Jocassee from the Foothills Trail. JOHN CLARK PHOTO

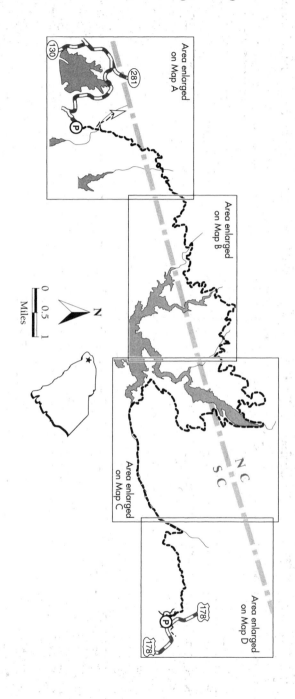

Finding the trailhead: To reach the Laurel Valley (eastern) trailhead from Pickens, go north on U.S. Highway 178 for 16.7 miles. The Foothills Trail crosses US 178 just past the highway bridge over Eastatoe Creek. At the Laurel Valley Lodge sign, turn left onto Laurel Valley Road just past the creek, then take a right onto Horsepasture Road at the fork and go 0.3 mile to the Foothills Trail parking area, on the left.

To reach the Bad Creek (western) Trailhead from Laurel Valley, go 8.3 miles south along US 178, then turn right (west) on South Carolina Highway 11. Travel 14.6 miles west, passing Keowee-Toxaway State Natural Area and the bridge over Lake Keowee, then turn right (north) on SC 130 and drive 10 miles to the entrance to Duke Power's Bad Creek Hydroelectric Station Visitor Center, on the right just before the North Carolina state line. Register at the guard gate, then enter the Bad Creek property and follow the signs about 2 miles to the parking lot for Lower Whitewater Falls and the Foothills Trail.

The Foothills Trail Conference arranges vehicle shuttles to trailheads for those with only one vehicle. Hoyett's Grocery and Tackle, near the entrance to Devil's Fork State Park, also provides this service, as well as boat shuttles to access points on the Horsepasture and Toxaway rivers.

The hike: This hike is entirely within the Jocassee Gorges area of South and North Carolina formerly owned by Duke Power Company, whose hydroelectric projects resulted in the creation of Lake Keowee, Lake Jocassee, and Bad Creek Reservoir. Duke has now sold most of the property north and east of 7,565-acre Lake Jocassee to federal and state agencies, which intend to provide various levels of permanent protection. The South Carolina Department of Natural Resources has acquired the largest single portion, 32,000 acres. Duke Power retains much of the land in the Bad Creek Reservoir area.

The Blue Ridge Escarpment, called the Blue Wall by the Cherokees, jags its way across the area, creating a land of waterfalls and river gorges as streams from the north plunge over the escarpment in their rush to Lake Jocassee and lower-lying lands in South Carolina. The Jocassee Gorges receive abundant rainfall (more than 80 inches annually in some areas), and they offer great biodiversity, including a host of rare mosses and ferns, the

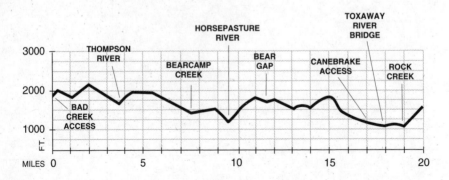

Foothills Trail, Jocassee Gorges Segment Map A

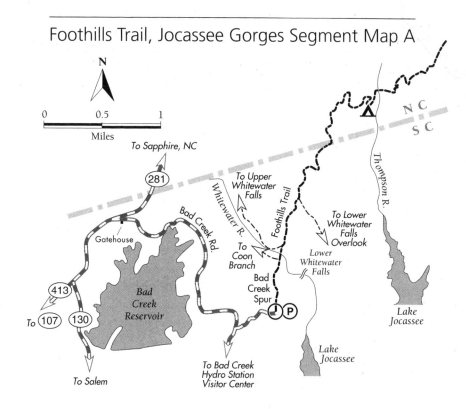

endemic and rare Oconee bell, the rare showy orchis, and many other wild-flower species.

From the Bad Creek (western) Trailhead, follow the blue-blazed Bad Creek spur 0.6 mile over a ridge, across two footbridges over the Whitewater River, past the Coon Branch turnoff to the left (north) to the intersection with the Foothills Trail. Turn right (east) on the Foothills Trail, and hike toward the Thompson River, 3 miles away. (The left fork leads northwest to Upper Whitewater Falls.)

After a mild ascent of less than 1 mile, the blue-blazed spur forks right (southeast) to Lower Whitewater Falls, 0.9 mile away. Continue on the Foothills Trail, which heads north into North Carolina, ascending and then descending past small falls and streams and through lush hemlocks, locust

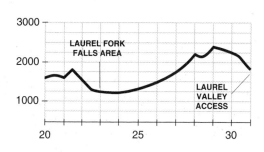

trees, mountain laurels, rhododendrons, and galax to the stunningly beautiful Thompson River gorge. The river rushes swiftly over and around boulders as it passes under the sturdy footbridge that carries you east across the stream to the foot of the bluff on the other

Foothills Trail, Jocassee Gorges Segment Map B

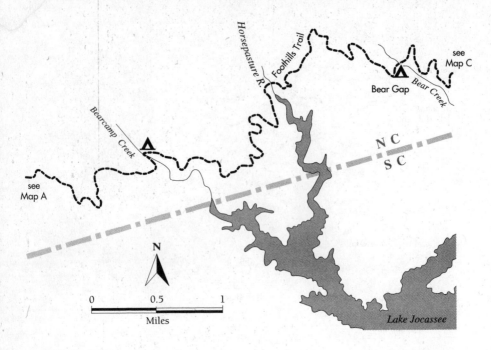

side. Campsites on either side of the bridge are limited, but they make idyllic layover points.

On the east side of the bridge, you encounter a steep, 400-foot climb up the bluff on the way to the campsite at Bearcamp Creek, 3.5 miles away. Much of the trail follows old logging roads as it winds along a ridge and descends slowly toward the creek valley. Just across the creek a 0.3-mile spur heads north to Hilliard Falls. The Foothills Trail follows Bearcamp Creek south for more than 0.5 mile before veering away to the east and making an abrupt 500-foot descent to the banks of the National Wild and Scenic Horsepasture River, 2.7 miles beyond the Bearcamp Creek campsite.

The west bank of the river offers great picnicking sites and some areas adequate for camping. The river, which flows into Lake Jocassee a few yards to the south, mirrors the greenery of the steep surrounding bluffs and provides a serene spot of beauty. This is one of the Foothills Trail's boat access points.

Cross the impressive 50-foot arch bridge over the Horsepasture River, then climb stairs and steep slopes 500 feet to continue along a ridge toward Bear Gap and Bear Creek 2.4 miles away. The ridge provides very good views of the gorge of the Horsepasture River and the mountains beyond. The trail crosses a short suspension bridge over a small gorge, rolls up and down through other ravines, and offers views of Lake Jocassee to the south

Foothills Trail, Jocassee Gorges Segment Map C

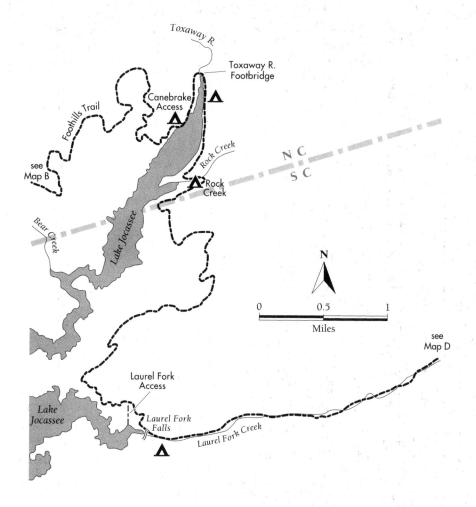

before descending 200 feet to the Bear Gap campsite area and the 30-foot bridge over Bear Creek.

From Bear Gap, the trail follows a rugged series of ups and downs for more than 4 miles before making a long descent to the Canebrake boat landing on the western shore of the Toxaway River, 5.3 miles from Bear Gap. Along the way, you cross Cobb Creek, a site noted for the rare Oconee bell, as well as dog hobble and wild ginger.

Lake Jocassee stretches away to the south of Canebrake boat landing, a designated boat access point for the Foothills Trail. The next short stretch of the trail follows the Toxaway River north, passing an old home site. The work of beavers can be seen along this section, and the level terrain is suitable for

Foothills Trail, Jocassee Gorges Segment Map D

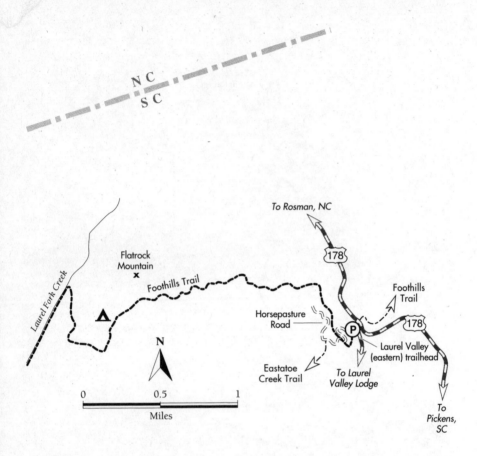

camping. After 0.5 mile, the trail ascends briefly then heads down a series of wooden stairs before crossing an impressive, 220-foot suspension bridge 25 feet above the Toxaway River.

Several feet beyond the eastern end of the bridge, cross a shorter suspension bridge over rapidly flowing Toxaway Creek, then pass south through a 0.5-mile stretch lined with hemlocks. There are a few campsites near the eastern bank of the Toxaway River.

Next, you must negotiate almost 300 torturous steps that rise 200 feet straight up a bluff. About halfway up the rhododendron-shrouded climb a bench appears, allowing you to rest and enjoy panoramic views of Lake Jocassee. At the top, the trail continues a short distance along a ridge, with the lake on the right (west) and a deep ravine on the left (east). At the southern end of the ridge, you have a bird's-eye view of Rock Creek as it flows into the Toxaway River. The trail then descends sharply, partly on stairs, for about 100 feet and continues on to the foot bridge and campground at Rock

The Thompson River. JOHN CLARK PHOTO

Creek. Rock Creek is only 1.3 miles from the Toxaway River bridge, but it is an extremely rugged 1.3 miles.

The trail ascends 600 feet and then drops 500 feet in the 4 miles from Rock Creek to Laurel Fork Falls. The trail moves away from the river and crosses back into South Carolina after about 0.5 mile. Much of this section of the trail makes use of old roadbeds. It is easy to miss turns, so pay especially close attention to the white blazes. To the west, you can catch occasional glimpses of the Toxaway River as it pours into Lake Jocassee. The trail here affords frequent signs of the area's plentiful wild turkeys. Near the end of this section, a 0.3-mile spur departs to the right for the Laurel Fork boat access on Lake Jocassee.

In the next 0.5 mile several excellent views open up on the right of the Laurel Fork Falls' 80-foot tumble into a cove of the lake. Just past the top of the falls, a small suspension bridge on the right allows you to detour to the south side of Laurel Fork Creek, where you can visit a camping and picnic area. Watch from water level as Laurel Fork Creek flows serenely along, then suddenly plunges over the precipice.

The next 4 miles of the Foothills Trail follow and crisscross both Laurel Fork Creek and the rough, rocky road that also follows and crisscrosses the stream. In the past, the road has been used seasonally by four-wheel-drive and all-terrain vehicles. These noisy machines can destroy the sense of solitude of the previous 23 miles, but the South Carolina Department of Natural Resources has proposed closing the road to motorized vehicles to prevent further erosion problems. In any event, the trail builders have created a pathway that for the most part stays some distance from the road, while winding through a rich green river valley thick with mountain laurels, rhododendrons, hemlocks, white pines, ferns, and Oconee bells.

Four miles beyond the falls, the trail crosses West Laurel Fork Creek and continues 4 more miles to Laurel Valley, passing through the Laurel Fork Heritage Preserve to ascend the south flank of Flatrock Mountain. After reaching a point 1,100 feet above the Laurel Fork Falls area, the trail descends a swift 700 feet to the Foothills Trail parking area at Laurel Valley. This section of the trail crosses several logging roads and offers good winter views to the south and southwest.

Facilities: None at eastern trailhead; portable toilets and pay phone at western trailhead.

Lodging and amenities: Campsites are available at Table Rock, Devil's Fork, and Oconee state parks, and at Cherry Hill Recreation Area and Keowee-Toxaway State Park. Primitive camping is allowed along the trail. Commercial lodging and camping is available at Laurel Valley and along SC 11. Limited services are available at Pickens and Walhalla, and full services are available at Easley, Clemson, and Seneca.

For more information: Foothills Trail Conference; Heritage Trust Program, South Carolina Department of Natural Resources; Duke Power Company; Hoyett's Grocery and Tackle. See Appendix A: For More Information.

12 Lower Whitewater Falls and Coon Branch Natural Area

General description:	Half a day's hike to an observation deck overlooking beautiful Lower Whitewater Falls and a walk through a virgin forest area alongside the Whitewater River.
General location:	North of Walhalla, in the northwest corner of the state.
Distance:	4.6 miles round trip.
Difficulty:	Moderate.
Trail conditions:	Conditions are good. Traffic is moderate.
Best time to go:	Year-round.
Maps:	Foothills Trail, Duke Power; Reid and Cashiers USGS quads. See Appendix A: For More Information.
Fees:	None.

Finding the trailhead: From the intersection of South Carolina Highway 28 and SC 11 just south of Walhalla, follow SC 11 (also known as the Chero-kee Foothills Scenic Highway) northeast 12 miles, then turn left (north) on SC 130 and travel 10 miles to the entrance to Duke Power's Bad Creek Hydroelectric Station, on the right (east) just before the North Carolina state line. Register at the guard gate, then enter the Bad Creek property and fol-low the signs about 2 miles to the parking lot for the Lower Whitewater Falls and Foothills trails, on the left (northeast).

The hike: The first part of the trail is the 0.6-mile blue-blazed Bad Creek spur that connects the parking lot with the Foothills Trail. The spur moves through fields to the top of a ridge, revealing good views of Lake Jocassee and the flatlands to the south. A young cedar forest surrounds the trail as you near the crest of the ridge and head down toward the Whitewater River. Just before a bridge about 0.5 mile from the trailhead, the 0.9-mile Coon Branch Trail forks left.

Turn left (north) at this junction for a 1.8-mile (round-trip) side trip to the Coon Branch Natural Area. The trail goes through a thick forest, crossing a series of five bridges over tributaries. Although you don't reach the virgin forest until the end of the trail, there are pockets of old-growth vegetation all along the way. Towering hemlocks, aging hardwoods, and emerald rhodo-dendrons highlight the way. The undergrowth harbors squawroot, fairy wands, May apples, wood lilies, trilliums, and many other wildflowers.

This area teems with wildlife. Raccoons and beavers are in evidence along the water, and feral hogs, bobcats, white-tailed deer, and black bears inhabit the forest. The sounds of warblers, tanagers, vireos and flycatchers filter down from overhead, and woodpeckers thrive here.

Lower Whitewater Falls and Coon Branch Natural Area

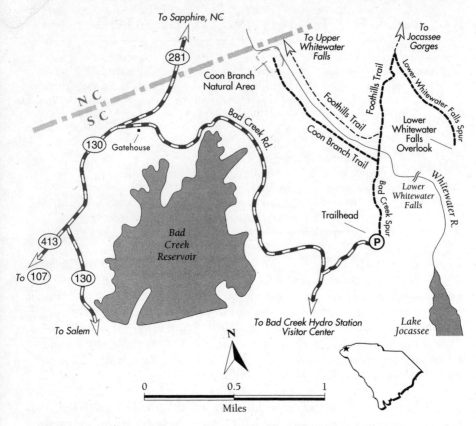

After the fourth bridge you enter the Coon Branch Natural Area, a 20-acre grove at the end of the trail. It is a treasure of never-felled timber, a glimpse of what this area looked like centuries ago before the arrival of Europeans. The largest Fraser magnolia in the state grows here, 6 feet around and 86 feet tall. Giant tulip poplars, hemlocks, and chestnut oaks abound. The trail moves through the grove and over one last bridge before ending.

After returning along the Coon Branch Trail to the intersection with the spur trail, turn left (north) and cross the two footbridges over the Whitewater River. The bridges offer a good view of the Whitewater, an unusually clear and pristine stream with native populations of rainbow and brown trout, unusual for South Carolina streams, which rely heavily on stocking with hatchery-reared fish.

About 0.1 mile from the Coon Branch Trail junction, the spur trail from the parking lot intersects the white-blazed Foothills Trail. Bear right and proceed to the northeast on the Foothills Trail, following the white blazes that appear concurrently with the blue blazes of the Lower Whitewater Falls Trail. (The left turn leads northwest to the Upper Whitewater Falls in North Carolina, a 1.7-mile climb.)

After a walk of about 0.5 mile through a forested area (a farm half a century ago) and along a moderate ascent up a ridge, the Lower Whitewater Falls Trail branches right (southeast), away from the Foothills Trail, which continues on to the Thompson River and Jocassee Gorges. The Lower Whitewater Falls Trail moves along paths and old roadbeds through woodlands filled with wildflowers and birds. The trail descends fairly steeply for the last 0.25 mile to an observation platform that offers a distant, but quite rewarding, view across the river gorge to the 400-foot Lower Whitewater Falls. The Upper and Lower Whitewater Falls, which together plunge 800 feet through six cascades into Lake Jocassee, form one of the highest series of falls in eastern North America.

Facilities: Portable toilets and pay phone at trailhead parking lot. No water.

Lodging and amenities: There are campsites at Cherry Hill Recreation Area, Keowee-Toxaway State Park, Devil's Fork State Park, and Oconee State Park. Primitive camping is allowed along the Foothills Trail. Lodging and other services are available at Walhalla, Seneca, and Clemson.

For more information: Duke Power Company. See Appendix A: For More Information.

13 Keowee-Toxaway State Park

General description:	This half-day loop offers fairly steep ascents and descents, impressive rock outcrops, and good views of the Blue Ridge Mountains and the northern portion of Lake Keowee.
General location:	West of Pickens, in the northwest corner of the state.
Distance:	Raven Rock Trail, 4.2 miles, loop.
Difficulty:	Moderate to strenuous.
Trail conditions:	Conditions are average to difficult. Traffic is light to moderate.
Best time to go:	Year-round. More difficult in wet weather.
Maps:	Trail maps available at Interpretive Center; Salem and Sunset USGS quads. See Appendix A: For More Information.
Fees:	None.

Finding the trailhead: From Pickens, travel 7 miles west on Secondary Road 32 to Shady Grove Junction. At Shady Grove Junction, turn right (north) on South Carolina Highway 133 and go 3.4 miles to SC 11 (Cherokee Foothills Scenic Highway). The park entrances are 0.25 mile to the left (west) on SC 11. The south entrance leads to the Interpretive Center and picnic areas.

Keowee-Toxaway State Park

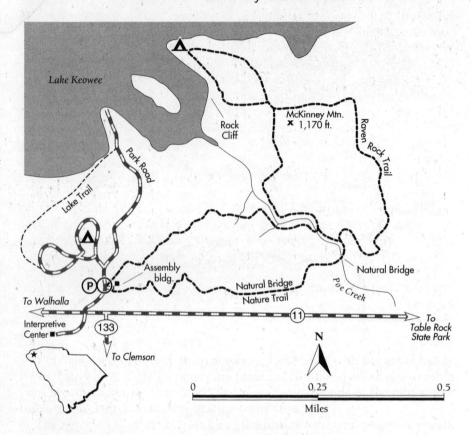

The north (right) entrance leads to the hiking trails, lake access, and camping area. Park in front of the Assembly building, on the right (east), just inside the north park entrance.

From Clemson, travel 20 miles north on SC 133 to SC 11 and continue as indicated above. From Walhalla, travel 20 miles northwest on SC 11. The entrances are just across the bridge over Lake Keowee.

The hike: In the Cherokee language, keowee means "land of the mulberry groves" and toxaway means "land of no tomahawks." Lake Keowee is manmade, created when the Duke Power Company flooded the Keowee River valley, much of which was home to Cherokee Indians for centuries. The British built Fort Prince George near here in 1753, and the area became a center of trade and cultural exchange between settlers and the Cherokee Indian Nation. In the 1790s, settlers moved into Cherokee territory and drove the tribe into the North Carolina mountains. Cherokee history and culture is explored in exhibits at the park's Interpretive Center and by informational kiosks along a 0.25-mile trail on the south side of the 1,000-acre park. Park hours are 9 A.M. to 9 P.M., April through October; 9 A.M. to 6 P.M., Saturday through Thursday, and 9 A.M. to 8 P.M., Friday, November through March.

The hike begins behind the Assembly building. The first 0.5 mile is a fairly level walk through oak forest with a dense understory that shelters mountain laurels, blueberries, and Bowman's root. The trail descends to Poe Creek, which flows under the path and emerges with a rush through boulders on the left side of the trail. Shortly thereafter, the Raven Rock Trail forks right (northeast) and embarks on a steep climb. The Natural Bridge Nature Trail continues along the creek for 0.1 mile, where it joins the Raven Rock Trail on its return route.

The Raven Rock Trail ascends over and around boulders, eventually emerging on a rocky ridge with a clear understory. The trail follows a series of ups and downs around McKinney Mountain. A rocky area near the top allows you an excellent view west to the Blue Ridge Mountains. Farther along, another vista overlooks Lake Keowee.

After this last vista, the trail begins a steep plunge to the lake shore. Halfway down, an option presents itself: You can turn left (south) and return to the trailhead or continue down (northwest). A few yards farther down is another fork. The lower (left-hand) portion of the trail is a short loop that eventually returns to this point. We recommend you descend to the northwest, on the steeper, right-hand path and return on the left-hand trail. Both this fork and the previous one are confusing and not well marked, so proceed through this area with care.

The final, extremely steep descent leads to a large, flat, pine-shaded point of land that juts into the lake. This area makes a very good campsite, and the views to the north are excellent. You may want to swim or fish (for bass, bream, crappie, catfish or carp) here.

The uphill return is demanding but scenic. For a while, the trail leads upward over stone ridges with attractive views of the lake, an adjacent island, and distant mountains before turning through a forest heavily damaged by storms. It emerges at the two intersections you passed on the way down. Bear right (east) at both forks. The trail continues to ascend along a mountain-side ridge before beginning its descent toward Poe Creek.

You hear wonderfully musical Poe Creek several minutes before it comes into view through the understory lush with ferns, wild geraniums, and hemlocks. The upstream view of the cascading creek is inspiring, and the trail follows the creek upstream through thick greenery, over moist terrain, and past a couple of rudimentary campsites. After about 0.25 mile, the Raven Rock Trail meets the Natural Bridge Nature Trail and turns right (west); cross the creek using boulders as steppingstones.

The trail briefly follows the creek downstream, then turns uphill for the return to the trailhead. The final 0.5 mile is a moderately strenuous 230-foot ascent over ridges and across several brooks, with a final steep stretch to the parking lot in front of the Assembly building.

Facilities: Rest rooms, water, and picnic shelters available at Interpretive Center. Rest rooms and water at campground.

Lodging and amenities: The park has 24 campsites, and primitive camping is allowed along the hiking trails. Campsites are also available at nearby Devil's Fork and Table Rock state parks, as well as at nearby Mile Creek County Park. Walhalla and Pickens offer limited lodging and services. Full services are available at Seneca, Clemson, Easley.

For more information: Keowee-Toxaway State Park. See Appendix A: For More Information.

---

14 Eastatoe Creek Trail

General description:	Half a day's hike through a mountain cove to a beautiful, secluded stream.
General location:	North of Pickens, in the northwest corner of the state.
Distance:	3.5 miles round trip.
Difficulty:	Strenuous.
Trail conditions:	Conditions are generally good. Traffic is light.
Best time to go:	Spring, with summer and autumn close behind. Rocks slippery during wet weather.
Maps:	Heritage Trust Program brochure; Eastatoe Gap USGS quad. See Appendix A: For More Information.
Fees:	None.

Finding the trailhead: Go north 8.3 miles on U.S. Highway 178 from its intersection with South Carolina Highway 11 (8.4 miles north of Pickens). Cross the bridge over Eastatoe Creek and turn left (southwest) at the Laurel Valley Lodge sign. This road forks immediately; take the right, unpaved fork. Go to the Foothills Trail parking area, which is uphill and ahead on the left. Walk up the dirt road about 0.1 mile and turn left (south) onto an old logging road blocked to vehicles by a cable.
The trail begins on the old logging road.

The hike: This trail is essentially a big climb down, and then a big climb back up. However, the destination makes it worthwhile. Eastatoe (pronounced "EAST-a-toe-ee") Creek is a beautiful stream untrammeled by development, whose waters are so pristine that rainbow trout reproduce naturally, making it an exceptional case in South Carolina.

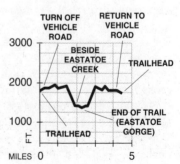

Eastatoe Creek Trail

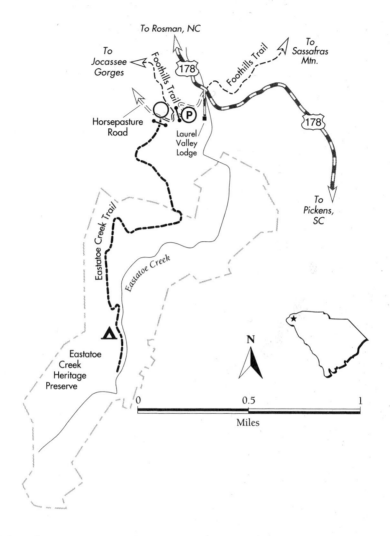

Within the Eastatoe Creek Heritage Preserve's 373 acres (managed by the Heritage Trust Program of the South Carolina Department of Natural Resources), the Eastatoe tumbles 600 feet, concluding between the walls of Eastatoe Gorge. Here, the 15-foot wide creek pours into a rock sluice 3 feet wide, creating both an impressive flume and sufficient humidity for some very rare plants.

Three ferns generally associated with the tropics occur at Eastatoe Creek, including the Tunbridge fern, which is found nowhere else in North America. The park-like area at the end of the trail features a spectacular wildflower show in the spring.

The trail first passes through an area recovering from heavy logging. This is a good spot to see white-tailed deer, and birds such as the prairie warbler and the rufous-sided towhee thrive here. After the trail enters the preserve, it runs level for about 0.5 mile, then descends swiftly. However, the descent is made relatively easy by the judicious use of switchbacks. The path crosses numerous streams, each bridged by several logs. You hear Eastatoe Creek before you see it.

Soon, the switchbacks end and the trail drops precipitously down a set of stairs. For a while, the trail borders a 100-foot drop-off to the roaring creek below.

Suddenly, you emerge upon the rain forest habitat in Eastatoe Gorge. At the end of the hike, by the side of the creek, there is a primitive camping area. The blaze markings are somewhat confusing, but all you need to know is that when you come to a triple blaze, you should turn around. The trail is impassable beyond this point.

Exercise great caution when exploring the rocks beside the creek at the end of the trail. The spray from the rock sluice can make boulders slippery and treacherous. Across the creek, a remarkable cliff forms the wall of the gorge; there is a small cave at water level. An adjacent waterfall is attractive, and the flume is quite dramatic.

Hike out the way you came.

Facilities: None.

Lodging and amenities: Laurel Valley Lodge, near the trailhead, offers lodging, camping, and a restaurant. Primitive camping is available at a designated camping area at the end of the Eastatoe Creek Trail, and along the Foothills Trail. Campsites are available at Keowee-Toxaway State Park and at Table Rock State Park. Limited services are available at Pickens, and full services are available at Greenville.

For more information: Heritage Trust Program, South Carolina Department of Natural Resources. See Appendix A: For More Information.

15 Foothills Trail, Sassafras Mountain Segment

General description:	A one- or two-day hike to the summit of South Carolina's highest mountain and down to Laurel Valley and the Jocassee Gorges area.
General location:	North of Pickens, in the northwest corner of the state.
Distance:	14.1 miles one way.
Difficulty:	Moderate to strenuous.
Trail conditions:	Conditions are good. Traffic is moderate to heavy.
Best time to go:	Year-round.
Maps:	Guide to the Foothills Trail, Foothills Trail Conference; Table Rock, Eastatoe Gap USGS quads. See Appendix A: For More Information.
Fees:	$2 per vehicle at Table Rock State Park. No fee at the Laurel Fork trailhead.

Finding the trailhead: To reach the Table Rock State Park (eastern) trailhead from Pickens, go north on U.S. Highway 178 for 8.4 miles to the junction with South Carolina Highway 11; turn right (east). It is 4.4 miles on SC 11 (Cherokee Foothills Scenic Highway) to the turnoff for Table Rock State Park's west gate, on the left (north). From the west gate, follow signs to the nature center, which serves as the trailhead.

To reach the Laurel Valley (western) Trailhead from Table Rock State Park, proceed west on SC 11 for 4.4 miles to US 178, turn right, and follow US 178 north 8.3 miles. The Foothills Trail crosses US 178 just past the highway bridge over Eastatoe Creek and follows a dirt road. Turn left (west) onto this dirt road just past the creek, take a right (west) turn at the fork, and follow this dirt road (Horsepasture Road) 1,500 feet to the Foothills Trail parking area on the left (south).

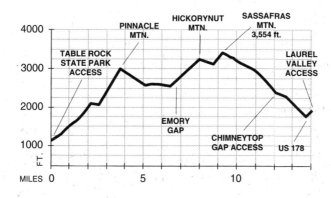

Foothills Trail, Sassafras Mountain Segment Overview

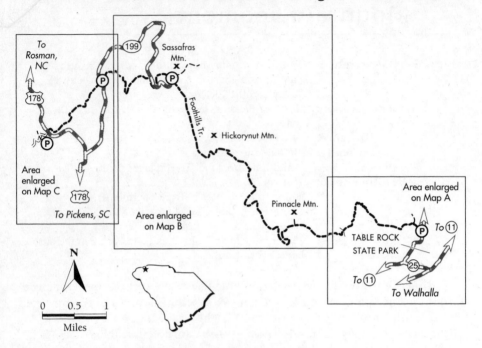

The hike: We describe the trail from east to west. From the north side of the nature center at the eastern trailhead, follow the yellow-blazed trail along Carrick Creek toward Pinnacle Mountain over gently ascending, lushly forested terrain. After 0.3 mile, stay left (west) where the Carrick Creek Nature Trail veers right. The first 1 mile is easy walking, then the trail climbs sharply, crisscrossing rocky Carrick Creek and its tributaries. The dense foliage is almost like a rain forest, and partridgeberry complements the ever-present rhododendron and mountain laurel. The creek tumbles swiftly and noisily downward, providing a continually rushing auditory background.

At 2.7 miles, bear left (west) where the trail to Table Rock Mountain, marked by a sign and blazed red, veers right (north). About 0.1 mile thereafter, the trail leaves the creek and moves through mixed hardwoods. Half a mile farther, as you are still heading steeply up, you encounter Bald Rock, a series of rocky outcrops which provide great views of the hills and plains to the south and of Table Rock Mountain.

The yellow-blazed Table Rock State Park section of the trail ends at 3.8 miles. Here the yellow-blazed trail continues to the right (north), toward the peak of Pinnacle Mountain, 0.2 mile away. The Foothills Trail bears left (west) along a white-blazed path, leaving the park and entering the former Duke Power Company property acquired by the South Carolina Department of Natural Resources (DNR) as part of the Jocassee Gorges

Foothills Trail, Sassafras Mountain Segment Map A

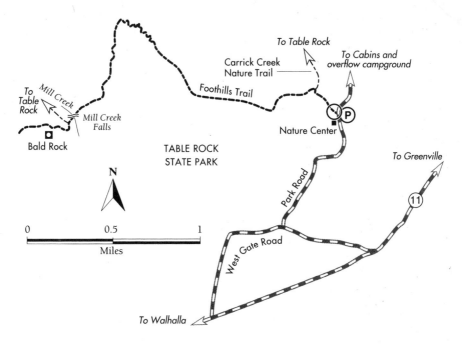

purchase. The remainder of this hike traverses DNR property along a white-blazed trail.

The trail begins a gentle descent and, at 4.2 miles, reaches the top of Drawbar Cliffs, with sweeping views west to Lake Keowee. The trail descends Drawbar Cliffs, which form the flank of Pinnacle Mountain, on switchbacks, then levels out along old logging roads before beginning the ascent of Hickorynut Mountain. At 5.7 miles, the trail passes the Marion Castles Rock House, an outcropping where a fellow by the name of Marion Castles hid out during the Civil War to avoid conscription into the Confederate Army.

The trail continues along a section of the old Emory Gap toll road, then upward through hemlocks and rhododendrons to the ridgetop of Hickorynut Mountain Gap at 7.8 miles. The trail then descends gently, passing the chimney and other remnants of the home of John L. Cantrell, one of the earliest settlers of this area. This is an excellent camping spot, only 1.2 miles away from the road access at the top of Sassafras Mountain.

The trail remains fairly level as it passes through galax, rattlesnake plantain, pink lady's slipper, trailing arbutus, holly, sourwood, and mountain laurel, then ascends again to bring you near the top of 3,554-foot Sassafras Mountain, South Carolina's highest peak, 9.4 miles from the Table Rock State Park Trailhead.

Foothills Trail, Sassafras Mountain Segment Map B

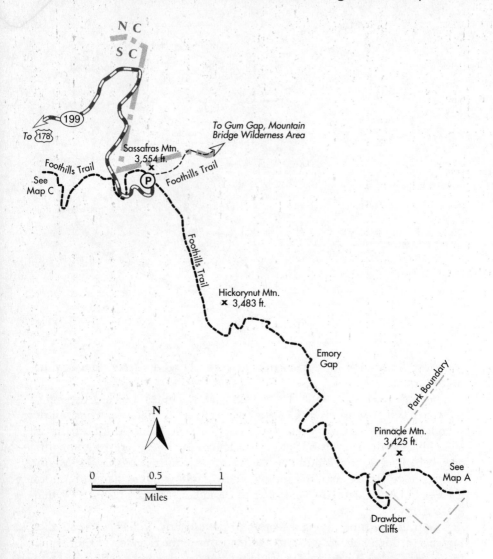

The trail emerges on a paved road, across from a parking area. The parking area is at the end of Secondary Road 199 (F. Van Clayton Memorial Highway), 4.2 miles from Rocky Bottom on US 178. (Behind the radio tower across the road from the parking lot is the trailhead for the 12-mile Gum Gap Segment of the Foothills Trail that links Sassafras Mountain with Caesars Head, Raven Cliff Falls, and the rest of the Mountain Bridge Wilderness Area, all the way to Jones Gap, 20 miles away.)

The trail heads right (northeast) about 0.1 mile up a dirt road to the Sassafras Mountain summit, where there is a lot of sassafras and great vistas all

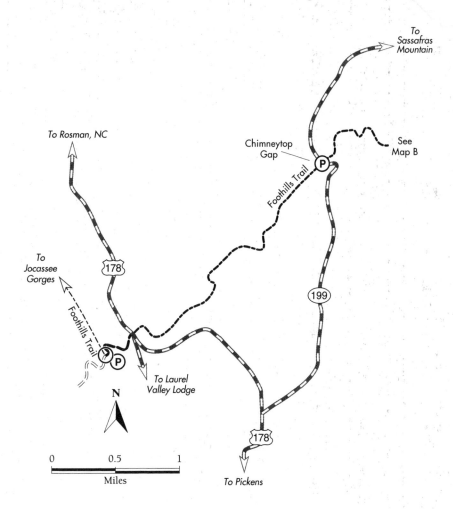

To Sassafras Mountain

To Rosman, NC

Chimneytop Gap

See Map B

Foothills Trail

To Jocassee Gorges

178

199

Foothills Trail

To Laurel Valley Lodge

N

178

0   0.5   1

Miles

To Pickens

around. Sassafras Mountain is a fruitful birding area. Species include ruffed grouse; raven; dark-eyed junco; Carolina chickadee; pileated woodpecker; solitary vireo; and chestnut-sided, Swainson's, black-throated blue, worm-eating, and blackburnian warblers.

The trail winds down from the summit, emerging on SR 199 for about 0.1 mile downhill. Signs on the left (south) side of the road indicate where the Foothills Trail plunges down into the forest toward Chimneytop Gap, 2.5 miles away. Follow the trail.

The forest is composed of white pines, maples, tulip poplars, locusts, black birches, witch hazels, and many varieties of oak, including chestnut oak. A large section along the trail was harvested in 1971 by Duke Power and replanted with white pine. The undergrowth is sparse, allowing visibility to

93

View from Graybar Cliffs. JOHN CLARK PHOTO

stretch for significant distances, even in summer. Vegetation includes mountain laurels, rhododendrons, Fraser magnolias, grapevines, spotted wintergreens, Christmas ferns, galax, and running-pines.

The trail undulates downward along ridges and across ravines. There are several excellent westward vistas. At the 10.7-mile mark, in Rogers Gap, stand a number of large tree stumps, remnants of the chestnut blight that decimated this forest in the 1930s.

The trail crosses paved SR 199 (F. Van Clayton Memorial Highway) and arrives at Chimneytop Gap, 2,400 feet above sea level, at the 12-mile mark. There is a Foothills Trail sign here and a parking area on the west side of the road, a few hundred feet uphill (north).

For the next 1 mile, the trail ascends and descends gently as it clambers over and around ravines and streams. Large hemlocks join the mixture of oaks and other hardwoods. Underneath are spike lobelias, goldenrods, pokeweeds, large grapevines, and closed gentians. Huge rocks, some with caves, tower above. After 1 mile, the trail plunges steeply. The density of the vegetation increases, and Fraser magnolias, mountain laurels, rhododendrons, Christmas ferns, partridgeberries, wild ginger, Christmas ferns, and galax abound.

At 13.9 miles, the trail crosses US 178 at an elevation of about 1,700 feet, then proceeds uphill along a dirt road to a parking lot on the left, at the 14.1-mile mark. A left turn just as you begin on the dirt road carries you the few hundred feet to the Laurel Valley Restaurant and Lodge, a quaint, locally flavored complex on the banks of Eastatoe Creek.

Facilities: Rest rooms, drinking water, refreshments, and interpretive center at Table Rock trailhead. No public facilities at Laurel Valley trailhead.
Lodging and amenities: Campsites are available at Table Rock State Park, and primitive camping is allowed along the trail outside the park. Commercial lodging is available at Laurel Valley and along SC 11. Limited services are available at Pickens, and full services are available at Easley, Clemson, and Greenville.

For more information: Table Rock State Park; Foothills Trail Conference. See Appendix A: For More Information.

16 Table Rock State Park

General description:	A very difficult but immensely rewarding day hike featuring spectacular views from the top of the dramatic cliffs of Table Rock Mountain, as well as a visit to the summit of Pinnacle Mountain.
General location:	Northwest of Greenville, in the northwest corner of the state.
Distance:	10 miles, loop.
Difficulty:	Highly strenuous.
Trail conditions:	Conditions are good. Traffic is heavy.
Best time to go:	Year-round, though footing may be treacherous in icy conditions.
Maps:	Table Rock State Park brochure; Table Rock USGS

View eastward from the top of Table Rock. John Dantzler photo

Table Rock State Park

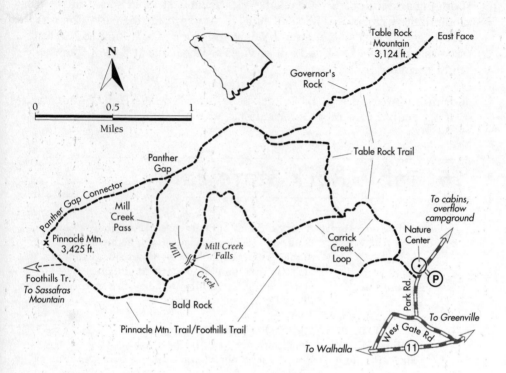

N

0   0.5   1
Miles

East Face

Table Rock
Mountain
3,124 ft.

Governor's
Rock

Table Rock Trail

Panther
Gap

Panther Gap Connector

Mill
Creek
Pass

Pinnacle Mtn.
3,425 ft.

Mill Creek
Falls

Mill Creek

Carrick
Creek
Loop

To cabins,
overflow
campground

Nature
Center

P

Foothills Tr.
*To Sassafras
Mountain*

Bald Rock

Pinnacle Mtn. Trail/Foothills Trail

Park Rd.

To Greenville

West Gate Rd

11

To Walhalla

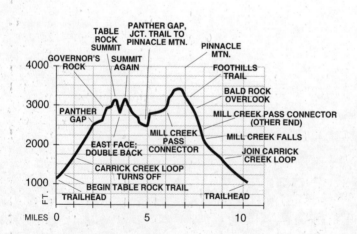

Table Rock State Park. John Clark photo

quad. See Appendix A: For More Information.

Fees: $2 per vehicle.

Finding the trailhead: From Pickens, go north 8.4 miles on U. S. Highway 178 to the junction with South Carolina Highway 11. Turn right (east) and go 4.4 miles on SC 11 (Cherokee Foothills Scenic Highway) to the turnoff for Table Rock State Park's west gate, on the left (north). From the west gate, follow the signs to the nature center, which serves as the trailhead.

The hike: Table Rock is one of South Carolina's most popular state parks. The imposing granite dome of Table Rock, the pristine mountain lake, the excellent network of trails—all draw visitors from far and near. The mountain got its name from Cherokee legend. The Cherokees believed that the Great Spirit used Table Rock as a dining table and the shorter mountain, The Stool, as a seat. The trail system at Table Rock State Park has been designated a National Historic Trail. The park is open daily from 7 A.M. to 9 P.M., all year.

The park presents a marvelous menu of choices, and we recommend a particularly excellent one: Climb Table Rock Mountain, follow the link trail to Pinnacle Mountain, and return via the Pinnacle Mountain Trail, an eastern terminus of the Foothills Trail.

The 3.4 mile trail up Table Rock Mountain is rugged, but it is also very wide and well marked most of the way to the top. Boulders fallen from the Rock add interest to the climb, with decorating help from asters and goldenrod in the autumn and galax in the spring.

It is exciting to walk across the giant rockface that has graced so many pictures, posters, and postcards. The trail in fact carries you across three major outcroppings, including Governor's Rock, roughly halfway up, and the east and south faces of Table Rock Mountain. Beyond the summit there are brilliant views of Slicking Falls to the northeast and of Caesars Head across the Greenville Watershed. At Panther Gap, on the way back down from the summit of Table Rock Mountain, pick up the 1.9-mile connector trail to Pinnacle Mountain.

At 3,425 feet, Pinnacle Mountain is the highest mountain entirely within the borders of South Carolina. While views from its summit are completely obscured by trees and the climb to and from the top is extremely steep, it is less than 1 mile on the trail down to Bald Rock, another marvelous outcropping with wonderful vistas, including one of the finest views of Table Rock Mountain. (Between the summit of Pinnacle Mountain and Bald Rock overlook is the turnoff, to the right, for the Foothills Trail to Sassafras Mountain.)

The climb down from Pinnacle Mountain is long and difficult, but enlivened by lovely Mill Creek Falls, 1.3 miles from the summit. There is enough space between the slats of the rickety bridge over Mill Creek to unnerve anyone with small feet. Exercise great care. Beyond Mill Creek, boulders and outcroppings abound until Carrick Creek and its wondrous rock sluices take over. You descend rapidly as you cross back and forth over fast-flowing Carrick Creek and its tributaries, eventually passing a left (northeast) turnoff for the Carrick Creek Nature Trail loop, which leads back to the Table Rock Trail. Stay right (southeast) as the trail eases into a gentle slope downward over the last 1 mile, taking you along Carrick Creek back to the trailhead at the nature center.

Facilities: Drinking water, rest rooms, nature center, park store, lake swimming area, bathhouse, and boat rentals.

Lodging and amenities: Table Rock State Park has 100 campsites with hookups, 14 cabins, and a restaurant at the east gate. Motel accommodations and other services can be found outside the park along SC 11, and at Pickens, Easley, and Greenville.

For more information: Table Rock State Park. See Appendix A: For More Information.

17 Foothills Trail, Gum Gap Segment

General description:	A day-long hike to the highest point in South Carolina, with great views of the Blue Ridge Mountains.
General location:	North of Greenville in the northwest corner of the state.
Distance:	12 miles one way.
Difficulty:	Moderate to strenuous.
Trail conditions:	Good to fair conditions. Traffic is light.
Best time to go:	Year-round. Take care during hunting seasons.
Maps:	Mountain Bridge Wilderness Area map, available at Caesars Head State Park; Table Rock and Eastatoe Gap USGS quads. See Appendix A: For More Information.
Fees:	None.

Finding the trailhead: The eastern trailhead is on the Raven Cliff Falls Trail. The Raven Cliff Falls parking lot is 1 mile north of Caesars Head State Park and 35 miles northwest of Greenville on U.S. Highway 276. The trailhead is across the highway from the parking lot. Be sure to register before setting out.

The western trailhead is at the top of Sassafras Mountain. From the intersection of US 178 and South Carolina Highway 11 (11.2 miles west of the western intersection of US 276 and SC 11 at the base of Caesars Head; 8.4 miles north of Pickens on US 178), continue northward on US 178 for 7.4 miles to the community of Rocky Bottom. Turn right (northeast) on Secondary Road 199 (F. Van Clayton Memorial Highway) and drive 4.8 miles to the parking area just below the summit. The trailhead is directly across SR 199 from the parking lot.

The hike: The 12-mile Gum Gap Segment of the Foothills Trail comprises a 7.5-mile spur of the Foothills Trail from Sassafras Mountain to Gum Gap, near the boundary of Watson Heritage Preserve, plus 4.5 miles of the Gum Gap and Raven Cliff Falls trails, which are part of the Mountain Bridge Wilderness Area network of trails. Some authorities refer to this hike as the Caesars Head Spur of the Foothills Trail.

This hike is easy to moderate for about 75 percent of its length and tremendously arduous for the balance. You walk through a portion of the Mountain Bridge Wilderness Area, including Watson Heritage Preserve, then pass through Gum Gap and follow the North Carolina border, finally climbing Sassafras Mountain, the highest mountain in South Carolina. This trail is easier from west to east, but only slightly. At the western end, there are sharp ascents and descents in both directions.

Foothills Trail, Gum Gap Segment

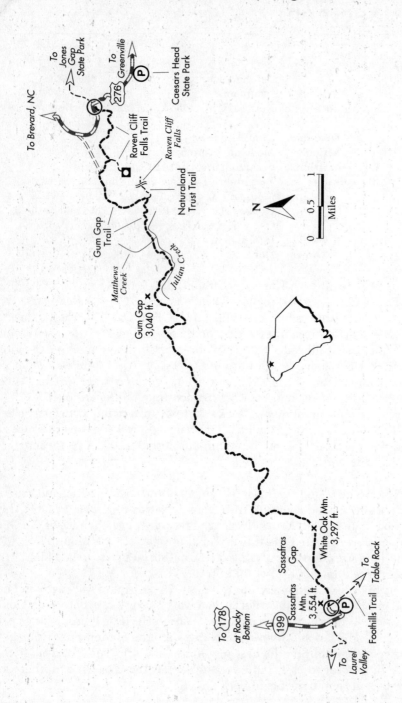

To Jones Gap State Park

To Greenville

276 (P)

Caesars Head State Park

To Brevard, NC

Raven Cliff Falls Trail

Raven Cliff Falls

Naturaland Trust Trail

Gum Gap Trail

Matthews Creek

Julian Creek

Gum Gap 3,040 ft.

N

0   0.5   1

Miles

White Oak Mtn. 3,297 ft.

Sassafras Gap

To Table Rock

Sassafras Mtn. 3,554 ft.

199

To 178 at Rocky Bottom

Foothills Trail

To Laurel Valley

The hike mainly follows old logging roads. Begin on Raven Cliff Falls Trail then turn right (northwest) onto blue-blazed Gum Gap Trail after 1.4 miles. After 1.5 miles on the Gum Gap Trail, you reach a junction with the Naturaland Trust Trail. (The Naturaland Trust Trail leads from here 0.4 mile to the bridge across Raven Cliff Falls, one of the more spectacular hiking experiences in South Carolina.)

At 0.1 mile past the junction with the Naturaland Trust Trail, you enter Watson Heritage Preserve, which harbors the only montane bog habitat in South Carolina. South Carolina's sole population of federally listed threatened swamp pink takes shelter here, as do eight other rare and significant plants, including painted trillium and climbing fern. In the late spring and early summer, this is one of the best places anywhere to view rhododendron. Also look for white pine, eastern hemlock, pink lady's slipper, galax, and running-pine. Along the trail, white-tailed deer and wild turkey are often seen, and ruffed grouse can be heard. Black bears are present in the area, but shy away from humans.

You hear Matthews Creek rushing over the rocks down the ravine on the left (south) before you see it. The creek parallels the trail for 0.3 mile then goes on to form Raven Cliff Falls downstream. The trail is 20 to 30 feet above the stream, while the opposite bank is much higher. This stretch of the trail is very pleasant. The crossing at the confluence of Matthews and Julian creeks can be difficult, and after heavy rains the only option is wading. (There are numerous small streams on the Watson Heritage Preserve property, but don't worry—the rest are easy to cross.) Native brook trout, now rarely found in South Carolina, live wild in Julian and Matthews creeks.

At the western border of the Heritage Preserve is a sign identifying the spot as Gum Gap, 4.5 miles from the beginning of the hike. From here, Sassafras Mountain is another 7.5 miles along the Foothills Trail. The trail turns left (south) onto a dirt road that is still used by vehicles. Almost immediately, a fork heads to the right (south). Turn here.

Immediately after Gum Gap, the road climbs fairly steeply for 0.5 mile. In general, the trail provides excellent winter views. The rest of the hike follows the state line, with Greenville Watershed property (strictly no trespassing) on the left (south). The trail continues to be blazed blue. The section after Gum

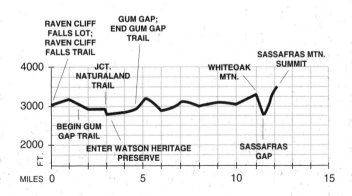

The view into North Carolina from a bluff on the Gum Gap Segment of the Foothills trail.
JOHN CLARK PHOTO

Gap passes through a series of gorges. Although it involves some moderate ascents and descents, it is not a difficult trail until it nears Sassafras Mountain.

A highlight of the section beyond Gum Gap is Bursted Rock, 1.5 miles south (left) of Gum Gap, a rock outcropping at the top of a mountain. Two miles beyond Gum Gap, at the top of a 0.2-mile climb, a rock outcropping on the right-hand side provides a tremendous view of the French Broad River valley and the Blue Ridge Mountains. After another 0.2 mile, the trail leaves the logging road. It heads off to the left (south) into the woods. This turn is easy to miss. Watch first for the red blazes of the Greenville Watershed property line, then the double blue blazes that indicate the turn.

A brief sojourn in the forest introduces you to a lot of galax, a view of a rock outcropping to the left of the trail, and a slippery but short descent of a steep hillside. Even here, the trail skirts the border of the Greenville Watershed. Turn left (south) when you come back to the road.

The next-to-last ascent begins a little more than 3 miles past Gum Gap. At a large roadside hunt camp, the trail leaves the road again. At a bend, it heads straight up a mountainside. Watch carefully for blue blazes. This is a short, steep ascent, followed by a steeper descent. At 3.4 miles from Gum Gap, bear right into a boggy area, from which the most difficult climb starts. The steepest part is short, but nearly vertical. The trail continues ascending afterward, but at a more moderate pitch.

The western end of the trail leads you through another short ascent, a long, steep descent to the former roadbed of centuries-old Emory Gap Toll Road at Sassafras Gap, 6.7 miles from Gum Gap. From Sassafras Gap, you begin an extremely strenuous climb up Sassafras Mountain, unrelieved by switchbacks or other such niceties. The climb up Sassafras is 0.8 mile, of which the final 0.2 mile is the worst.

The trail ends at the top of the mountain, on SR 199 (F. Van Clayton Memorial Highway), across from the parking lot which serves as the trailhead.

Facilities: Caesars Head State Park, 1 mile south of the eastern trailhead, has rest rooms, drinking water, cold drink machines, a park store, and good information, including an excellent diorama of the Mountain Bridge Wilderness Area trails. There are no facilities at the western trailhead on the top of Sassafras Mountain.

Lodging and amenities: Primitive camping is permitted in Watson Heritage Preserve, provided the campsite is 100 feet from both water and the trail. Camping is also permitted between Gum Gap and Sassafras Mountain, so long as the campsite is on the north side of the trail. Camping within the Mountain Bridge Wilderness Area is by permit only. Table Rock State Park has campsites. Full services are available at Brevard, North Carolina, and at Greenville, South Carolina.

For more information: Mountain Bridge Wilderness Area; Foothills Trail Conference. See Appendix A: For More Information.

18 Raven Cliff Falls

General description:	A day hike to one of the highest and most scenic cascades in the eastern United States.
General location:	North of Greenville, in the northwest corner of the state.
Distance:	Overlook option: 4 miles, round trip. Bridge option: 6.6 miles, round trip.
Difficulty:	Moderate.
Trail conditions:	Conditions are good. Traffic is often heavy.
Best time to go:	Year-round, but avoid the coldest days of winter.
Maps:	Mountain Bridge Wilderness Area map, available at Caesars Head State Park; Cleveland and Table Rock USGS quads. See Appendix A: For More Information.
Fees:	None.

Finding the trailhead: The Raven Cliff Falls parking lot is 1 mile north of Caesars Head State Park and 35 miles northwest of Greenville on U.S. Highway 276. The trailhead is across the highway from the parking lot. Be sure to register before setting out.

The hike: Raven Cliff Falls was an extraordinarily popular hiking destination even before a swinging footbridge was recently built across it. You are now faced with two intriguing options: You can go to the overlook for a spectacular, if slightly distant, view of the gorgeous falls; or you can walk to the suspension bridge and stand right above the falls. There is no wrong choice.

If you want to go to the overlook, follow the markers to stay on the red-blazed Raven Cliff Falls Trail all the way to the overlook, a distance of 2 miles. If you would rather head to the bridge, follow Raven Cliff Falls Trail for 1.4 miles, then fork right (northwest) onto the Gum Gap Trail. After 1.5 miles on Gum Gap Trail, take the left fork (southeast) onto the Naturaland Trust Trail and go 0.4 mile to the bridge.

Raven Cliff Falls Trail, which leads to the scenic overlook, is an old buggy road that took honeymooners to the falls at the beginning of the 20th century.

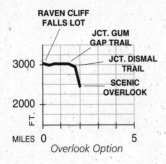

Overlook Option

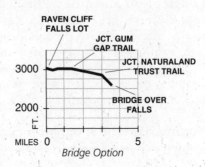

Bridge Option

Raven Cliff Falls

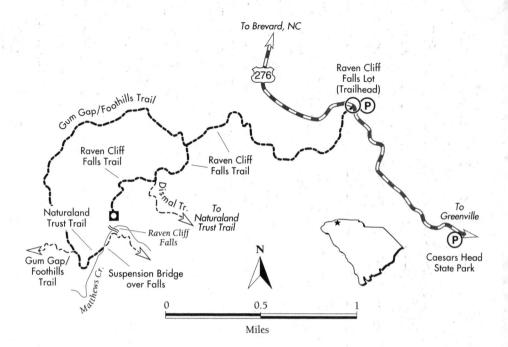

Although eroded in places, it generally makes for easy footing. On a clear day, you can see all the way to Greenville, 35 miles away, but marvelous views of the Blue Ridge Escarpment are available anytime. The last 0.5 mile before the overlook is the only relatively steep part of this hike, and switchbacks help ease the descent.

The falls themselves are the great attraction. Matthews Creek drops 420 feet over Raven Cliff Falls, forming one of the highest cascades in the East. The total height of all the tiers of the waterfall is close to 1,000 feet. Whether you view them from the observation deck across the gorge or from the bridge, where you can feel their spray, the falls are truly an awesome experience, and a pleasure to hike.

Rhododendron and mountain laurel are everywhere and put on quite a show in spring and summer. Two of the more exotic and spectacular varieties of rhododendron, pinxter flower and flame azalea, are well-represented. Chestnut oak predominates in an oak-hickory mix. The spray area of the falls harbors a rare species of wildflower, monkshood, found at only a few locations in South Carolina.

Hawks soar overhead, as do the ravens who gave the falls their name. Other bird species found here include black-and-white warbler, worm-eating warbler, hooded warbler, solitary vireo and scarlet tanager. Above Raven Cliff Falls, Matthews Creek is home to the native brook trout, now rare in South Carolina.

Raven Cliff Falls. SUSAN NELLE PHOTO

The beauty of the falls and their accessibility make them extremely popular. The parking lot is nearly always overflowing. Arrive as early as you can. If you have enough time and energy, you should hike to both the bridge and the overlook, in that order (about 7.8 miles total), and picnic at the latter. The overlook is large enough to accommodate several parties comfortably.

This hike is entirely within Mountain Bridge Wilderness Area. Raven Cliff Falls, formerly privately owned, was acquired by the state in the 1980s.

Facilities: None at trailhead. Caesars Head State Park, with rest rooms, drinking water, cold drink machines, a park store, and good information, is 1 mile down US 276.

Lodging and amenities: Primitive camping is available at Jones Gap State Park and along Jones Gap and Naturaland Trust trails, with prior permission, and full-service campsites are available at Table Rock State Park. Full services are available at Brevard, North Carolina and Greenville, South Carolina.

For more information: Mountain Bridge Wilderness Area. See Appendix A: For More Information.

19 Bill Kimball–Coldspring Branch Loop

General description:	The playful waters of Coldspring Branch offer a nice counterpoint to the overwhelming views of the rock dome called El Lieutenant, the key attraction of this half-day loop.
General location:	North of Greenville, in the northwest corner of the state.
Distance:	4.6 miles, loop.
Difficulty:	Very strenuous.
Trail conditions:	Conditions are rugged. Traffic is light.
Best time to go:	Spring, summer, and autumn. Do not attempt in icy conditions.
Maps:	Mountain Bridge Wilderness Area map, available at Caesars Head State Park; Cleveland USGS quad. See Appendix A: For More Information.
Fees:	None.

Finding the trailhead: The Raven Cliff Falls parking lot is 1 mile north of Caesars Head State Park and 35 miles northwest of Greenville on U.S. Highway 276. The trailhead for the Coldspring Branch Trail, which leads to the Bill Kimball Trail, is at the south end of the parking lot.

The hike: The loop hike described here is a combination of two Mountain Bridge Wilderness Area trails. The Bill Kimball Trail is the more difficult and spectacular, while Coldspring Branch Trail is the more restful. Together, they create a dynamite, but difficult, loop trail. This hike is recommended only for experienced

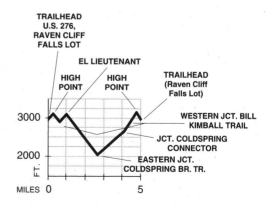

Bill Kimball–Coldspring Branch Loop

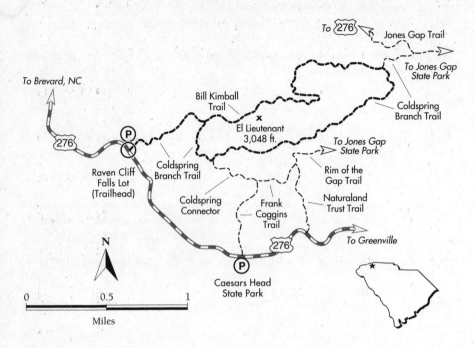

hikers with appropriate equipment, because parts of the Bill Kimball Trail are steep, rocky, and uneven.

The star of this hike is a huge rock dome. Its resemblance to the famous El Capitan of Yosemite National Park has led trail-builders to dub it El Lieutenant. Coldspring Branch harbors now-rare native trout, while ravens, seldom encountered in South Carolina, hang out at El Lieutenant. Broad-winged hawks soar overhead. Of course, Coldspring Branch has plenty of rhododendron and mountain laurel, but the stream is also noted for its spring wildflowers. Trees along the way include northern red oak, scarlet oak, white oak, chestnut oak, white pine, Fraser magnolia, and hickory. Carolina hemlock grow on El Lieutenant.

Start from the Raven Cliff Falls parking lot on Coldspring Branch Trail, which exits the lot at its southern end. This initial section, constructed in 1996, plunges down a ravine and climbs up again, but keeps you off the shoulder of US 276. Before 1996, hikers had to walk along the highway to connect with the old roadbed that constitutes most of the Coldspring Branch Trail.

The trail ascends immediately from US 276, then levels before plunging to the bottom of another slope to meet the Bill Kimball Trail at 0.6 mile from the trailhead.

Bear left (northeast) onto the Bill Kimball Trail, which is blazed pink. There are more Mountain Bridge Wilderness markers along the trail than there are pink blazes. Overall, trail marking is adequate. The Bill Kimball Trail starts off by going up, then flattens out to run along a ridge. It continues generally upward, but not at a steep pitch.

After cresting the ridge, the trail descends steeply. You enjoy excellent winter views of cliffs on the far side of Jones Gap, and the sound of falling water resonates. Switchbacks and a few sets of stairs are provided for the toughest part of the descent.

A chain helps you down past the first rock face. There is a tiny cave under the rock outcropping. The switchback is somewhat difficult. The trail continues switchbacking downward past other excellent boulders and outcroppings. From time to time, however, seepage from the rocks creates a boggy mess.

The other faces of El Lieutenant are more impressive. After a substantial descent, the trail ascends again to a spectacular rockface. Brave trees grow out of a steep slope in the middle of the rock. Other trees, mainly Carolina hemlocks, grow at the top. Many boulders have fallen to the foot of this rocky slope, and the trail threads its way among them. A chain again helps you negotiate the way.

But this rockface is only the appetizer. The final view of the face of El Lieutenant is jarring in its hugeness. This rock dome totally dominates its surroundings, the 300-foot sheer cliff making an unforgettable visual impact. From El Lieutenant, the trail heads downward. Even the switchbacks are steep and rocky. After the switchbacks end, the trail, well decorated with rhododendron, continues to descend, though not as steeply. The Middle Saluda River roars nearby.

El Lieutenant. John Dantzler photo

The trail meets the stream, and sometimes runs up the middle of it. If you stay on the rocks, you will stay dry. The stream flows through jungle-like vegetation; ferns, hemlocks, mountain laurel, and rhododendrons predominate. The rapids are both lovely and noisy.

The trail gradually evolves into a very heavily eroded roadbed, though no vehicle could negotiate it at its beginning. Eventually, it becomes a passable road. The trail twice crosses a small stream on logs and rocks. It crosses the next, very messy tributary on logs and ends at Coldspring Branch Trail, which branches left and right. Don't continue left (north) to Jones Gap Trail (0.2 mile away); instead turn right (southeast) to return to the trailhead.

It is all uphill from here, but the first part is the worst. Over its entire length, the trail crosses Coldspring Branch some eight times, nearly always over rock fords, and there are also crossings of tributaries. After 1.5 miles, the Coldspring Branch Trail meets the Coldspring Connector, on the left. (The Coldspring Connector connects to the Frank Coggins Trail, which in turn connects Caesars Head State Park with the Rim of the Gap and Naturaland Trust trails.) Bear right (west), staying on Coldspring Branch Trail. From this point, the ascent becomes steeper. After another 0.5 mile, the trail returns you to the western intersection of the Coldspring Branch Trail and the Bill Kimball Trail. From here, bear left (northwest) and return 0.6 mile to the parking lot.

Facilities: None at trailhead. Caesars Head State Park, 1 mile down US 276, has rest rooms, drinking water, cold drink machines, a park store, and good information, including an excellent diorama of Mountain Bridge Wilderness Area trails.

Lodging and amenities: Primitive camping is available at Jones Gap State Park and along some Mountain Bridge Wilderness Area trails, and full-service campsites are available at Table Rock State Park. Full services are available at Brevard, North Carolina and at Greenville, South Carolina.

For more information: Mountain Bridge Wilderness Area. See Appendix A: For More Information.

20 Naturaland Trust Trail

General description:	A rugged day-long hike from the top of Caesars Head through a cove forest, looping around to cross Raven Cliff Falls on a swinging footbridge.
General location:	North of Greenville, in the northwest corner of the state.
Distance:	9.5 miles, one way.
Difficulty:	Very strenuous.
Trail conditions:	Conditions are good. Traffic ranges from light to heavy.
Best time to go:	Year-round.
Maps:	Mountain Bridge Wilderness Area map, available at Caesars Head State Park; Table Rock USGS quad. See Appendix A: For More Information.
Fees:	None.

Finding the trailhead: The eastern trailhead is across the highway from Caesars Head State Park, 35 miles northwest of Greenville on U.S. Highway 276. The western trailhead is 1 mile farther north on US 276, on the left. Parking for the western trailhead is at the Raven Cliff Falls parking lot, across the highway on the right.

The hike: The Naturaland Trust Trail and its access trails make almost a complete circle from the summit of Caesars Head, along the way passing beneath a rock formation called the Cathedral and over a bridge across roaring Raven Cliff Falls.

The Naturaland Trust Trail is named for the Naturaland Trust, a Greenville land trust responsible for the preservation of much of the Mountain Bridge Wilderness Area and for the construction of many of the trails here, including this one.

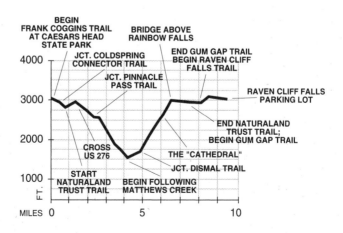

Naturaland Trust Trail

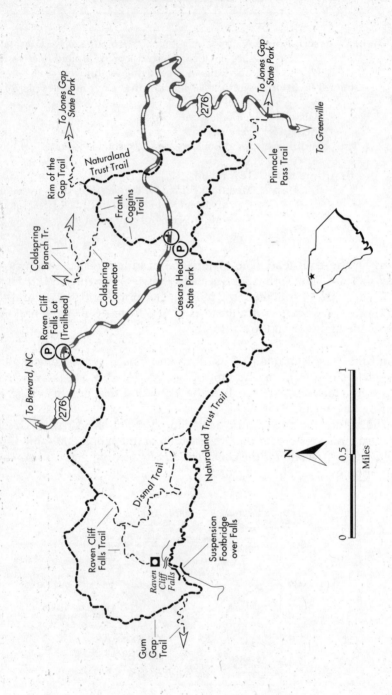

Author John Dantzler on the trail. Susan Nelle PHOTO

To hike the Naturaland Trust Trail from Caesars Head State Park, cross the highway and follow the purple-blazed Frank Coggins Trail. Only 0.8 mile long, this trail ends at Cliff Falls and the junction with the Naturaland Trust and Rim of the Gap trails. Turn right (southeast) onto the pink-blazed Naturaland Trust Trail. Down the trail 0.3 mile you come to 20-foot Firewater Falls, named for the remains of a moonshine still at the top. From here the trail continues 0.2 mile to US 276, which should be crossed carefully. Turn left (south) and proceed along the highway for 0.1 mile.

Because the Naturaland Trust Trail is so lengthy, some hikers prefer to cut off the first 1.3 miles, a loop on the north side of US 276. To make this shortcut, simply head south on US 276 from Caesars Head State Park 0.5 mile, turning right at a road blocked to traffic by a pipe gate. Trail markers also show the place to turn.

Once off the highway, the Naturaland Trust Trail circles the Caesars Head rock formation under sometimes massive cliffs. Rockcliff Falls, a 40-foot cascade, sits 0.3 mile from the highway. The trail takes you scrambling over rocks rather frequently, and along the way you pass an impressive official campsite under an immense rock.

113

Wildflowers put on a good show in the spring and include Ohio spider-wort, violets, phlox, wild hydrangea, foxglove, rattlesnake plantain, black-berry, wild azalea, partridge pea, butterfly pea, and sunflower, as well as the omnipresent mountain laurel and rhododendron. Trees include tulip poplar, sassafras, sourwood, hickories, and oaks, particularly chestnut oak. Ferns of every make and model grace the trail. White-tailed deer abound, while bird species you are likely to see include broad-winged hawk, Carolina chickadee, Carolina wren, and raven.

About 1 mile from the highway the Naturaland Trail intersects Pinnacle Pass Trail, to the left (east). In winter, the profile of Caesars Head can be seen from this point. Continue to the right (west), descending into the Dismal, a forest of mature hardwoods that runs from beneath Caesars Head to Table Rock Reservoir in the southwest. The steepness of the terrain here has made logging difficult, and the forest cover is thus relatively pristine. As the trail descends, Table Rock Mountain becomes visible to the west.

At 2.7 miles from the US 276 highway crossing, Matthews Creek, fresh from tumbling over Raven Cliff Falls, joins the trail. After another 0.8 mile from US 276, you reach the junction with the purple-blazed Dismal Trail, to the right (north).

From the junction with the Dismal Trail, it is 0.2 mile to the first crossing of Matthews Creek. The setting is less dramatic than that of the later crossing at Raven Cliff Falls, but when the water is high, this one is fairly dramatic as well: You cross on two metal cables, one for the feet, one for the hands. When the water is low, the stream can be forded by stepping across rocks.

The Cathedral is 0.7 mile farther. This massive rock formation looms 120 feet directly above the trail and has to be seen to be believed. The trail climbs steeply up steps, ladders, and switchbacks right alongside Raven Cliff Falls, which unfortunately is screened from view by heavy ground cover. At the top of the climb a spectacular swinging bridge crosses the falls (see Hike 18).

Beyond the bridge, the Naturaland Trust Trail continues 0.4 mile to its end, where you should turn right onto the blue-blazed Gum Gap Trail. The remaining 2.9 miles of the hike follow Gum Gap Trail (see Hike 17) and the red-blazed Raven Cliff Falls Trail (see Hike 18) to Raven Cliff Falls parking lot.

Facilities: Caesars Head State Park has rest rooms, drinking water, cold drink machines, a park store, and good information, including an excellent diorama of Mountain Bridge Wilderness Area trails.

Lodging and amenities: Primitive camping is available at Jones Gap State Park and along this trail at designated sites with prior permission (ask at Caesars Head or Jones Gap state park), and full-service campsites are available at Table Rock State Park. Full services are available at Brevard, North Carolina, and at Greenville, South Carolina.

For more information: Mountain Bridge Wilderness Area. See Appendix A: For More Information.

21 Rainbow Falls

General description:	A short, steep hike down a sheer cliff for spectacular bottom-up views of a 100-foot waterfall.
General location:	North of Greenville, in the northwest corner of the state.
Distance:	1.8 miles round trip.
Difficulty:	Strenuous.
Trail conditions:	Conditions are generally good. Traffic is heavy.
Best time to go:	Fall, winter, and spring. Summer access is limited.
Maps:	Standingstone Mountain USGS quad. See Appendix A: For More Information.
Fees:	None.

Finding the trailhead: The trailhead is on the property of Camp Greenville, a 1,600-acre YMCA conference center and youth camp located about 40 miles north of Greenville, just off U.S. Highway 276. Travel 2.4 miles past Caesars Head State Park on US 276 and turn right (east) at Camp Greenville Road, just at the North Carolina state line. Camp Greenville Road winds into North Carolina, then back into South Carolina. The camp office is 4.3 miles east of the US 276 turnoff. From the camp office, follow the signs toward Symmes Chapel. At the fork in the road, where signs point to the chapel on the right (east) fork and the Airnasium and cabins to the left (north), park in the small gravel parking area on the right (south) side of the road. Backtrack about 10 yards and enter the trail between two large marker stones at the head of a short stairway.

The hike: The trail is on the private property of Camp Greenville, and all visitors must obtain permission at the camp office before hiking to the falls. It is best to call for permission in advance (864-836-3291). During summer, the camp is heavily used by youth groups and access to outside hikers is necessarily limited.

The footing on the extremely steep, 400-foot descent is treacherous in rainy or icy conditions. Whatever the weather, you should wear footwear with adequate ankle support and soles appropriate for walking on slippery surfaces.

From the trailhead, you move down quickly through rhododendron and mountain laurel, and within minutes you can hear the rush of Cox Camp Creek pouring out of the North Carolina mountains. Depending on the season and the density of the foliage, you soon encounter views of the powerful stream galloping out of plateau forest, dancing through rocky rapids, and then dropping in a dead fall to the floor of the V-shaped gorge.

During the fall migration of songbirds and raptors, this cliff is an excellent vantage point from which to view warblers, vireos, ravens, peregrine falcons, and bald eagles.

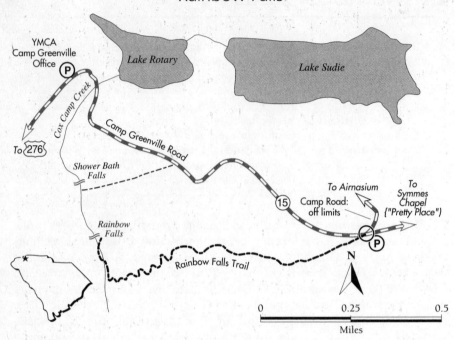

Rainbow Falls

YMCA
Camp Greenville
Office ⓟ

Lake Rotary

Lake Sudie

Cox Camp Creek

To (276)

Camp Greenville Road

Shower Bath
Falls

Rainbow
Falls

Rainbow Falls Trail

⑮ Camp Road:
off limits

To Airnasium

To
Symmes
Chapel
{"Pretty Place"}

ⓟ

N

0   0.25   0.5

Miles

You follow a trail of very steep descents, sometimes with the aid of heavy ropes. Fairly level ledge sections punctuate the climb and allow you to catch your breath and enjoy the views. The way down the side of the cliff sometimes passes beneath massive granite overhangs.

The narrow valley at the bottom of the trail is a magical place. You walk through hemlocks, oaks, and lush ferns to cross the stream by treading across boulders while grasping a sturdy cable for balance as you edge along a large fallen tree. Once on the west side, you pick your way upstream a few yards and choose the best spot from which to enjoy the upward vista of plummeting Rainbow Falls. You can cross back to the east side of the creek to get closer to the base of the falls and experience the refreshing spray (occasional falling rocks make it dangerous to get too close, however). On sunny days, rainbow prisms glisten from the mist.

During seasons when daylight is short, time your visit so you arrive at the bottom of the falls in the middle of the day, since the high-walled, south-facing gorge receives only a few hours of sunlight each day. Some level ground and many boulder surfaces offer delightful picnic sites, and you may wish to explore the floor of the gorge downstream of the falls.

Needless to say, the trip back up the cliff takes more time and effort than the downward journey, but as you ascend and rest along the various ledges, you have a stronger appreciation of the falls, which are intermittently visible in the distance.

After returning to the trailhead, walk or drive several hundred feet up

Author John Clark on the trail to the falls. Yvonne Michel photo

the paved road to Symmes Chapel, popularly known as Pretty Place. This covered stone structure on the edge of the Blue Ridge Escarpment commands a panoramic view of the section of the Middle Saluda River valley known as Jones Gap. The chapel, ringed by 49 inspirational plaques, is a popular wedding site. It is open to the public when not reserved for private use.

Facilities: Facilities at Camp Greenville are for the use of groups registered to use the camp. The nearest public rest rooms, water fountains, and vending machines are available at Caesars Head State Park.

Lodging and amenities: Primitive camping is available at Jones Gap State Park and along some Mountain Bridge Wilderness Area trails, and full-service campsites are available at Table Rock State Park. Full services are available at Brevard, North Carolina, and at Greenville, South Carolina.

For more information: YMCA Camp Greenville. See Appendix A: For More Information.

117

Rainbow Falls. JOHN CLARK PHOTO

22 Jones Gap Trail

General description:	A relatively easy day hike along the scenic Middle Saluda River from Jones Gap State Park to Caesars Head State Park.
General location:	North of Greenville, in the northwest corner of the state.
Distance:	5.3 miles one way.
Difficulty:	Moderate.
Trail conditions:	Conditions are generally good. Traffic is moderate to heavy.
Best time to go:	Year-round.
Maps:	Mountain Bridge Wilderness Area map available from Jones Gap and Caesars Head state parks; Standingstone Mountain and Cleveland USGS quads. See Appendix A: For More Information.
Fees:	None.

Finding the trailhead: The eastern trailhead is at Jones Gap State Park, about 30 miles northwest of Greenville off U.S. Highway 276/South Carolina Highway 11. At 1.4 miles past the eastern intersection of US 276 and SC 11, turn right on River Falls Road (Secondary Road 97). After 3 miles, the road name changes to Jones Gap Road. It is an additional 3 miles to Jones Gap State Park. From the parking area at Jones Gap State Park, cross a bridge over the Middle Saluda River and head toward the park buildings. The trailhead is beyond the park buildings and is reached via a short path past the second bridge across the Middle Saluda.

From the US 276/SC 11 turnoff to Jones Gap State Park, the western trailhead is 13.3 miles farther up US 276. It is located at a brown pipe gate on the right side of the road 2 miles beyond Caesars Head State Park, and 1 mile past the Raven Cliff Falls parking lot on US 276. Hikers are required to register at boxes located at the trailheads.

The hike: The Jones Gap Trail is full of delights, chief of which is the relative ease of the hike, surprising in a trail that ascends 1,600 feet over its 5-mile length. The trail was built in the 1840s by Solomon Jones as a toll road. Legend says that Jones chose his route by releasing a pig and following it, knowing it would take the easiest path. The story is certainly apocryphal; what Jones followed was the Middle Saluda River, knowing that the stream finds the easiest way down. And so it proved.

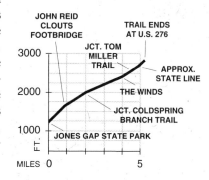

Jones Gap Trail

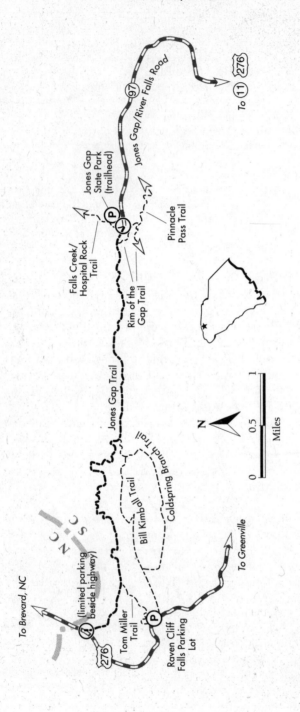

The Solomon Jones Road operated as a toll route until about 1910. In the 1930s, it was considered as a route for the road that is now U.S. Highway 276, but fortunately this option was rejected. Today, Jones Gap Trail has been accorded official status as a National Recreation Trail. The trail also serves as the easternmost segment of the Foothills Trail. The river it follows, the Middle Saluda, was the first to be designated a State Scenic River.

Jones Gap Trail is not only easy to hike, but also easy to follow. Blazed blue, it stays next to the Middle Saluda River for almost its entire length, crossing and recrossing the river several times. One of the best crossings occurs at about the 1-mile point, where an excellent footbridge overlooks pretty cascades on either side. The trail offers excellent views of Cleveland Cliff and Little Rich Mountain, especially in the wintertime.

Jones Gap Trail affords a number of loop opportunities. Be forewarned that all of these loops have stretches that are much more difficult than any part of the Jones Gap Trail itself. Near the eastern trailhead, the Rim of the Gap Trail turns off to the left (south); access to the Pinnacle Pass Trail is also reached this way. Both of these trails are very long and very strenuous, and not recommended as part of a loop with Jones Gap Trail.

Coldspring Branch Trail turns off from Jones Gap Trail to the left (south) at 2.1 miles from the eastern trailhead. This one is more manageable as part of a loop. (Coldspring Branch Trail also makes an excellent loop hike when combined with the Bill Kimball Trail; see Hike 19). Coldspring Branch Trail runs to US 276 at the Raven Cliff Falls parking lot, where you may pick up the Tom Miller Trail to continue the loop. The latter is short (0.7 mile), but tough. It is much easier to handle when traveled west to east, i.e. making this loop clockwise from the other direction. (After the Tom Miller Trail loops around to intersect the Jones Gap Trail, you can continue east along the Jones Gap Trail 4.5 miles to Jones Gap State Park.)

The beauty of the Middle Saluda River beggars description, but landmarks are few and far between. Even the landmarks are actually watermarks; for instance at 3.3 miles the stream drops about 15 feet into a deep ravine to the left of the trail. Fortunately, because the trail hugs the river so tightly, landmarks are little needed. You can focus on the river as it tumbles, rushes, or roars and not worry about losing the trail.

At 3.9 miles from the eastern trailhead, there is a sign for the Winds. The original road became so tortuous here that people in carriages had difficulty negotiating it. The trail ascends on a number of switchbacks, the first of which is somewhat difficult to see. Do not hike straight up the hill, as this leads to soil erosion. The songbirds in the trees here are so numerous they create a cathedral of pleasing sounds.

Birds are abundant throughout the hike. You may be able to spot ravens, red-tailed hawks, red-bellied woodpeckers, Carolina chickadees, tufted titmice, white-breasted nuthatches, downy woodpeckers, and hermit thrushes. Swainson's warblers, usually hard to find in the mountains, may be encountered on this trail.

The river is the primary attraction, but not the only one. The forest shading the Middle Saluda is rich and varied and features eastern hemlock, mountain laurel, rosebay rhododendron, beech, sweet gum, and tulip poplar. Wildflowers and other interesting plants include strawberry bush (hearts-a-bursting), rattlesnake plantain, Christmas fern, beechdrops, partridgeberry, foamflower, and yellow violet.

Facilities: Jones Gap State Park features rest rooms, showers, drinking water, cold drink machines, and an environmental education center. Caesars Head State Park has rest rooms, drinking water, cold drink machines, a park store and good information, including an excellent diorama of Mountain Bridge Wilderness Area trails.

Middle Saluda River. Susan Nelle photo

Lodging and amenities: Primitive camping is available at Jones Gap State Park and along this trail and Naturaland Trust Trail at designated sites. Trailside campers must register and pay a fee at the park office. Full-service campsites are available at Table Rock State Park. Full services are available at Brevard, North Carolina and Greenville, South Carolina.

For more information: Mountain Bridge Wilderness Area. See Appendix A: For More Information.

23 Rim of the Gap Trail

General description:	Outstanding views of Jones Gap, including Cleveland Cliff and Rainbow Falls, combine with spring wildflowers and autumn colors to make this linear trail one of the finest day hikes in the state.
General location:	North of Greenville, in the northwest corner of the state.
Distance:	5.2 miles one way.
Difficulty:	Very strenuous.
Trail conditions:	Conditions are good, though rugged. Traffic is light to moderate.
Best time to go:	Year-round. Avoid the coldest part of winter.
Maps:	Mountain Bridge Wilderness Area map, available at Jones Gap and Caesars Head State Parks; Cleveland, Standingstone Mountain, Table Rock USGS quads. See Appendix A: For More Information.
Fees:	None.

Finding the trailhead: The western trailhead is at Caesars Head State Park, about 35 miles northwest of Greenville. Caesars Head State Park is on the left (south) side of U.S. Highway 276, 6.3 miles north of the western intersection of US 276 and South Carolina Highway 11. Directly across US 276 from Caesars Head State Park is the trailhead for the Frank Coggins Trail, which is also the trailhead for this hike.

The eastern end of the trail is at Jones Gap State Park, 16.6 highway miles from Caesars Head State Park. Turn east on River Falls Road (Secondary Road 97), 4.3 miles east of the western intersection of US 276 and SC 11. After 3 miles, the road name changes to Jones Gap Road. It is an additional 3 miles to Jones Gap State Park. From the parking lot at Jones Gap State Park, take a short trail that crosses the Middle Saluda River, passes the park buildings, and crosses the river again to reach the Jones Gap Trailhead. Register at the trailhead. The Rim of the Gap Trail is 100 yards down Jones Gap Trail to the left.

Rim of the Gap Trail

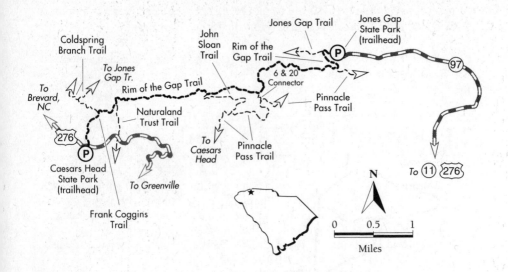

The hike: The Rim of the Gap Trail is quite accurately named. For much of its length it hugs the southern rim of Jones Gap, offering magnificent views of this ancient cleft. The latter part of the trail passes through mountain cove and river cove forests rich in species diversity, including spring wildflowers.

The Rim of the Gap Trail starts about 1 mile east of Caesars Head State Park. It is reached via the purple-blazed Frank Coggins Trail, an old roadbed.

After 0.5 mile's walk on the Frank Coggins Trail you reach the Coldspring Connector, which connects to Coldspring Branch Trail (see Hike 19). Continue ascending. At 0.8 mile, on the other side of pretty Cliff Falls, you reach the intersection of the Frank Coggins, Naturaland Trust, and Rim of the Gap trails.

Follow the yellow-blazed Rim of the Gap Trail and cross the rock sluice that is a lower section of Cliff Falls via a cable over slick rocks. Afterward, you cross a bridge; be sure to hold onto the cable here also, as the bridge can be very slippery. People have fallen off before. The trail passes big rock outcroppings. Many of these feature a lot of seepage, so the footing can be very wet. The trail is icy in winter and not recommended during cold spells, especially at the higher elevations toward Caesars Head.

The trail follows switchbacks down the mountain. There is another cable crossing of Cliff Falls a short distance from the bottom. Next, you cross a smaller waterfall, this time fording on rocks. A switchback passes beneath another rock outcropping and rock sluice, and then passes by another one.

The trail goes up rocks. Some seepage moistens the trail; exercise extra care after rains. The many stairs and ladders are a challenge. One outcropping features a good-sized cave.

A mile along the Rim of the Gap Trail, 1.8 miles from the western trailhead, there is a rock with a beak-like overhang, somewhat similar to the famous outcropping at Caesars Head. This is a good place to rest; a fairly strenuous climb follows. Watch the blazes, as the trail makes some sudden turns.

The trail passes through two tight clefts, one shin-high and one knee-high, before reaching Weight Watcher's Rock after 1.4 miles on the Rim of the Gap Trail (2.2 miles from the western trailhead). A giant boulder balanced on several other boulders, Weight Watcher's Rock gives you a small rectangular gap to squeeze through. It might better be called Height Watcher's Rock, as the low bridge aspect is more pronounced than the narrowness. If you're carrying a large backpack, take it off and hand it through the gap, or simply walk around on the bypass trail to the left.

The trail's best view of Jones Gap comes 0.1 mile after Weight Watcher's Rock. Take a side trail from one of the switchbacks 20 feet or so through the mountain laurel. You can see the entire length of Jones Gap, including Rainbow Falls on the north rim.

Return to the Rim of the Gap Trail to continue the hike. At the top of the climb the trail becomes relatively level. The old roadbed you follow for much of the rest of the hike begins here. The trail intersects with the John Sloan and 6 & 20 trails, both short connectors to the Pinnacle Pass Trail (at 1.7 and 2.4 miles, respectively, from the start of Rim of the Gap Trail), making numerous loop hikes possible.

The remainder of the Rim of the Gap Trail offers spring wildflowers and good late autumn and early spring views of Rainbow Falls. The roadbed traversed by the trail passes through a cove forest, then a river cove forest. You pass the scar from a major 1978 landslide. The trail is heavily eroded on the way down to Jones Gap State Park.

When you reach the intersection with Pinnacle Pass Trail (3.9 miles from Frank Coggins Trail), you are nearly at the eastern trailhead. It is 0.4 mile to Jones Gap State Park from this point. The final section holds some nifty rock outcroppings and giant boulders (one reminiscent of the statuary at Easter Island) and an extremely dramatic ravine. At the end of the Rim of the Gap Trail, turn right on Jones Gap Trail for a hundred yards. The park buildings are just across the bridge over the Middle Saluda River, and the parking lot is slightly beyond.

Facilities: Jones Gap State Park features rest rooms, showers, drinking water, cold drink machines, and an environmental education center. Caesars Head State Park has rest rooms, drinking water, cold drink machines, a park store, and good information, including an excellent diorama of Mountain Bridge Wilderness Area trails.

Lodging and amenities: Primitive camping is available at Jones Gap State Park and along Jones Gap and Naturaland Trust trails with prior permission, and full-service campsites are available at Table Rock State Park. Full services are available at Brevard, North Carolina and Greenville, South Carolina.

For more information: Mountain Bridge Wilderness Area. See Appendix A: For More Information.

24 Pinnacle Pass Trail

General description:	A rugged, one- to two-day hike up and over a number of mountains and ridges, punctuated by a spectacular vista of Jones Gap.
General location:	North of Greenville, in the northwest corner of the state.
Distance:	13 miles one way.
Difficulty:	Very strenuous.
Trail conditions:	Conditions are good, but rugged. Traffic is generally light.
Best time to go:	Year-round. Avoid the coldest days of winter.
Maps:	Mountain Bridge Wilderness Area map, available at Jones Gap and Caesars Head State Parks; Cleveland USGS quad. See Appendix A: For More Information.
Fees:	None.

Finding the trailhead: The eastern trailhead is at Jones Gap State Park, about 30 miles northwest of Greenville off U.S. Highway 276/South Carolina Highway 11. At 1.4 miles past the eastern intersection of US 276 and SC 11, turn right on River Falls Road (Secondary Road 97). After 3 miles, the road name changes to Jones Gap Road. It is another 3 miles to Jones Gap State Park. Hikers are required to register at the eastern trailhead. From the parking area, take a short trail past the park buildings, crossing the Middle Saluda River twice on bridges. On the other side of the second bridge is the Jones Gap Trailhead. Follow the Jones Gap Trail for a few hundred feet to where the yellow-blazed Rim of the Gap Trail turns off to the left (south). After several hundred feet on the Rim of the Gap Trail, take the left (east) fork onto the Pinnacle Pass Trail.

The western trailhead is at Caesars Head State Park, 10.6 miles up US 276 from the US 276/SC 11 turnoff to Jones Gap. From the parking area, walk down US 276 the way you came 0.5 mile. Here, at a brown pipe gate

Pinnacle Pass Trail

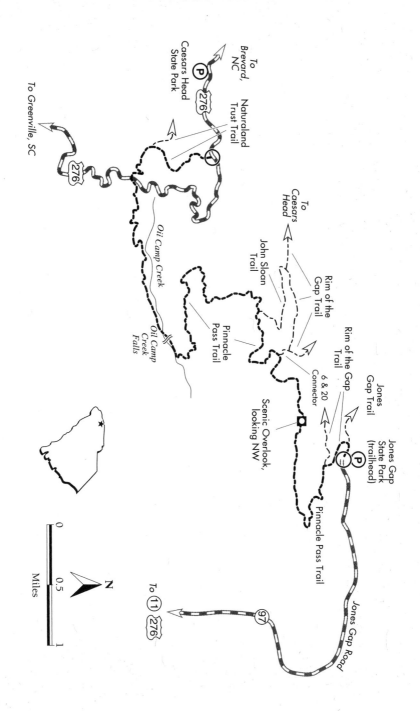

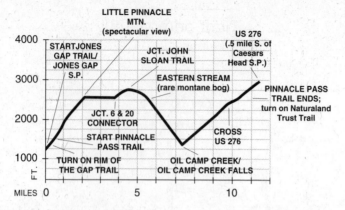

on the right (southwest) side, the Naturaland Trust Trail heads into the forest, meeting the western terminus of the Pinnacle Pass Trail after 0.9 mile.

The hike: The best view in South Carolina, possibly in the eastern United States, is less than 2 miles from popular Jones Gap State Park. The trail runs mostly uphill, but the view is an experience well worth the climb. From a rocky precipice, the hardy gaze down on an unforgettable panorama of the length and breadth of Jones Gap, bisected by the Middle Saluda River and towered over by dramatic mountains.

Interesting rock outcroppings, rock sluices, and excellent autumn colors and views of Cleveland Cliff make for a delightful hike. An old moonshine whiskey-still provides local color. After a rugged climb, the trail drops 10 or 20 feet, and a railing and chain protect you from the 2,000-foot drop-off. Here is the vista that makes the climb worth the effort. You are 2.2 miles from Jones Gap State Park and standing atop a crest of Little Pinnacle Mountain.

The hike continues for a total of 13 miles, all the way to Caesars Head State Park. Along the way, the Pinnacle Pass Trail intersects two very short connector trails, the 6 & 20 Connector and the John Sloan Trail (3.7 and 4.5 miles, respectively, from the beginning.) Each connects with the Rim of the Gap Trail, and each makes possible numerous exciting and difficult loop hikes on the longer Pinnacle Pass and Rim of the Gap trails.

About 0.7 mile past the intersection with the John Sloan Trail, the Pinnacle Pass Trail leaves the rugged roadbed it has so far followed and plunges to the left (south) down a narrow path through the forest. The markers are very subtle, so keep a wary eye.

After a lengthy descent, you reach the midway point on Pinnacle Pass Trail (5.4 miles), where you see an unusual plant community called a cataract bog. Tread lightly; it harbors a number of very rare plants, including mountain pitcher plant, grass-of-Parnassus, and Indian paintbrush.

Beyond the cataract bog, the trail crosses a wide expanse of granite. You are still atop Little Pinnacle Mountain (which should perhaps be renamed

Long Skinny Mountain.) The way is marked by blazes painted on the outcropping and by one cairn. The climb down (over the next 1.7 miles) is rugged.

Along the trail, trees include a large variety of oaks (especially chestnut, northern red, scarlet, and white), hickories, cucumber tree, eastern hemlock and rarer Carolina hemlock, mountain laurel, and rhododendron. Also present are wild ginger, wild hydrangea, large grapevine, and rattlesnake plantain.

This is one of the highest trails in the state, so don't be surprised to encounter such mountain birds as raven, ruffed grouse, rose-breasted grosbeak, and worm-eating warbler, as well as more cosmopolitan species such as broad-winged hawk and pileated and downy woodpeckers.

Ravines, more waterfalls (including lovely Oil Camp Creek Falls), and more breathtaking views await the adventuresome who complete the entire hike. The last third of the trail runs mostly on unpaved Oil Camp Creek Road. (The trail turns right to join the latter 7.2 miles from Jones Gap State Park.) It is also within a wildlife management area, so take care during hunting season. As the old road makes its gradual climb to Caesars Head, it curls back on itself in majestic switchbacks that are attractions unto themselves. Over 2.5 miles, Oil Camp Road (and the trail) climbs over 800 feet, but the switchbacks make it easy.

After these 2.5 miles, the trail turns off Oil Camp Creek Road in order to cross US 276. The final 0.7 mile of Pinnacle Pass Trail is quite strenuous. The Pinnacle Pass Trail ends at the Naturaland Trust Trail. Turn right on to the latter and proceed north 0.9 mile to US 276 and turn left (west) onto the highway. Caesars Head State Park is 0.5 mile uphill.

Lodging and amenities: Primitive camping is available at Jones Gap State Park and along some Mountain Bridge Wilderness Area trails, and full-service campsites are available at Table Rock State Park. Full services are available at Brevard, North Carolina, and at Greenville, South Carolina.

For more information: Mountain Bridge Wilderness Area. See Appendix A: For More Information.

25 Falls Creek Trail–Hospital Rock Trail

General description:	An extremely rugged day hike along a mountain trail with great views, particularly of splendid Falls Creek Falls.
General location:	North of Greenville in the northwest corner of the state.
Distance:	6.1 miles one way.
Difficulty:	Very strenuous.
Trail conditions:	Conditions are fair, but rugged. Traffic is very light.
Best time to go:	Year-round. Avoid the coldest days of winter.
Maps:	Mountain Bridge Wilderness Area map, available at Jones Gap State Park; Standingstone Mountain, Cleveland USGS quads. See Appendix A, For more information.
Fees:	None.

Finding the trailhead: To reach the eastern trailhead, go 1.4 miles past the eastern intersection of U.S. Highway 276 and South Carolina Highway 11 and turn right on Secondary Road 97 (River Falls Road). After 3 miles, the road name changes to Jones Gap Road. Go 1 more mile and turn right onto Duckworth Road at the sign for Palmetto Bible Camp. After 0.7 mile, turn right again, onto Falls Creek Road, at another sign for the bible camp. Go another 0.4 mile (passing Palmetto Bible Camp) and cross a small bridge and waterfall; the trailhead is just to the left (north).

The western trailhead is at Jones Gap State Park, at the end of SR 97. From the parking lot, head toward the park buildings on a short trail that crosses the Middle Saluda River. At the fish pond of the former Cleveland Fish Hatchery, bear right (north). The trailhead is straight ahead, marked by a hiker registration station. All hikers are required to register at Jones Gap State Park. There is no registration box at the Falls Creek end of the trail.

The hike: This is a tough one, one of the most difficult hikes in South Carolina. The rewards, however, are great. Falls Creek Falls is a wonder, and Falls Creek above the falls makes a gloriously peaceful picnic spot. Hospital Rock is only one of numerous dramatic rock outcroppings encountered along the hike, which follows two trails: Falls Creek Trail and Hospital Rock Trail. Both are blazed in orange.

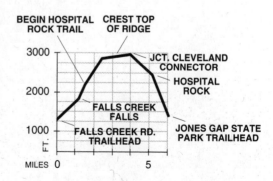

Falls Creek Trail–Hospital Rock Trail

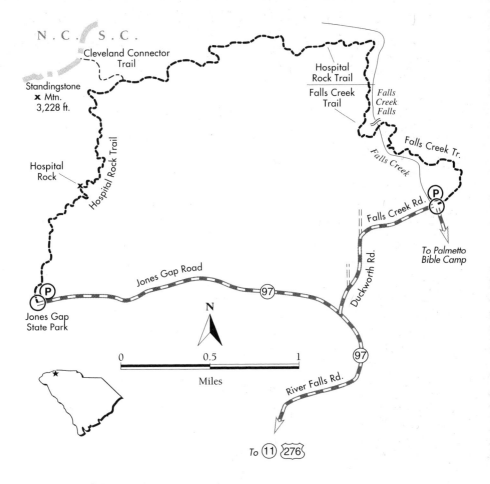

The flora and fauna here resemble those found elsewhere in the mountains, but, whether flora or fauna, there seems to be more of it. The chestnut oak and Fraser magnolia are taller; the mountain laurel and rhododendron come up even thicker. Other trees include hickory, tulip poplar, northern red oak, red maple, white pine, eastern hemlock, sassafras, holly, redcedar, beech, and Carolina silver bell. Among the wildflowers, expect to see galax, white snakeroot, rattlesnake plantain, closed gentian, violets, spotted wintergreen, wild hydrangea, wild ginger, beautyberry, and a variety of asters. Other plants include fox grape, switch cane, Christmas fern, and bracken. The heavy foliage makes birds difficult to spot, but you may see red-shouldered hawk, pileated woodpecker, or chickadee.

Between October 1 and January 1, and during the month of April, wear fluorescent orange. Parts of the trail pass through a wildlife management area, and hunting is allowed during these months.

The hike starts off on orange-blazed Falls Creek Trail and follows an old logging road—straight up. Gigantic boulders and a nice ravine add interest to the climb. Eventually, the logging road thins out, becoming a narrower and often highly eroded track. Pay close attention to trail blazes, as there are many turnings which are rather easy to miss. The trail crosses several small streams, including Little Falls Creek at 0.7 mile.

Climbing up on switchbacks, you hear but don't see Falls Creek Falls 1.2 miles from the trailhead. To get down to the falls, use the guide chain. At the stream itself, a guide cable helps you cross the very slippery rocks. Viewed from the bottom, Falls Creek Falls are a glory. They are one of the finest waterfalls in the Mountain Bridge Wilderness Area.

After the waterfall, you ascend Falls Creek Trail on narrow switchbacks. These continue through another zone of big boulders. In late autumn or early spring you may be able to see Fall Creek Falls from a big boulder to the right of the trail at 1.5 miles. The trail then takes you up and over the boulders. Suddenly, the trail almost levels out, passing through a thicket of mountain laurel and rhododendron with a chestnut oak canopy. There is a neat little rock sluice. Here, above the waterfall, Falls Creek is a lovely mountain brook. The area is dark, cool, and peaceful; it is a superlative place to be in the summertime. There is a sea of hemlock.

At another old logging road, turn right (north) and sharply uphill. When the trail leaves Falls Creek, it becomes the Hospital Rock Trail. Nothing marks this fact; the blaze even stays orange. This is also roughly the point where the trail enters the Jones Gap State Park boundary.

One of the rewards of all this climbing is a huge, submarine-shaped rock outcropping. Actually, there are a number of outcroppings. After these, the trail climbs to the top of the ridge 0.5 mile from the start of Hospital Rock Trail. At the top, the forest is quite pleasant, with good views to either side in late autumn and early spring. At the ridgeline, the trail again becomes an old logging road.

While the roadbed continues straight with a pink blaze, the Hospital Rock Trail, well blazed with orange, turns to the left (west) on a much smaller path, heading downward. Along this stretch, several oak trees display big goiters (burls), and rhododendron abounds. A stream runs in the ravine to the left. Footing is rocky and uncertain. The trail levels out for a nice stretch as it passes to the right of an immense thicket of mountain laurel.

Hospital Rock Trail crosses numerous tributaries of Headforemost Creek on wet rocks between 1 and 1.5 miles from Falls Creek. The stream does a good deal of flowing under, around, and over the trail. Hospital Rock Trail ascends and turns right. At the junction with the Cleveland Connector, a Mountain Bridge Wilderness Area signpost says that Hospital Rock is another 1.2 miles on the Hospital Rock Trail (via the left, or southwest, fork), that Camp Greenville is 0.5 mile on the Cleveland Connector (the right fork, up the hill), and that it is 2.4 miles back the way you came to Falls Creek Trail.

Continue on the trail to Hospital Rock, where you pass a huge, beautiful, bowl-shaped ravine with virtually no undergrowth (on the left). While the trail here is an old logging road, time has allowed the forest to reclaim it somewhat. When the trail leaves the roadbed, it goes straight down, crossing another rhododendron-bordered stream on rocks. As you descend with the stream on your left, you come to a large rock that is very difficult to negotiate; a chain is provided to help you.

The trail levels off, skirting a ridge. Views range from excellent to spectacular, particularly in autumn. The level part sadly does not last, and at 2.9 miles the trail goes back to making you scramble down rocks. Jones Gap itself makes for a lovely view. There are many interesting outcroppings and the grapevines are quite large. You must do a great deal of slipping and sliding to get down to several switchbacks, which make the descent more manageable.

Don't try to stay at the informal campsite at Hospital Rock; camping is not allowed on this part of the trail. Legend says that Confederate deserters hid out here during the Civil War, and there is certainly room enough—the cavern under the rock is high enough for people to stand.

A sign at the rock informs you that it is 1.1 miles to Jones Gap State Park. After Hospital Rock, the trail turns a corner and heads upward. After a short distance, the trail starts down again on switchbacks. The tough stuff now is mainly climbing up and down the rock-lined ravines that punctuate the trail. The trail passes under high-tension power lines at 3.9 miles, then reaches another stream; in the midst of all the switchbacks is a nifty rock sluice. The trail crosses on rocks just below the sluice and follows the stream down.

The final portion of the trail is easy, and passes old plumbing for the former Cleveland Fish Hatchery, now Jones Gap State Park, and several primitive campsites, ending at the state park facilities.

Facilities: Jones Gap State Park features rest rooms, showers, drinking water, cold drink machines, and an environmental education center.

Lodging and amenities: Primitive camping is available at Jones Gap State Park and Jones Gap and Naturaland Trust trails at designated campsites with prior permission. Full-service campsites are available at Table Rock State Park. (Campsites at end of Hospital Rock Trail are so near the park that they don't really qualify as trailside camping.) Full services are available at Brevard, North Carolina, and at Greenville, South Carolina.

For more information: Mountain Bridge Wilderness Area. See Appendix A: For More Information.

26 Paris Mountain State Park

General description:	A rugged half day's hike on a mountain trail at the edge of South Carolina's largest metropolitan area.
General location:	Just north of Greenville, in the northwest corner of the state.
Distance:	6 miles, loop.
Difficulty:	Strenuous.
Trail conditions:	Conditions are generally good. Traffic is moderate to heavy.
Best time to go:	Spring, summer, and fall.
Maps:	Park brochure; Greenville NW and Greenville NE USGS quads. See Appendix A: For More Information.
Fees:	$2 parking fee in summer.

Finding the trailhead: From Interstate 385, take Exit 40. Go north on South Carolina Highway 291 (Pleasantburg Drive) 1.6 miles. At U.S. Highway 29, take a hard left (west) to continue on SC 291.

After another 2.5 miles, turn right (northeast) on SC 253 (Paris Mountain Road). Continue 2.7 miles, turning left (north-northeast) onto Secondary Road 344, which leads to Paris Mountain State Park. From the entrance, Sulphur Springs Picnic Area is a little more than 1 mile, on the left (west). The trailhead is in the picnic area, adjacent to shelter 6.

The hike: Paris Mountain is a monadnock, an immense rock that endured when the mountains around it weathered away. This area has been protected since the 1890s. Due to the steepness of the terrain, much of the park has never been logged. Two reservoirs add beauty to the park. Both were originally built to provide drinking water to the city of Greenville. Now they provide recreation and scenic vistas.

Paris Mountain State Park features three long trails. Two combine to form a single long hiking loop, while the third is mainly for mountain biking. Additionally, a 1-mile nature trail circles Lake Placid, the park's swimming lake. The Sulphur Springs and Brissey Ridge trails are best approached as a loop (6 miles total), although the Sulphur Springs Trail alone forms a loop of 4 miles. Both trails are rather challenging.

From the trailhead at the picnic area, the Sulphur Springs Trail follows a pleasant stream through mountain laurel and rhododendron. This first stretch of the trail is wide and well worn.

At a gazebo about 0.1 mile from the trailhead, the trail forks. A sign reading simply "Trail" points to both forks. Either fork takes you to the dam that holds back Mountain Lake, where the routes meet again 0.1 mile later. Of the two, the left-hand fork is much more interesting, but exercise caution, as it is not well maintained and the last few hundred feet offer fairly

Paris Mountain State Park

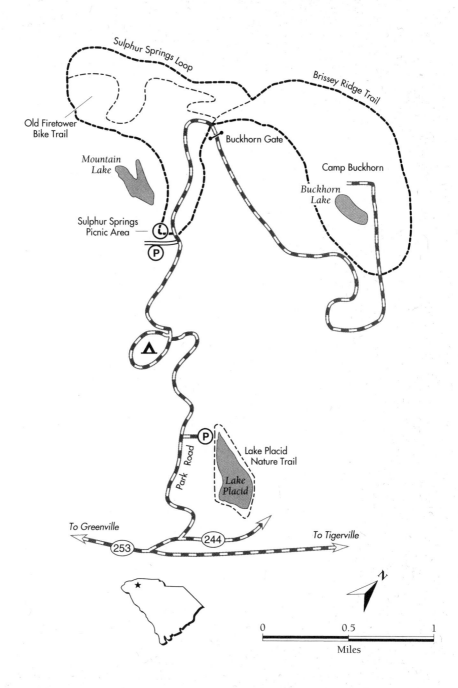

Mountain Lake Dam. John Dantzler photo

treacherous footing. The right-hand fork, which goes by the gazebo on a wide set of stairs, is the official trail, and is wider and more road-like.

Mountain Lake was created in 1898 as one of the two lakes built in the park to provide drinking water for Greenville. The dam is very impressive, and the waters of the lake are lovely. The trail, blazed white, runs along the eastern edge of the lake. The footing becomes difficult as the trail narrows to little more than a path across rocks. The rock formations overhanging this arm of the lake provide great scenic interest. The trail continues to skirt the lake on the east until the latter narrows to the stream again. Slabs of rock lying across the stream mark where the trail crosses. The trail becomes wider again after the crossing. A cute waterfall peeks at you before diving under a boulder.

For a stretch, the trail runs nearly level alongside the creek, then ascends, straight up, with the creek on hand immediately to the right laughing at you. The stream does not again form a waterfall, though, until almost the top of the climb, where the stream plunges 10 feet. Below this, the trail crosses on some logs.

The trail descends into a mountain laurel thicket and crosses the stream again. On the other side, there is more climbing to do. At a T intersection 1.4 miles from the trailhead, continue straight, following Sulphur Springs Trail to the Brissey Ridge Trail; this route also leads to Buckhorn Gate. To your right (east) the Old Firetower Bike Trail goes straight down. The bike trail leads to Buckhorn Gate, 1.6 miles away.

As you continue toward the Brissey Ridge Trail, the trail appears to fork at the top of the first ascent, about 0.3 mile past the junction with the bike trail. Bear right. The trail now descends fairly gently. You are on an old road running along a ridgeline, and the hiking is easy and pleasant. If you want to do only the Sulphur Springs Loop, turn right for Buckhorn Gate and the return trip along the Sulphur Springs Trail to Sulphur Springs Picnic Area; this section of trail goes straight down initially.

The Brissey Ridge Trail, blazed yellow, descends quite rapidly. You see a number of large, interesting trees along this trail; one of these comprises two trunks growing out of an older, larger trunk with an immense hole in its middle.

Signs posted along the way keep you on the proper trail and prevent you from turning onto side paths. The trail levels off, then heads down again, briefly following an old logging road. Once off the logging road, the trail heads downhill on a reasonably steep grade.

Cross the main park road after 1.3 miles on Brissey Ridge Trail and continue toward Buckhorn Gate, 1 mile away. The trail follows a stream, then crosses the stream on a log and goes steeply up. Next, the trail—never straight and never level, with a great deal of up and down—snakes along the side of an undulating ridge toward Buckhorn Gate. After 0.5 mile, the trail trends generally downward until it reaches a gorge bisected by a small stream. Cross the stream on logs, and then ascend again to arrive at Buckhorn Gate.

Buckhorn gate, there is a turning circle and parking area. The mountain bike trail and the Sulphur Springs Loop converge here with Brissey Ridge Trail, although neither is conspicuously marked.

To return to the trailhead, cross the road to pick up the continuation of the trail, now the Sulphur Springs Loop again. A sign informs you that Sulphur Springs Picnic Area is 1 mile away.

The trail ascends, crests the ridge, and heads steeply down. You eventually reach a cool mountain brook, which you cross twice over sturdy bridges. You'll need to make a third crossing as well, this time via either logs or by fording.

From this point, the trail heads up again, then down, emerging across the road from the Sulphur Springs Picnic Area and the trailhead, almost directly opposite the driveway. This end of the trail is unmarked from the point of view of visitors at the picnic area except for a blaze and a sign reading "Buckhorn Gate, 1 mile," both 100 feet up the hill.

Facilities: Rest rooms, drinking water, swimming, picnic areas.

Lodging and amenities: The park has 50 campsites. All services are available at Greenville.

For more information: Paris Mountain State Park. See Appendix A: For More Information.

Midlands

The Midlands region stretches across the central part of the state and comprises many subregions. Most of the Midlands region is part of the Piedmont geological province. All of the Sandhills are in the Midlands. Another subregion, the Savannah River Valley, stretches for 200 miles along the state's western border, from the Chattooga River in the Mountains all the way across the Coastal Plain to the Atlantic Ocean, but most of the valley's hikes described in this book are in the Midlands. The Savannah River Valley is also sometimes described as the state's Freshwater Coast due to the recreation opportunities offered by Lakes Hartwell, Russell, and Thurmond.

The 15 hikes featured in this region range from the hilly trails in the Long Cane Ranger District of Sumter National Forest in the western part of the state, near Georgia, to the flat terrain of Congaree Swamp in the center of the state, to the Sandhills belt near Cheraw and the state's northeastern border.

The upper portion of the Midlands offers a rolling landscape and includes several monadnocks, solitary prominences that rise several hundred feet above the land around them. Remnants of ancient mountain ranges, they are made of much harder rock than that of the surrounding area. When the rest of the ancient mountain ranges weathered away, the monadnocks, such as Parson's Mountain, were left to stand alone. You will find easier hikes on the flatter trails along and below the Sandhills.

Major points of departure for Midlands hikes include Abbeville, Edgefield, and Aiken in the west; Columbia and Newberry in the central region; Rock Hill in the north-central area near Charlotte; and Sumter and Cheraw in the east.

The wonderfully diverse and far-flung Midlands is not so much a region as an apt name for most of the area between the mountains and the coast. Hills and ravines characterize the hikes at Poinsett and Kings Mountain state parks, and in the Long Cane and Enoree/Tyger ranger districts of Sumter National Forest. Peachtree Rock Heritage Preserve, Harbison State Forest, Carolina Sandhills National Wildlife Refuge, and Cheraw State Park perch across the center of the state, offering a variety of perspectives on the sandhills, the state's ancient seashore. In the north-central part of the state, between Columbia and Charlotte, the Anne Springs Close Greenway and Landsford Canal State Historic Site offer scenery and history while Congaree Swamp National Monument and Santee State Park offer watery tranquillity and easy hiking at the upper edge of the coastal plain.

The Midlands trails are mostly accessible from interstates 20, 26, and 77, which converge at Columbia, South Carolina's capital, located in the center of the state. Additionally, I-85 provides a jumping-off point for Kings Mountain State Park. Carolina Sandhills National Wildlife Refuge and Cheraw State Park are a short distance north of the Florence exit of I-95, and Santee

State Park is just north of the Santee exit of I-95. Another roadway, U.S. Highway 1, passes right by Cheraw State Park and Carolina Sandhills National Wildlife Refuge. US 1 is within 45 minutes' drive of 13 of the region's 15 hikes as it crosses the state from northeast to southwest, from North Carolina to Georgia.

All Midlands hikes are within easy reach of the accommodations and services in the Columbia area and along the interstate highways. The region is also blessed with an abundance of attractive small towns that offer history, good food, and comfortable bed-and-breakfast facilities. These towns include Abbeville, McCormick, Edgefield, and Blackville in the west; Newberry, Winnsboro, Chester, and Rock Hill in the north-central portion; and Camden, Hartsville, Cheraw, and Bennettsville in the east.

27 Long Cane Trail

General description:	Two to three days of hiking on a long loop trail through well-watered and rolling terrain, featuring the tall trees of Long Cane Scenic Area.
General location:	Just south of Abbeville, in the western part of the state.
Distance:	22 miles, loop.
Difficulty:	Moderate.
Trail conditions:	Trail conditions range from excellent to poor. Traffic ranges from light to moderate.
Best time to go:	Year-round. Take care during fall hunting season.
Maps:	Forest Service trail map; Verdery and Abbeville East USGS quads. See Appendix A: For More Information.
Fees:	None.

Finding the trailhead: From Abbeville, take South Main Street south until it turns into a lovely country lane, Secondary Road 33. After 8 miles, bear left (northeast) on SR 47. Fell Hunt Camp is another 1.5 miles, on the right (east). The trailhead is across the road from the entrance to the hunt camp.

To reach the same trailhead from Greenwood, proceed south 8 miles on South Carolina Highway 10 and, at Verdery, turn right onto SR 47. The trailhead is 3.5 miles, on the right (west).

The trail can also be joined at Parson's Mountain Recreation Area and at several crossings of Forest Service Roads.

The hike: The Long Cane Trail, an equestrian and hiking trail, passes through the ancient hills and valleys that abut the upper Savannah River. "Ancient" here is no exaggeration; some of the vegetation in the Long Cane Scenic Area, through which the trail passes, is very unusual, remnant of the long-ago era when these hills were a spur of the Appalachian Mountains.

Long Cane Trail

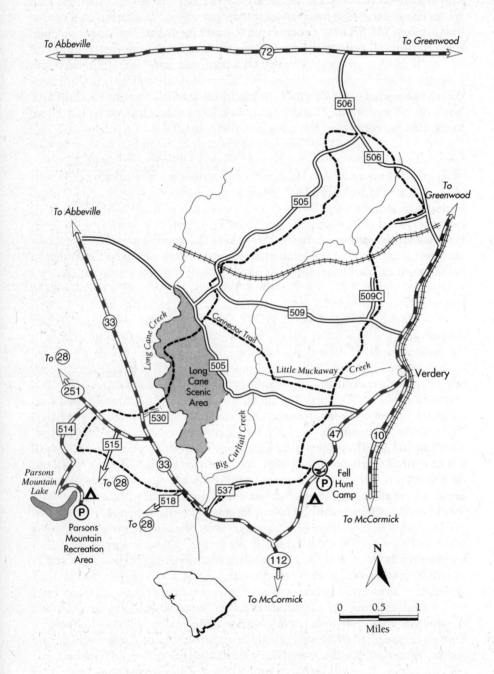

To Abbeville

To Greenwood

72

506

506

506

505

To Greenwood

To Abbeville

33

509C

To 28

509

251

Long Cane Creek

Connector Trail

Little Muckaway Creek

Verdery

514

505

Long Cane Scenic Area

515

530

47

10

Big Curltail Creek

To 28

33

Fell Hunt Camp

To 28

518

537

To McCormick

112

To McCormick

N

0   0.5   1
Miles

The Long Cane Trail passes through lands mostly forested with pine, but there are plenty of hardwoods, too. Trees include baldcypress, hickory, red maple, tulip poplar, dogwood, and several species of oaks. The huge river cane explains the names of the trail, scenic area, and creek.

Hunters come here for the deer and wild turkey. While you may not encounter these elusive creatures, you will surely see their tracks. The calls of the red-shouldered hawk and pileated and downy woodpeckers fill the air.

From Fell Hunt Camp, cross the road to the trailhead, where there are two signs featuring color maps of the trail. Of the two, the one farther from the paved road is newer, clearer, and more accurate. Continue along the trail, which at this point is an old road. It narrows and passes recently clearcut land to the right and mature mixed forest to the left. The trail turns into a red clay track much churned by horses, and footing can be difficult.

The trail emerges into a clearing. A pleasant and well-blazed path turns off to the left; do not follow it. It is a former trailbed, and while it leads past an interesting old smokehouse to a lovely little creek, it eventually fades away into the woods.

Instead, bear right (north). You pass several more clearcuts, ford a small creek, cross a petroleum pipeline right of way, traverse some lovely stretches of older forest, and pass a lone aging oak in an old homesite clearing before meeting Forest Service Road 505, once an Indian trail known as the Virginia Path. In 1825, the Charleston Road was built on this path and for many years, regular stagecoach service operated along the route.

Cross FS 505 to continue the hike. From this point, the terrain shows many dips and rises. After about 0.25 mile, you may continue straight ahead on the main trail or choose to turn left (west) on a 2.6-mile connector trail which will shorten the overall mileage of the hike by 7 miles. (See the discussion of this variation at the end of this hike description.)

Past the connector trail turnoff, the primary loop trail fords Little Muckaway Creek. You will need to wade after heavy rains. On the opposite bank, the trail ascends steadily and passes along and across numerous old roads as the forest gradually becomes older and the hardwood character more pronounced. The trail crosses FS 509 and follows FS 509-C to that road's end, about 1 mile farther on. At the end of FS 509-C, the trail turns left (north) onto an old logging road.

At Gray's Creek, the remains of an old bridge facilitate an easy ford. Immediately afterward, the trail passes under a still-used railroad trestle. The vegetation on either side of the trail is alive with birds. The trail ascends briskly from the trestle and moves through a wisteria-filled forest, passing an ancient cemetery, marvelous old hickory and maple trees, and a massive hybrid white oak.

The trail follows a spur of FS 506 before heading west toward Big Curltail Creek. On this northernmost portion of the hiking loop, you may want to follow FS 506 instead of the trail, about 1.5 miles northwest to just past its intersection with FS 505, where you can pick up the forest trail again. This detour allows you to avoid brambles, a heavy concentration of fire ant nests,

Big Curltail Creek. John Clark photo

brambles, a heavy concentration of fire ant nests, and a difficult fording of Big Curltail Creek.

After the second crossing of FS 506, the trail passes over varied terrain under old hardwoods, mostly white and blackjack oaks. There is a splendid ravine on the right.

In another 1 mile, the trail crosses FS 505 again, then moves southwest to reemerge on FS 505 once more, about 3 miles farther along. Turn left (south) onto FS 505 and continue along the road about 0.3 mile to cross a railroad track. After continuing on the road another 0.3 mile, the trail heads off to the right (west) for a short trek through pine forest before crossing FS 505 yet again and plunging back into the forest for about 0.7 mile. The trail passes another intersection with the 2.6-mile connector mentioned earlier before crossing FS 505 for the last time.

Here the trail enters the Long Cane Scenic Area. The scenic area is a special place. Left unlogged and largely undisturbed, it grows as nature intended. Through it winds Long Cane Creek—dark, mysterious, and beautiful.

The trail wends its way through old hardwoods. It passes the state's largest shagbark hickory, which is in fact the second-largest of its species in the world.

The trail crosses Long Cane Creek's substantial stream over a unique bridge—an iron plank that arcs downward in the middle. While it lacks rails, the edges are raised a few inches, in the manner of a sliding board.

In a grassy wetland on the western side of the river, the trail becomes very difficult to discern, but it emerges clearly on the far side of the wetland.

The trail crosses SR 33 and SR 251 to enter Parson's Mountain Recreation Area. Parson's Mountain Lake comes within sight at a clearing. Leaving the recreation area, the trail crosses FS 515 at a point which was once the site of the largest white oak in South Carolina; the tree is now gone, but the huge stump remains.

The trail ascends gradually through numerous ravines and emerges on gravel FS 518 just south of paved SR 33. Here you should turn right (east) on SR 33 and walk 0.6 mile, crossing the highway bridge over Long Cane Creek and turning left (northeast) at FS 537.

The trail moves away from the road and Long Cane Creek, into the woods. It follows babbling Stillhouse Branch, briefly joining a motorcycle trail at a creek crossing. At the crossing, a paved ramp leads down to the water's edge. You can jump across here or ford on rocks and logs. High water presents problems.

The rest of the way to Fell Hunt Camp is mostly uphill, but enlivened by attractive ravines. The trail is marked sporadically with brown wands that protrude from the ground, but trail finding can be a challenge at times.

Although there are some disadvantages to sharing a trail with horses, inconveniences on Long Cane Trail are minimal, and horse activity helps keep the trail discernible. Equestrian use is heaviest in the area nearest Fell Hunt Camp, the trailhead. There is very little concentrated equestrian use on most other parts of the trail, except for the connector trail.

Variation: The connector trail can shorten the overall loop from 22 to 15 miles, but it presents numerous difficulties. It also offers several special attractions, foremost of which is the opportunity to walk along restful Little Muckaway Creek.

After following Little Muckaway Creek west a short distance, you reach a dirt road that runs steeply uphill, away from the water. The trail, not well marked at this point, passes the road and follows the creek for about another mile. Cross the creek on two fallen trees that form a makeshift bridge, the upper tree serving as a handrail.

In another 0.25 mile, after skirting private property, the trail comes out at a petroleum pipeline and its dirt service road. Turn right onto the service road and follow the right of way to Big Curltail Creek. The underbrush alongside the pipeline harbors unbelievable numbers of songbirds.

Big Curltail Creek is quite wide, and to cross you will need to wade, swim, or find a fallen tree. On the other side, continue following the right of way. Head uphill and turn left (northwest) at the next plastic marker pointing that way. From here, the trail moves 1 mile through forest to reconnect with the main loop.

Facilities: Drinking water and rudimentary toilet facilities at Fell Hunt Camp; rest rooms and drinking water at Parson's Mountain Recreation Area.

Lodging and amenities: Primitive camping is allowed at Fell Hunt Camp and along the trail. Parson's Mountain Recreation Area offers 23 campsites. Full services are available at Greenwood and charming, historic Abbeville.

For more information: Long Cane Ranger District of Sumter National Forest. See Appendix A: For More Information.

28 Parson's Mountain

General description:	A morning or afternoon walk up Parson's Mountain and around a lake.
General location:	Just south of Abbeville, in the western part of the state.
Distance:	4 miles, loop.
Trail conditions:	Trail conditions are very good. Traffic is light.
Difficulty:	Moderate.
Best time to go:	Year-round.
Maps:	Parson's Mountain Recreation Area map, Forest Service; Verdery USGS quad. See Appendix A: For More Information.
Fees:	$3 per vehicle.

Finding the trailhead: From Abbeville, take South Carolina Highway 28 south for 2.1 miles. Turn left (southeast) on Secondary Road 251 and proceed 1.5 miles to the entrance on the right. Follow Forest Service Road 514 past the swimming area and the camping area, across the causeway over Mountain Creek (Parson's Mountain Lake is to your right), and to the boat ramp. The trailhead is at the boat ramp parking lot.

The hike: At 800 feet, Parson's Mountain is not especially high, but it dominates its relatively flat surroundings and offers a commanding view from its summit. It also offers hikers a surprisingly spirited climb. Gold was mined here during the Civil War, and the mine shafts are a highlight of the trail.

Wading birds, including great blue heron, frequent the lake, and redheaded and other woodpeckers are common in the forest.

The woods are rich in flowering plants, including wild ginger, hepatica, dogwood, cat brier *(Smilax)*, sparkleberry, redbud, and rattlesnake plantain. Big beeches grow near the lake and watercourses, including one by the lake that still stands though the base of its trunk is split in half.

The mainly clay-surfaced trail crosses an old road and descends to cross a stream. On the right you see a bridge marked by a double white blaze; the trail around the lake crosses this bridge and we recommend it for the return segment of this hike. The main trail continues across FS 515, which also ascends to the top of Parson's Mountain.

From the road, the trail to the fire tower trends mostly up, passing abandoned gold mine shafts from the Civil War era along the way. South Carolina was an important gold producer in the early 1800s. Even today, the Carolina slate belt, just inland from the Sandhills, is home to four working gold mines.

At the summit, swifts dart about the 80-foot fire tower. Near the fire tower an impressively large chestnut tree, probably a hybrid, is especially popular with the caterpillars.

Return down the mountain to the bridge and turn left (northwest) for the loop around the lake. The bridge leads over a serene brook. The trail enters a fern forest and crosses several small streams. At a marker by a white oak, the trail forks. Continue right to head clockwise around the lake, emerging at the circle road for the swimming area. Turn right on the road to get down to the swimming area. Exit the swimming area at the east end to pick up the trail again. Follow the trail past the campground and across the road to the trailhead.

Facilities: Rest rooms and drinking water at the swimming area and campground. There is a portable toilet near the fire tower at the summit.

Lodging and amenities: Parson's Mountain Recreation Area has 23 campsites, and primitive camping is available at nearby Fell Hunt Camp. Other campsites are at Lick Fork Lake Recreation Area and a variety of public and private locations along lakes Russell and Thurmond. Lodging and other

Parson's Mountain

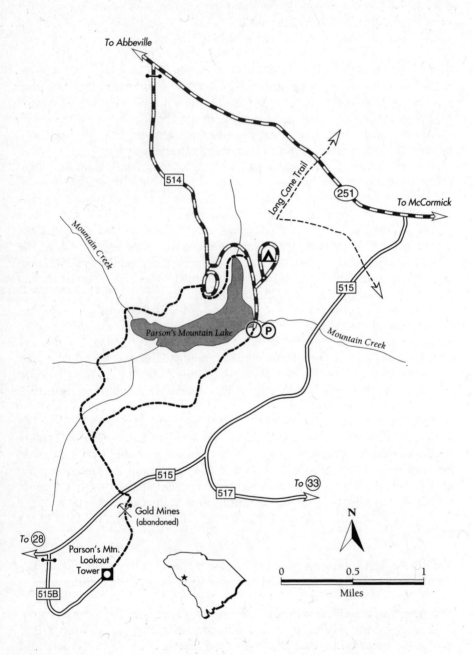

amenities are available at the beautiful and historic town of Abbeville, as well as at Greenwood.

For more information: Long Cane Ranger District of Sumter National Forest. See Appendix A: For More Information.

---

29 Turkey Creek Trail

General description:	A one- to two-day hike on a linear trail following the banks of Wine, Turkey and Stevens creeks in the Savannah River Valley, featuring great cypress trees, slippery beaver runs, and scenic river views.
General location:	North of Augusta, in the western part of the state.
Distance:	12.5 miles one way.
Difficulty:	Moderate.
Trail conditions:	Trail conditions range from good to poor. Traffic ranges from light to heavy.
Best time to go:	Year-round. Avoid during hunting season and after heavy rains.
Maps:	Free map available from Long Cane Ranger District; Parksville and Clarks Hill USGS quads. See Appendix A: For More Information.
Fees:	None.

Finding the trailhead: The northeastern trailhead is at a small parking lot on South Carolina Highway 283, about 14 miles northeast of Edgefield. From Edgefield, follow SC 23 west for 2 miles, then turn right (northwest) onto Secondary Road 35. Go 5 miles to the intersection with SC 283. Turn left (west) at the intersection and drive 7 miles to a small parking lot on the left (south). (The parking lot is 2 miles west of the SC 283 bridge over Turkey Creek.)

The middle trailhead at Key Bridge is on SR 227/68. (Because it crosses a county line, the road is designated as SR 227 north of Key Bridge, and as SR 68 south of the bridge.) From the northeastern trailhead, drive west about 0.5 mile on SC 283 and turn left (southeast) on SC 138. Follow SR 138 1.5 miles and turn left (south) on SR 227. From this intersection, Key Bridge, an old steel girder structure, is 2.3 miles. The trail crosses SR 227 about 0.1 mile north of the bridge. Parking is on the shoulder of the road.

To reach the southwestern trailhead from the northeastern trailhead, drive west about 0.5 mile and turn left (southeast) on SR 138. Follow SR 138 about 3.5 miles and turn left (south) onto Forest Service Road 617, which is unpaved. Drive 0.7 mile on FS 617 and take the first right (west) onto FS 617A. The southwestern trailhead is at the end of FS 617A, 0.6 mile from the junction with FS 617.

Turkey Creek Trail

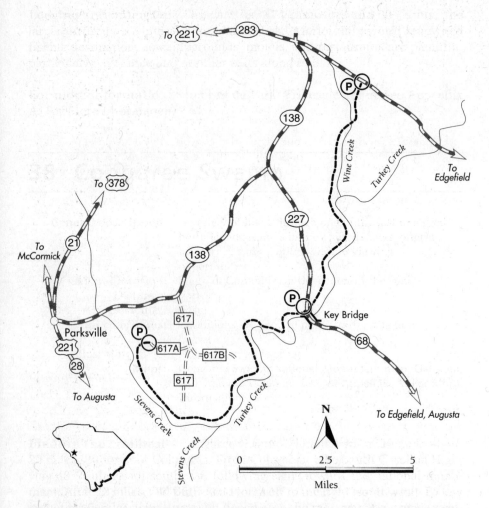

The hike: Large, climax-stage hardwood forests, dotted with massive oaks and tall baldcypresses and their sleek cypress knees, characterize the area bordering Turkey and Stevens creeks, dark rivers that range from 40 to 80 feet wide. White-tailed deer and wild turkeys are plentiful, as are a variety of nongame birds, wildflowers, and butterflies.

On the McCormick County (west) side of Turkey Creek, the Turkey Creek Trail has three major entry points and can be hiked in two segments. The 5.2-mile northern segment begins at a small parking lot on SC 283 and ends at Key Bridge on SR 227/68. The terrain and vegetation on this lightly traversed segment are more rugged than on the southern segment, but you are rewarded with more elevated views and greater solitude. Because of the dense vegetation in the middle of this segment, you should wear long pants.

The trail begins in a forest of pine, oak, maple, and dogwood. It soon begins to follow, and then crosses, Wine Creek, a shallow, rocky stream about 10 feet wide, decorated with moss and ferns and amply populated with small reptiles and amphibians.

After about 2 miles, you reach the confluence of Wine and Turkey creeks. Impressive views of Turkey Creek reveal themselves intermittently as you hike along high bluffs. By and large Turkey Creek is a quietly flowing stream, though whitewater churns a few places along this section. You walk around and through deep ravines leading to the river, sometimes aided by footbridges and sometimes, when they have been damaged or carried away by gully washers, having to cope without them.

Tree stumps and steep, slippery paths down to the riverbank provide evidence of the area's large beaver population. Brier and cane thickets cause difficulty in places, especially at and around the pipeline right of way clearing at the 3.2-mile mark.

When you reach the trailhead just north of Key Bridge, be sure to walk down the road and onto the bridge, which offers a great vantage point to enjoy the river as it lumbers along below you.

The 7.3-mile southern segment, which hikers often share with mountain bikers, undulates more gently and has fewer ravines. The vegetation is less dense, except along the final 2.3 miles. The southern segment begins near Key Bridge and ends in a parking area at the end of FS 617A.

Views through hickory, oak, and cypress along Turkey Creek alternate with jaunts on high ground away from the river and through the margins of pine forest and evidence of recent clearcutting to the right (northwest).

The confluence of Turkey and Stevens creeks, about 5 miles from Key Bridge, offers easy access to the riverbank and the opportunity to wade or swim. At this point, the terrain slopes gently to a sandy area at the water's edge.

The trail follows Stevens Creek upstream. After about 0.1 mile, you encounter a sign and a fork in the trail. Turn left (west) and continue another 2 miles along Stevens Creek, then walk 0.3 mile through pine forest to the parking area that marks the end of FS 617A. The sign pointing in this direction reads, "Modoc 7.5 miles," but the trail traverses only the 2.3 miles to FS 617A, not to Modoc. (Alternatively, you can take the right fork and walk 0.2 mile to the end of FS 617.)

Some parts of this final trail section offer scenic travel along the banks of Stevens Creek. However, when the trail moves away from the stream, usually to pass around and through ravines, dense vegetation often impedes the way. During the final 1 mile, be careful not to mistake the frequent beaver paths for right (north) turns of the trail.

Facilities: No rest rooms or drinking water at the trailheads.

Lodging and amenities: Camping with basic amenities is offered at nearby Lick Fork Lake and Parson's Mountain recreation areas, as well as at several

Turkey Creek. JOHN CLARK PHOTO

state, federal, and private facilities on Lake Thurmond. The nearby communities of Edgefield and McCormick offer food and lodging, including bed-and-breakfast facilities, and unique shops.

For more information: Long Cane Ranger District of Sumter National Forest. See Appendix A: For More Information.

30 Lick Fork Lake

General description:	A day hike around a small lake, along a creek, and through a mixed pine and hardwood forest.
General location:	North of Augusta, in the western part of the state.
Distance:	The recommended hike is 6.6 miles. The Lick Fork Lake Trail is 1.7 miles, loop. Horn Creek Trail is 5.4 miles, loop.
Difficulty:	Easy to moderate.
Trail conditions:	Trail is unobstructed and clear. Traffic is moderate.
Best time to go:	Year-round. Take care during hunting season (late fall).
Maps:	Forest Service map of Lick Fork Recreation Area; Colliers USGS quad. See Appendix A: For More Information.
Fees:	$3 per vehicle admission fee for day use.

Finding the trailhead: From Edgefield, take South Carolina Highway 23 south 8.2 miles, then bear left (south) on SC 230. Drive 0.5 mile to Secondary Road 263, turn left (east), and drive 1.9 miles to Forest Service Road 639, the Lick Fork Lake Recreation Area entrance road, on the right.

From the north parking area, walk though the picnic area and down to the lake. On the north side of the grassy beach, on the right as you face the swimming area, a sign marks the beginning of the Lick Fork Lake Trail. The trailhead for the Horn Creek Trail is adjacent to the parking lot adjacent to the south parking lot, just east of the dam (at the south end of the lake).

The hike: The Lick Fork Lake Trail heads north beside a stream that feeds the lake. Watch carefully for a sign indicating a 90-degree turn to the left (west). This turn carries you down to a small brook which you must ford by hopping across slippery rocks. (The initial path continues straight ahead upstream (north) for some distance before fading out, so it is important to watch carefully for the left turn.)

The trail now heads south, first along the stream and then along the west side of Lick Fork Lake. There are many scenic vistas. The trail crosses several brooks and gullies, some by means of small footbridges. The mixed forest has a clear understory and contains white oak, beech, northern red

Lick Fork Lake

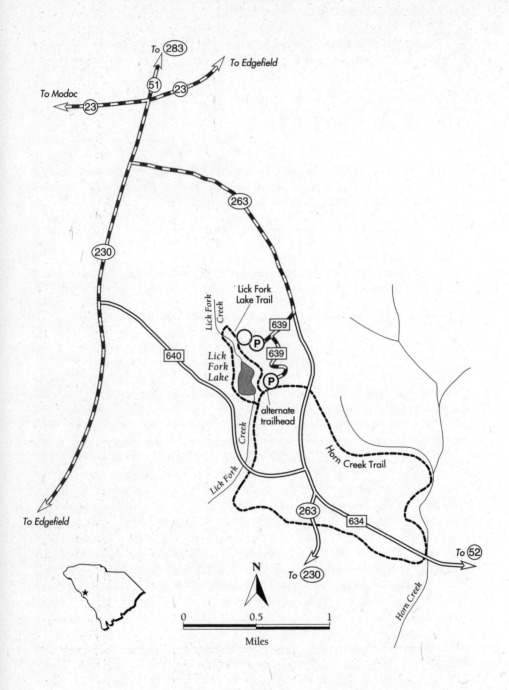

oak, dogwood, red maple, hickory, sourwood, and both loblolly and short-leaf pines. Underneath grow holly, ferns, and a variety of wildflowers. Watch for signs of beaver activity.

At the south end of the lake, beyond the dam, the Lick Fork Lake Trail crosses sonorous Lick Fork Creek over boulders to intersect the Horn Creek Trail at 1.2 miles. If you do not want to continue on the Horn Creek Trail, you may turn left (northeast) here and walk 0.5 mile to the south parking lot and north from there along the east side of the lake to the swimming area where the Lick Fork Lake Trail began.

Horn Creek Trail is well maintained by a local mountain biking organization. For most of the way a thick canopy provides shade and a clear understory for easy forest viewing. Wildflowers, grapes, and blackberries flourish in the understory. Wildlife includes red-cockaded and yellow-bellied sapsucker woodpeckers, pine warblers, nuthatches, Bachman's sparrows, chickadees, turtles, frogs, squirrels, deer, and fire ants.

The trail follows rocky Lick Fork Creek through a hardwood forest of ironwoods, maples, and sweet gums. It crosses FS 640 at 1.7 miles and, after crossing a footbridge over a tributary, heads up and over a ridge through an area that has been thinned by logging.

Author John Clark on the Horn Creek Trail. LEANN BROWN PHOTO

Horn Creek. John Clark photo

You cross SR 263 at 2.8 miles and head through a forest of pines and maples with a fairly dense understory. Crossing FS 634 at 3.4 miles, you encounter a bottomland marsh pond created by beaver activity on Horn Creek, to the right (east). Sycamores, swamp chestnut oaks, river birches, and water oaks replace the pines and hardwoods of the higher ground.

Crossing various tributaries along the way, the trail moves through more mixed forest, eventually leaving the creek to follow high ground through oaks, maples, and pines. After crossing SR 263 again at 5.9 miles, the trail ends back at the south parking lot.

From here, you may return to the swimming and picnic area near the north parking lot by passing the dam and boat ramp and following a lakeside trail. Walk by a pier and cross the footbridge (over a small lake branch) that connects the camping and picnic areas.

Facilities: Drinking water, rest rooms, and shower available in the swimming and picnic area. Rest rooms and drinking water are scattered throughout the camping area. A wheelchair-accessible fishing dock and short paved trail are located along the east side of the lake (access from the south parking lot).

Lodging and amenities: The North Augusta and Aiken exits on Interstate 20 have numerous facilities. There are attractive restaurant and bed-and-breakfast options in and around Edgefield and McCormick. Lick Fork Lake Recreation Area has 10 individual campsites, as well as a group campsite, and there are a large number of public and private campgrounds on Lake Thurmond.

For more information: Long Cane Ranger District of Sumter National Forest. See Appendix A: For More Information.

31 Peachtree Rock

General description:	A visit to prehistoric rock formations along two short loop trails through varied vegetation.
General location:	West of Columbia, in the central part of the state.
Distance:	2 miles, loop.
Difficulty:	Easy to moderate.
Trail conditions:	Conditions are good. Traffic is light to moderate.
Best time to go:	Spring, autumn, and winter.
Maps:	Nature Conservancy brochure; Pelion East USGS quad. See Appendix A: For More Information.
Fees:	None.

Finding the trailhead: From Columbia, follow South Carolina Highway 302 (Edmund Road) west, past the airport. Beyond the airport 16 miles, fork

Peachtree Rock

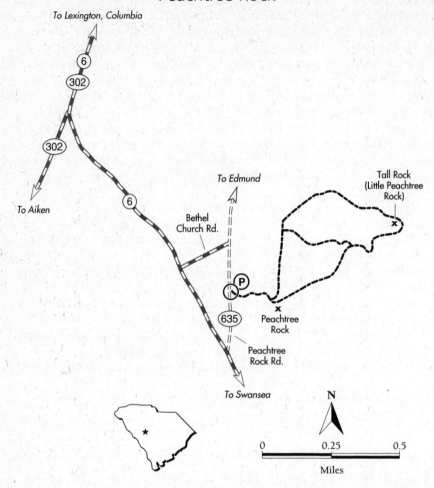

left (southeast) on SC 6. Follow SC 6 for 0.9 mile and turn left (north) onto Secondary Road 635 (Peachtree Rock Road), which is unpaved. The parking area is 0.2 mile, on the right. Be sure to lock your vehicle and secure all valuables, as the lot is secluded and unguarded. Follow the sign into Peachtree Rock Heritage Preserve.

The hike: Peachtree Rock Heritage Preserve is a 306-acre refuge dedicated to the protection of a number of unique sandstone formations and the flora and fauna surrounding them. Peachtree Rock, Little Peachtree Rock, and other interesting formations are the main attractions.

However, the flora and fauna are also unique and worth taking time to view. Even though the preserve lies in central South Carolina, many miles from the mountains, mountain laurel flourishes here. Moreover, one plant, the blueberry vine called Rayner's blueberry, is found nowhere else but

Author John Dantzler on a cliff along the trail. Walt Oliver photo

here in Lexington County. The trees are mostly turkey oak and longleaf pine, but others such as mockernut hickory dot the forest.

A variety of lizards, including eastern fence lizards, Carolina anoles, and various skinks, scramble underfoot. Birds are somewhat scarce, but pileated woodpeckers, tufted titmice, summer tanagers, and white-eyed and red-eyed vireos can usually be found.

About 0.1 mile from the trailhead sits Peachtree Rock, which looks something like an overturned pyramid balanced precariously on its apex. About 20 feet high, the sandstone rock is riddled with wormholes from the ancient days when South Carolina's Sandhills belt was the eastern seacoast. One ridge over, a smaller set of outcroppings looks like a set of extremely large teeth.

Near Peachtree Rock the only natural waterfall in central South Carolina drops 20 feet into Hunt Creek. This waterfall never forms a rushing torrent, but it cools the air and lends a mood of tranquillity to the scene.

Start at the waterfall and take the blue-blazed trail. In hotter weather, it is a good idea to hike both trails completely, ending each on Hunt Creek where it is much cooler and shadier. The rest of the preserve is very open, sunny, and sandy.

After about 0.25 mile, the trail turns right onto an old logging road. It turns (right again) off the road shortly thereafter. About 1 mile from Peachtree Rock, you find yourself at the top of a ridgeline with a panoramic view of the countryside. Just ahead sits Little Peachtree Rock (or Tall Rock), a skinnier version of Peachtree Rock. This rock is out in the open, unlike Peachtree Rock, so it is much easier to see and to photograph. The trail runs right by it.

The trail from here to Hunt Creek is fairly rugged. Mostly sand, it can be one of the hottest spots in South Carolina when the sun is shining. Desert plants, such as beargrass and prickly pear cactus, thrive here and the lizards are quite active.

Hunt Creek is a good place to cool off. This is the best area for bird viewing, and here you can observe a wider variety of plant life. Do not be surprised if you do not see the creek for some distance; it is largely subterranean.

Circle around back to Peachtree Rock and pick up the red trail. The "red trail," in fact blazed brown, is easy to follow. It too is only about 1 mile long, but it features other interesting rock formations, as well as galax, more commonly found closer to the mountains.

Facilities: None.

Lodging and amenities: The nearest public campground is at Dreher Island State Park. All services and amenities are available in the Columbia area.

For more information: The Nature Conservancy. See Appendix A: For More Information.

32 Buncombe Trail

General description:	A two- to three-day hike along a loop trail through mixed forest and hilly terrain.
General location:	Northwest of Columbia, in the north-central part of the state.
Distance:	27.5 miles, loop, plus 4.25 miles of shortcut trails.
Difficulty:	Easy to moderate.
Trail conditions:	Conditions are fair to good. Traffic is primarily equestrian.
Best time to go:	Year-round. Take care during hunting season and after heavy rains.
Maps:	Forest Service map of Enoree/Tyger Ranger District of Sumter National Forest; Forest Service map of Buncombe Trail; Newberry NW USGS quad. See Appendix A: For More Information.
Fees:	None.

Finding the trailhead: The trailhead is in the Brick House Campground of the Enoree/Tyger Ranger District of Sumter National Forest. From Interstate 26, take South Carolina Highway 66 east toward Whitmire for 3.5 miles. Turn right (south) onto Brick House Road. On Brick House Road, there is an open field on the left (east side) and a campground about 0.2 mile farther down the road, on the right (west side). The Buncombe Trail crosses Brick House Road between these two areas; this crossing serves as the trailhead. Park at the campground and walk back up the road to the trailhead.

The hike: The Buncombe Trail is a long loop through Sumter National Forest lands. The terrain is pleasantly hilly, with a myriad of wildlife viewing opportunities and a number of small streams to add interest (and sometimes challenge).

The Buncombe Road was once the main road between Columbia and Asheville (then Buncombe), North Carolina. The Brick House, on SC 66 across from Brick House Road, was an important inn in the 19th century.

This long trail is also used by equestrians. Riders almost invariably are friendly, polite, and happy to share the trail. Of course, there are disadvantages to hiking a horse trail: droppings and the chewing up of the trail by hooves. You can avoid the worst of these disadvantages by hiking on weekdays or during winter, when there is less horse activity. The heaviest equestrian activity is on the shorter loop that departs from the main route about 4 miles into the hike.

Since this is a horse trail, you should not be surprised by the numerous fords. Under low-water conditions, you can negotiate all of the fords without getting your feet or legs wet. When rains have been heavy, though, you may need to wade. Bring an extra set of dry clothes and keep abreast of weather conditions before visiting.

Apart from the ever-present pine, the forest includes dogwood, tulip poplar, cedar, maple, and baldcypress. Some of the wildflowers present are Queen Anne's lace, elephant's foot, wild mint, nettle, coreopsis, mimosa, buffalo clover, mullein, honeysuckle, and butterfly pea. Christmas fern is among the many ferns in low-lying areas, and blackberries are common in the clearcut spots where they receive large amounts of sunshine.

Deer tracks can be seen all along the trail, as can the tracks of wild turkeys. Cold-blooded residents include Carolina anoles and numerous frogs. A partial list of insects: tiger swallowtails (yellow and black forms, some immense), red-spotted purples (butterflies), large beetles, velvet ants, orb-weaver spiders, funnel-web spiders, and millipedes.

Start out heading west, following the trail counterclockwise. This portion of the trail is marked only by a sign indicating "No four-wheel vehicles allowed." The remainder of the east side of the trail loop is, however, well blazed with white symbols looking something like a lowercase *i*.

The trail moves past dogwoods scattered among the pines and into a primordial-looking forest of ferns to cross a small footbridge over Mulberry Branch. After you cross this tributary of Headley's Creek, red clay and hardwoods become more common.

The trail fords Headley's Creek about 1.5 miles from the trailhead, then winds toward Drysache Branch. After another 2.75 miles, the inner loop trail forks east, circling back across Headley's Creek and through 5 miles of forest to Brick House Campground, for an inner loop of 9.25 miles.

Buncombe Trail

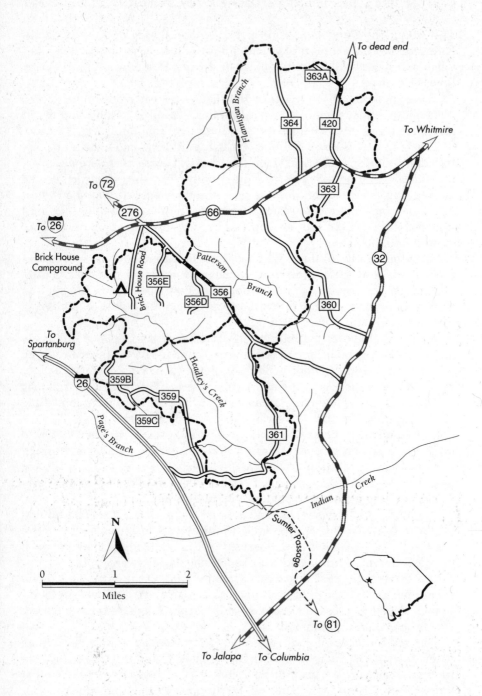

The outer trail continues to the southeast, paralleling Forest Service Road 359B (Page's Branch B), crossing FS 359C (Page's Branch C), at 5.75 miles and zigzagging through the forest before crossing FS 359 (Pond Road) at 7.25 miles.

Special attractions of this southwestern part of the trail are some especially large trees and the very numerous orb-weaver spider webs, especially numerous in early morning. This is the least traveled section of the trail, and undergrowth is a problem in places. The hum of traffic on I-26, to the west, reminds you that although your immediate surroundings seem rather isolated, you are not far from the turmoil of civilization.

From the first crossing of FS 359 the trail loops east, then south, and then back west to join FS 359 and follow it south across Page's Branch, all the way to FS 361, 8.5 miles from the trailhead.

The trail crosses FS 361 and loops southeast and then northeast, back up to FS 361 and another crossing of Headley's Creek, at 10.5 miles from the trailhead. Cross the creek, which has become much more impressive than it was at the 1.5-mile mark, via two FS 361 bridges. This southernmost curve of the Buncombe Trail is distinguished by a large clearcut and a right of way for a South Carolina Pipeline natural gas line. (This is also where the Sumter Passage of the Palmetto Trail leaves Buncombe Trail, heading south for SR 81.)

After crossing the bridges (heading northeast), look carefully on the right (east) side of the trail for a small post marked with a lowercase *i*. This post indicates the point at which the trail plunges back into the forest. It can be easy to miss.

The next 2.75 miles of trail runs north a short distance east of FS 361, the first 1 mile or so along private property fenced with barbed wire. Just prior to the intersection of FS 361 and FS 356 (Cromer Road), the trail turns east through forest to cross FS 356 slightly less than 0.5 mile east of this road intersection. A shortcut back to Brick House Campground turns left off the main trail at FS 356. After 0.75 mile, it joins the short loop mentioned above. The total length of this intermediate loop is 16 miles.

From FS 356, head northeast and downhill over rocky, boulder-strewn terrain. You ford a small tributary of Patterson Branch and then cross a bridge over Patterson Branch itself, reaching FS 360 (Flint Hill Road) at the 15-mile point. From FS 360, travel 2.75 miles northeast on red clay, through trees tall enough to look like old-growth forest, and across 3 tributaries of Patterson Branch before reaching SC 66. The last 1 mile before the highway parallels, but does not cross, FS 493, which runs along the east side of the trail.

After crossing SC 66, the trail turns sharply right (east). The next 2 miles run over mostly soft red clay. Sandy Branch flows along the bottom of a large ravine bordering the trail on the left (west). On the way down to this creek, the trail is highly eroded and fairly difficult. You cross Sandy Branch on a small bridge. This is an attractive area, dominated by old hardwoods, primarily oak. Beyond the bridge, you ascend again. Unfortunately, the track on this side is also heavily eroded.

The next stretch of trail follows an old road. Two miles after the trail crosses SC 66, turn right (north) onto FS 363. After 0.2 mile, a 20.6-mile marker indicates where the trail turns left (northwest) onto FS 363A. This sign is slightly inaccurate, as this is now almost exactly the 20 mile mark. FS 363A, though blocked by a gate, is still in use as a logging road. The trail turns left (west) off FS 363A after another 0.3 mile. The trail was widened recently along the next stretch (about 0.3 mile), which leads down to Mulberry Branch. This creek must be forded, and the crossing is difficult after rains.

After Mulberry Branch, you pass through a shady forest, then suddenly emerge into a clearcut, which leaves you without shade as you climb the upcoming ridge. The trail follows FS 364B closely, but the main track of the trail is always easy to distinguish.

FS 364 is the next gravel road you encounter, 1.5 miles after leaving FS 363. Turn right (northwest) and follow FS 364. The right (east) side of the road is private property. After a few hundred feet, an old clay road exits on the left (west) side. This is the trail. (If you reach a railroad trestle, you have gone too far on FS 364.) The trail is unmarked except for a few posts with double white stripes. The area you pass through here has recently been clearcut.

The next 2.5 miles are not the most enjoyable part of the Buncombe Trail. Trees are growing back from past clearcuts, but slowly. Near Flannigan Branch, the trail runs through old hardwoods that have been spared the saw. The trail crosses Flannigan Branch, then parallels it closely while crossing several tributaries. The stream provides a refreshing companion, and nice campsites are plentiful. One tributary, 0.25 mile before a 24-mile marker, is niftily bridged by granite slabs.

The trail turns right (west), away from Flannigan Branch. The sparse ground cover makes this section uncomfortable to walk during summer. You must traverse roughly 1.5 miles to cross SC 66 again, mostly uphill. The good news is that tracks along the trail indicate that you have an excellent chance of meeting white-tailed deer and wild turkeys along this stretch of small saplings and scrub brush.

Halfway between Flannigan Branch and SC 66, you meet and cross gravel FS 365 (Fremley Road). The trail sticks fairly near this road, but does not run alongside it. Crossing SC 66, you reenter a shady forest. The last stretch, which takes you back to Brick House Campground, is one of the nicest parts of the trail. Many small streams cross your path, all easily forded. Patterson Branch, 0.6 mile from SC 66, rates a bridge, built in 1977 by the U.S. Youth Conservation Corps.

The four-way trail intersection near Brick House Campground where the short loop meets the long loop is not well-marked. (On the map, it appears as a three-way intersection because one of the branches is not an official trail.) Turn north (right) to return to the trailhead in the Brick House Recreation Area. The short loop trail leads away to the south (left), while the eastern route takes you back the way you have come, along the long loop trail. If you head down the western trail (straight ahead), you come to a

Author John Dantzler on the Buncombe Trail. JOHN CLARK PHOTO

gravel road; if you turn north (right) here, you come to the main trail again and can follow it to the trailhead.

Facilities: Toilets, picnic tables, grills, and a water pump at the campground.

Lodging and amenities: Camping is available at Brick House Campground, but there are no hookups and minimal facilities. Camping is permitted along the trail. Motel accommodations are available at the Clinton and Newberry exits on I-26, and these two attractive college towns offer most services.

For more information: Enoree/Tyger Ranger District of Sumter National Forest. See Appendix A: For More Information.

33 Kings Mountain

General description:	A two-day hike through shaded hardwood forest, over ridges, down rocky ravines and across numerous brooks and streams.
General location:	West of Rock Hill, in the north-central part of the state.
Distance:	14.5 miles, loop; optional 1.5-mile battlefield loop and 1-mile roundtrip spur.
Difficulty:	Moderate.
Trail conditions:	Trail is generally in good condition. Traffic ranges from very light to heavy.
Best time to go:	Year-round.
Maps:	Free trail map available at Kings Mountain State Park entrance and at Kings Mountain National Military Park Visitor Center. Grover USGS quad. See Appendix A: For More Information.
Fees:	$2 fee per vehicle to enter Kings Mountain State Park.

Finding the trailhead: From York, drive north 4 miles on U.S. Highway 321, fork left on South Carolina Highway 161, and go 10 miles. At the intersection with SC 216, just before the North Carolina state line, turn left and go 1 mile; the entrance to Kings Mountain State Park is on the right. (To drive to the National Military Park Visitor Center, stay on SC 216.)

Enter the main area of the state park and drive straight ahead to the picnic area. Behind shelters 3 and 4, a maze of sandy paths leads down to the creek. The trail begins at the footbridge across the creek.

The hike: This hike runs through the southern portion of the Kings Mountain Range, a small series of granite outcroppings on the border between South Carolina and North Carolina. The hike goes through both Kings Mountain State Park and the adjacent Kings Mountain National Military Park, site of an important battle of the Revolutionary War. Here, in October 1780, a rag-tag force of rugged frontiersmen overwhelmed militia forces loyal to the British Crown, turning the tide of the war in the South in favor of the revolutionaries. Kings Mountain State Park is open from 7 A.M. to 9 P.M. April to October and 8 A.M. to 6 P.M. November to March.

You can begin at any of seven access points. The best trailhead is behind picnic shelters 3 and 4 in Kings Mountain State Park, where ample parking is available, as are rest rooms. The National Military Park Visitor Center also makes a good starting point, but the parking lot there closes at 5 P.M.

The trail connects Kings Mountain State Park with Kings Mountain National Military Park. You walk along streams under a dense, cool canopy of oak, hickory, and pine, wandering over rolling hills through an understory

Kings Mountain

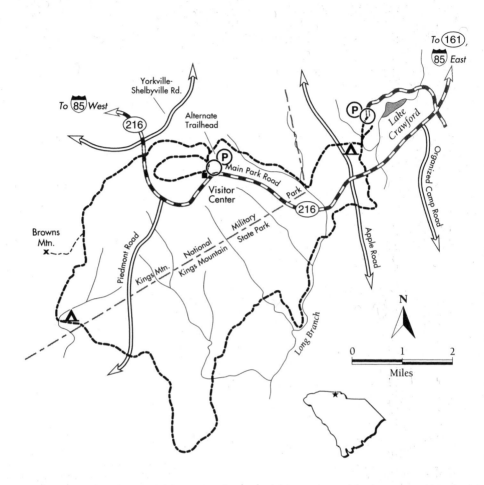

of mountain laurel, dogwood, fetterbush, wild ginger, Christmas fern, rattlesnake plantain, galax, and club moss.

From the picnic area at Kings Mountain State Park, follow any of a number of crisscrossing footpaths down to the creek; bear left (south) and cross a footbridge with handrails. The crisscrossing footpaths also allow you access to the creek's sandy shoals and to the nearby campground.

The trail forks on the other side of the bridge. A right (west) turn takes you counterclockwise around the loop, toward Kings Mountain National Military Park. About 0.2 mile along, you reach a primitive campsite with a water pump beside the intersection with a dirt road (Apple Road). After passing the boundary between the state and military parks, the trail meanders across and along a stream, which is in some places pooled and quiet, in others rocky and chatty.

After leaving the stream, you negotiate a gentle rise toward the Kings Mountain battlefield. At a fork, a sign indicates that the Kings Mountain National Military Park Visitor Center is 0.2 mile to your left (south), while Browns Mountain (2.4 miles) and Garner Creek Campsite (3.4 miles) are along the loop as it continues to the right (west).

If you take the left fork, you can cool your heels in the comfortable visitor center and view a short film about the Battle of Kings Mountain. Afterward, you can follow a 1.5-mile paved interpretive loop around and over the elongated plateau of the battlefield, which rises some 60 feet above the plain around it. Markers and monuments mingle with greenery in description and commemoration of the capture of the high ground by militia forces fighting for American independence. If you're looking for only a half-day outing, return to the picnic area at Kings Mountain State Park to complete a pleasant 6.5-mile hike.

If you continue on the western fork, you traverse ridges and gullies and cross a small stream before the trail widens over a relatively level area to emerge after 1 mile on Main Park Road (SC 216), near its intersection with Yorkville Road and Shelbyville Road.

Here the trail turns southwest, plunging into a green ravine thick with ferns, fetterbush, and yellow-root, then passing over three small footbridges. After the third bridge, the trail rises and, at 1.5 miles past Main Park Road, a sign indicates a one-way spur to the top of Browns Mountain (1,045 feet), a fairly steep 0.5 mile away. A fire tower once stood here, and its concrete foundations are still in place. The mountaintop provides an impressive view in cooler months, when trees are bare of leaves. There is little to see, however, when the trees are in full canopy.

The next portion of the trail travels through a clear understory and leads gradually down to a small tributary that must be forded by stepping across rocks. This area can be troublesome after heavy rains. Soon after this crossing, a boardwalk stretches over wonderfully babbling Garner Branch.

From the crossing of Garner Branch, the trail begins its southeast course, rising to a primitive campsite on top of a ridge. The trail again crosses the boundary between the military and state parks, continues for another 1 mile on high ground, and emerges at an obscurely marked point on Piedmont Road, a dirt extension of Secondary Road 731.

Between Piedmont Road and Apple Road (also unpaved) the trail stretches for 6.2 miles with no road access. This is one of the least hiked and most scenic sections, although there a few places where equestrians have strayed from nearby horse trails and churned up the path. The trail moves across rolling terrain and several streams, with a mainly hardwood forest canopy. Occasional dense vegetation in bottomland areas sometimes increases the trail's difficulty. A musical stream crossing about 1 mile west of Apple Road provides excellent camping and wading opportunities.

From Apple Road, the trail travels over high ground, crosses Main Park Road again, then gently descends alongside a brook to join the beginning of the loop and the footbridge back to the Kings Mountain State Park picnic area.

Facilities: Rest rooms, drinking water, picnic areas, and refreshments at the trailhead in Kings Mountain State Park. The state park also has lakes with fishing and swimming areas, and a "living" frontier farm. The Kings Mountain National Military Park Visitor Center has rest rooms and drinking water, as well as a gift shop and a theater with a short interpretive film.

Lodging and amenities: Kings Mountain State Park has a 119-site campground, and primitive camping is allowed at certain points along the trail. Food and lodging are available at nearby Rock Hill and Charlotte, and along I-85.

For more information: Kings Mountain State Park; Kings Mountain National Military Park. See Appendix A: For More Information.

34 Anne Springs Close Greenway

General description:	Moderately hilly trails through diverse terrain, from open fields to hardwood forest and rocky creek bottoms.
General location:	North of Fort Mill, in the north-central part of the state.
Distance:	Varies.
Difficulty:	Easy to moderate.
Trail conditions:	Conditions good on most trails. Traffic is light to moderate.
Best time to go:	Year-round.
Maps:	Anne Springs Close Hiking Trail Map, available at Greenway Headquarters and Greenway Nature Center; Fort Mill USGS quad. See Appendix A: For More Information.
Fees:	Free to Greenway members; $2 per person for nonmembers.

Finding the trailhead: Exit Interstate 77, 4 miles north of Rock Hill (9 miles south of Charlotte) onto South Carolina Highway 160 and head east toward Fort Mill. After 1 mile on SC 160, turn left (north) on U.S. Highway 21 Bypass. The main entrance is 1.5 miles from SC 160, on the right (east).

The hikes: Serving as a buffer between the town of Fort Mill and the Charlotte metropolitan area just to the north, the Anne Springs Close Greenway is a 2,300-acre preserve in the Steele Creek watershed. The preserve was opened in 1995 by members of the Close family, long-time advocates of the preservation and protection of South Carolina's natural heritage, on land owned by the family for 200 years.

Inside the Greenway, you can walk a section of the Nation Ford Road, once called the Great Waggon Road, built by settlers over the major Catawba Indian trading path that once extended from Pennsylvania to Florida. Trappers and traders walked this trail 300 years ago. When British Revolutionary War general Lord Charles Cornwallis led his troops down the Nation Ford Road and through this area in 1780, he said the countryside looked like an English park. At Springfield, a plantation home on the Greenway's northern boundary, Confederate President Jefferson Davis and his cabinet met for the last time, in April of 1865.

Special attractions at the Greenway include an interpretative nature trail around a scenic fishing lake, a nature center, a historic log cabin, and delightful swinging bridges. The Greenway has 14.6 miles of hiking trails, a few of which are shared with mountain bikers, plus 11.7 miles of equestrian trails that are also open to hikers. A sampling of a few of these trails is given below.

The mildly hilly Greenway trails offer views of a wide variety of trees and plant life common to the mixed hardwood forests in this part of the state. White oak, southern red oak, pignut hickory, shagbark hickory, and shortleaf and loblolly pines are all much in evidence.

The centerpiece of the hiking trails is a 1.5-mile interpretive nature walk around 30-acre Lake Haigler, which is stocked with bass, bluegills, shellcrackers, channel catfish, and aquatic weed-eating carp. To reach the Nature Trail, enter the preserve via the Dairy Barn entrance, pick up an interpretive brochure at the Nature Center at the end of the entrance road, then park in the lot on the right that is 300 yards south of the Nature Center. The Nature Trail begins at the parking lot. Follow the trail 200 yards to the south and bear right at the lakeside.

After another 100 yards, the trail crosses the western end of the lake over a land bridge which serves as a dam for the small incoming stream and for rain runoff. The undisturbed wetland pond to the right provides habitat for beaver, great blue heron, and wood duck. Water flows through pipes underneath the dam to feed Lake Haigler.

You walk through an open area filled with yellow-flowered medicinal woolly mullein plants growing to a height of 5 to 6 feet. You then pass a bat house, a structure which accommodates up to 200 bats enticed here to provide mosquito control. One bat can eat as many as 1,000 mosquitoes in a single night.

The trail continues on a gently rolling course around the lake, past more wetlands and evidence of beaver activity, and through a wide range of trees and other vegetation typical of the area. It crosses another bridge at the east end of the lake and connects with a trail that extends eastward to the Steele Creek bottomlands and on to the Springfield Loop Trail and the Complex–Avery Lake Loop Trail. The Nature Trail proceeds counterclockwise around the lake, past the camping area, and back to the parking lot.

The 2.3-mile Springfield Loop Trail begins in an orchard across from the intersection of US 21 Bypass and the entrance road for the Dairy Barn. This

Anne Springs Close Greenway

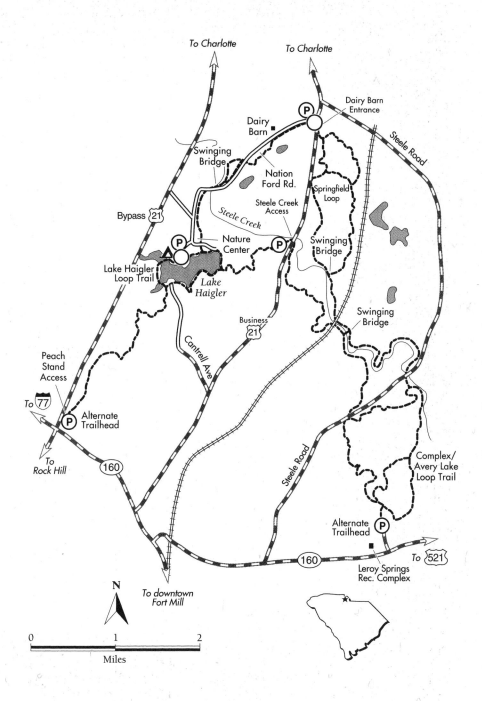

To Charlotte

To Charlotte

Dairy Barn Entrance

Dairy Barn

Steele Road

Swinging Bridge

Nation Ford Rd.

Springfield Loop

Steele Creek Access

Steele Creek

Bypass 21

Nature Center

Swinging Bridge

Lake Haigler Loop Trail

Lake Haigler

Swinging Bridge

Business 21

Cantrell Ave.

Peach Stand Access

To 77

Alternate Trailhead

To Rock Hill

160

Steele Road

Complex/ Avery Lake Loop Trail

Alternate Trailhead

To 521

Leroy Springs Rec. Complex

160

N

To downtown Fort Mill

0   1   2

Miles

gently rolling trail is highlighted by a bouncing, swinging bridge near its southernmost point, where a connector trail veers off toward the Complex–Avery Lake Loop Trail. The western side of the Springfield Loop is shared with mountain bikers and is quite clear. The eastern side, however, is closed to bikers and overgrown in places.

The 2.7-mile Complex–Avery Lake Loop Trail can be reached across from the Avery Lake Access turnoff on Steele Road, at the Steele Road bridge across Steele Creek, and north of the parking lot behind the Leroy Springs Recreation Complex on SC 160. Complex–Avery Lake Loop follows rocky Steele Creek for a short distance, making several crossings of picturesque tributaries. The trail offers significant elevation change and some challenge on the western side, which is closed to mountain bikers.

Additional trails run from the Dairy Barn across a swinging bridge to the north side of the Nature Trail, from the Peach Stand Access parking lot to the south side of the Nature Trail, and along Steele Creek connecting the three loop trails. The Peach Stand Access parking lot is beside US 21 Bypass, just north of its intersection with SC 160.

Facilities: Rest rooms, drinking water, and showers near the parking lot for Lake Haigler and the camping area. The Nature Center is housed in a 100-year-old home. Meeting facilities are available in an education center in the picturesque Dairy Barn, built more than 50 years ago.

Lodging and amenities: Camping is allowed at the Greenway (reservation required) All services are available at Rock Hill, South Carolina, and at Charlotte, North Carolina.

For more information: Anne Springs Close Greenway. See Appendix A: For More Information.

---

35 Landsford Canal State Historic Site

General description:	A stroll along the scenic Catauba River, featuring wondrous wildflowers, a wide variety of birds, and historic canal structures.
General location:	South of Rock Hill, in the north-central part of the state.
Distance:	3 miles round trip.
Difficulty:	Easy.
Trail conditions:	Conditions are good. Traffic is light to moderate.
Best time to go:	Year-round.
Maps:	Catawba USGS quad. See Appendix A: For More Information.
Fees:	None.

Landsford Canal State Historic Site

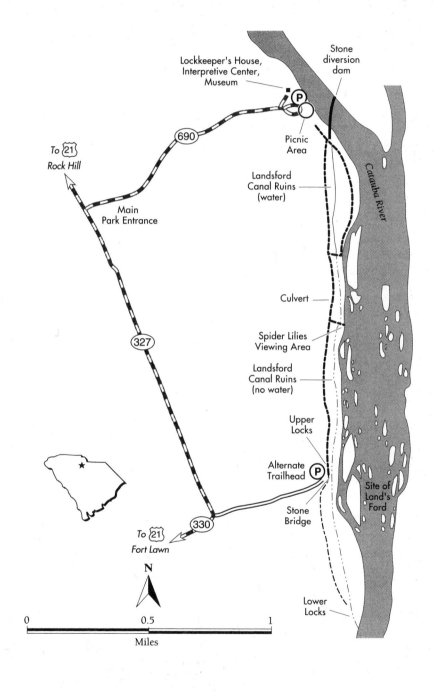

Lockkeeper's House, Interpretive Center, Museum

Stone diversion dam

690

To 21
Rock Hill

Picnic Area

Landsford Canal Ruins (water)

Catawba River

Main Park Entrance

327

Culvert

Spider Lilies Viewing Area

Landsford Canal Ruins (no water)

Upper Locks

Alternate Trailhead

Site of Land's Ford

330

To 21
Fort Lawn

Stone Bridge

Lower Locks

N

0   0.5   1
Miles

Finding the trailhead: From Interstate 77, take Exit 65 to South Carolina Highway 9 and head east. After 1.2 miles, turn left (northeast) onto SC 223. After 6.7 miles, merge onto U.S. Highway 21. Take a right (east) within 0.25 mile onto Secondary Road 330. After 2.2 miles, you reach the southern entrance to Landsford Canal State Historic Site, straight ahead. To reach the main entrance and trailhead, turn left (northwest) onto SR 327 and proceed 1.3 miles; the entrance is on the right. The main trailhead is at the site's picnic area, 0.5 mile past the main entrance.

The hike: Landsford Canal was built in the early 1800s to bypass the rapids on the Catawba River, as part of a plan to connect Charleston, South Carolina with the Mississippi River. The canal received heavy use for only about two years, and had been completely abandoned by 1846.

British Revolutionary War General Lord Cornwallis crossed the Catawba here at Land's Ford on his march from Charlotte to Winnsboro. Patriot General Thomas Sumter used the area as a camp and meeting place.

Tree stumps at the picnic area have been carved by Lancaster artist James "Smiley" Small into wonderful stylized faces. Officially, this hike comprises two trails. From the trailhead, you can take either, as they come together again after a relatively short distance. The nature trail runs along the wide Catawba River for about 0.5 mile, while the canal trail follows the remains of the old canal. The trails are equally appealing.

Start on the nature trail, and, at its end, bear left (south) onto the canal trail (bearing right returns you to the picnic area) to see the canal.

Nearly all of the original stonework from the canal is still intact, including the three locks. Most of the canal has filled with earth over time, although there are a few pleasant, tranquil stretches that still hold water.

Landsford Canal is famous for wildflowers. Wildflowers found in the park include cardinal flower, Jack-in-the-pulpit, crane-fly orchid, spicebush, spiderwort, Solomon's seal, fire pink, and yellow passionflower. The Catawba rapids feature the rare rocky shoals spider lily. A sign directs you to the left, up and down stairs, to the best viewing area for spider lilies. During May, the lilies' peak blooming season, they seem to fill the river. Return to the trail, and farther along you encounter the canal's locks, still impressive after more than 150 years. At the end of the canal trail, a bridge over the locks leads to a small picnic area and a boat put-in on the river. The stone bridge is interesting in and of itself, as it forms a flying arch.

Return as you came, by way of the canal trail.

Birds are well represented at Landsford Canal, especially during spring and autumn migrations. Osprey, yellow-billed cuckoo, green-backed heron, purple martin, ruby-throated hummingbird, assorted hawks and woodpeckers, and a great many varieties of warblers can be encountered here.

The park's museum and interpretive center, near the main entrance, is worth a visit. Built in the 1830s, it previously served as a lockkeeper's house. It was moved here from Rocky Mount Canal near Great Falls, and is the last lockkeeper's house still standing in South Carolina.

Facilities: Picnic area, rest rooms, water, interpretive center.

Lodging and amenities: All amenities are available in the Rock Hill area, and nearby Lancaster also offers a variety of services. Camping is available at Andrew Jackson State Park and Lake Wateree State Park.

For more information: Landsford Canal State Historic Site. See Appendix A: For More Information.

36 Harbison State Forest

General description:	A variety of undulating woodland trails in the midst of a major metropolitan area.
General location:	On the outskirts of Columbia, in the center of the state.
Distance:	Varies.
Difficulty:	Easy to moderate.
Trail conditions:	Conditions are excellent. Foot traffic is light to moderate.
Best time to go:	Year-round.
Maps:	Harbison State Forest brochure; Columbia Northeast USGS quad. See Appendix A: For More Information.
Fees:	None.

Finding the trailhead: From downtown Columbia, take Interstate 126/26 northwest toward Spartanburg. Exit after 5 miles onto Piney Grove Road. Head right (east) on Piney Grove Road for 1 mile, then turn left (north) on Broad River Road (U.S. Highway 176). Harbison State Forest is 1 mile farther, on the right.

The Firebreak Trailhead is at parking area 1, on the left immediately as you turn into the state forest property. To reach the other trailheads, continue on the entry road, which is gravel beyond the state forest's gate. To take the Eagle Trail, turn left (north) after 0.6 mile at the sign for the Gazebo and Eagle picnic shelters. The Eagle Trail starts next to the latter shelter. There are public rest rooms near the Gazebo shelter. To reach the Midlands Mountain Trailhead, return to the main gravel road and continue 1 mile farther to parking area 5. The Stewardship Trailhead is parking area 6, another 0.4 mile up the gravel road.

The hikes: Harbison State Forest is a special place for a variety of reasons. At 2,178 acres, it is the largest publicly owned and publicly accessible tract in the Dutch Fork–Irmo section of the Columbia metropolitan area. This land, once exhausted cotton field, has blossomed into an attractive urban forest whose trails afford pleasure and relaxation to hikers and mountain bikers. Bicyclists are allowed on three of the forest's six trails, but the pathways are generally wide enough to handle all users commodiously. A new trail is the Discovery Trail, which runs 0.4 mile from the Gazebo area to the Environmental Education Center. New trails are planned for the area around the Environmental Education Center.

Trees are the big attraction at Harbison State Forest. The forest is dominated by loblolly and longleaf pines, but there are plenty of oaks, hickories, red maples, hollies, and dogwoods. Wildflowers include flame azaleas, elephant's feet, spike lobelias, and butterfly peas.

Harbison State Forest is also a haven for wildlife. White-tailed deer, eastern box turtles, Carolina anoles, and wild turkeys are all likely to be encountered here. Other birds include eastern wood-pewees, and various woodpeckers, including downy, hairy, and pileated, and northern flicker.

The Firebreak Trail is a 4-mile loop, and a pretty good workout. The trail is blazed white (or silver) with diamond-shaped metal signs nailed to trees. The western flank of the trail generally runs parallel to Lost Creek Drive, so traffic noise is a petty annoyance. The terrain undulates nicely—interesting to the eye, but not too difficult for the legs. A bit less than 1 mile from parking area 1, the Firebreak Trail bears hard right (east). A new connector trail has been built here that continues north to connect with the Stewardship Trail. If you stay on the Firebreak Trail, after 1.2 miles, it passes into a busier area of the forest, where the picnic shelters are. However, a wilderness feel has been maintained, and the trail continues to be quite pleasant.

After 2 miles, the trail connects with the Midlands Mountain Trail. Turn right here for a pleasant 0.6-mile stretch of forest, then pick up the eastern flank of the Firebreak Trail to circle back to the parking lot through more interestingly varied terrain.

The Eagle Trail, an interpretive loop named for the Eagle Scouts who built it, is short but very worthwhile. It can be hiked as a loop of either 0.4 mile or 0.8 mile. For such a short trail, it is surprisingly challenging. It snakes up and down hills and ravines and offers a refreshing walk. Moreover, interpretive markers identify many tree species, helping you learn about indigenous flora and fauna. An interpretive guide is available at the trailhead kiosk and provides a key to the numbered signposts along the trail. Return the guide to the kiosk to be reused when you are done.

A barrier-free trail (barred to bicycles) has been developed in the Eagle Trail area. The 0.2-mile Historical Tree Grove Trail takes you on a tour of American history. Trees with significant historical value are planted in this area, and interpretive markers describe their roles in America's past.

The Midlands Mountain Trail (multiple use), a 2.7-mile loop with connector trails that bring it up to a total of 3.7 miles, is perhaps the finest trail at Harbison. The loop, blazed blue, was cleared in a remarkable four hours by a corps of 250 Boy Scouts. It provides a nice impersonation of a mountain trail. Perhaps its nicest feature is a 0.1 mile spur trail to Harbison Bluffs, about 1.5 miles from the parking area (whether you take the trail clockwise

Harbison State Forest

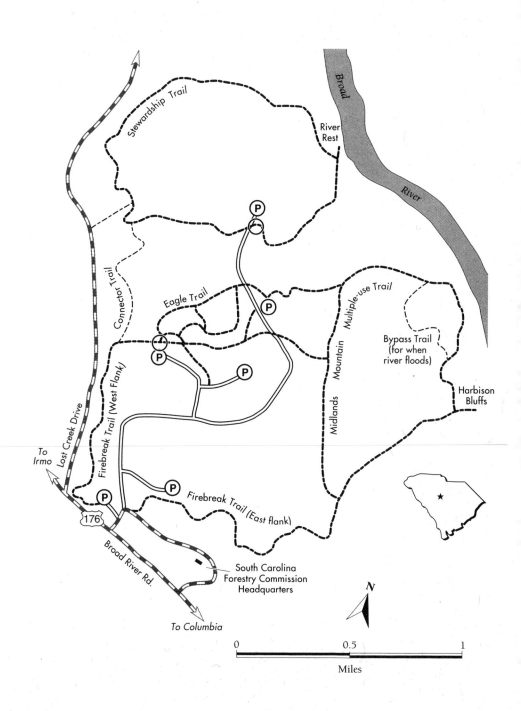

or counterclockwise—it is halfway around).

Harbison Bluffs offers a commanding wintertime view of the Broad River. To get a better view of the river, continue along the spur trail down the steep hill. The Broad River floodplain is another world, alive with vines and ferns and nice stands of pawpaw. A wider variety of trees is in evidence in the floodplain, where pines do not dominate to the degree they do elsewhere in the forest. The spur loops back up to Harbison Bluffs, but it is best to go back the way you came.

In wintertime, the Broad River floodplain often lives up to its name (particularly the "flood" and "broad" parts). Therefore, the Midlands Mountain Trail can be quite muddy as it approaches the floodplain. State forest managers have built a ridge trail that allows hikers to stay on higher ground when the river gets too rowdy.

The Stewardship Trail is another loop, this one 3 miles long. Unfortunately, in 1997 a devastating attack by southern pine beetles brought many trees down in this part of the forest. The bulk of the damage occurred on the eastern third of the trail, so you may prefer to hike the trail clockwise (cross the gravel road from the parking lot) as far as the River Reststop, and then turn around (which would make the hike 4.6 miles).

This trail is exceedingly popular with mountain bikers. Numerous small bridges over gullies and washes make riding easier. This is also the best area for viewing wildlife. The forest is mostly pine here, but red maple is heavily represented. The River Reststop consists of a couple of benches on a very short (100 yards) spur trail. Like the Harbison Bluffs spur, this spur runs all the way to the river, but it is much easier and shorter than the Harbison Bluffs spur.

Facilities: Picnic shelters, rest rooms, drinking water, environmental education center.

Lodging and amenities: The nearest public campsites are at Sesquicentennial State Park and Dreher Island State Park. All services and amenities are available throughout the Columbia area.

For more information: Harbison State Forest. See Appendix A: For More Information.

37 Santee State Park

General description:	Several short trails and one longer one along the shore of Lake Marion, famed for its bountiful fishing.
General location:	North of Santee, in the south-central part of the state.
Distance:	Varies.
Difficulty:	Easy.
Trail conditions:	Maintenance is generally good. Traffic is light.
Best time to go:	Year-round.
Maps:	Park brochure; Summerton and Vance USGS quads. See Appendix A: For More Information.
Fees:	$2 per vehicle in summer for day-use area.

Finding the trailhead: From Exit 98 on Interstate 95, take South Carolina Highway 6 west 1.2 miles through the town of Santee, turning right onto Secondary Road 105. After 2.4 miles, you reach the entrance to Santee State Park. Go straight to visit the western part of the park, where cabins, a fishing pier, and the Bike and Oak-Pinolly trailheads are located. Turn right to visit the eastern part of the park, including the day-use area (fee collected in summer), the swimming and picnic areas, and the trailheads for the Limestone Nature Trail and the Sinkhole Nature Trail.

The hikes: Santee State Park is the second most visited state park in South Carolina. This park is best known for its fishing, but its pleasant hiking trails are a happy surprise. The longest, the Bike Trail, is of course mostly used by mountain bikers, but it offers periodic glimpses of beautiful Lake Marion as well as a link between the shorter, more scenic trails. The park is open daily from 6 A.M. to 10 P.M.

Birds frequently seen along the trails include quail, eastern wood-pewee, wild turkey, brown thrasher, osprey, mourning dove, owls (great horned, eastern screech, and barred), Carolina wren, and several woodpeckers, including the rare red-cockaded.

At just 1 mile (round trip), the Oak-Pinolly Nature Trail is short but sweet. It starts next to the playground by the park restaurant. This trail is in the heart of the park, very much in the middle of things, but feels like a wilderness. It makes two small loops at its southern end, but is otherwise a linear trail. (It would be one loop, but the two arms of the trail have to come together to cross a footbridge over a small watercourse.) Blazed yellow, the trail is very easy to follow. There is a good array of birds, and deer are easy to spot.

The 7.6-mile (round trip) Bike Trail is available also to hikers. Sizable loblolly pines line the track. The trail is wide, so shade is at a premium; summer visits require a degree of fortitude, or at the least copious supplies of drinking water. There is a trailhead on the paved road in the western part of the park. A short spur of the trail also goes to the park campground, but there is no marked trailhead.

A heady aroma of what smells like roses pervades the air. However, it is most likely from the wax myrtle on both sides of the trail. The trail is near the lake; periodically you can see the lake and feel its pleasant breezes. Many ant mounds dot the trail, so walk carefully. Spanish moss is all around. Shortly after the 3-mile marker comes the trail's closest and best encounter with the lake. From this point, unofficial trails hug the shoreline to reach the park's picnic area, also our destination. However, please keep to official trails.

Exciting changes are in store for the Bike Trail. Park managers are completing additional trail segments which will create a 7-mile loop, plus connectors. Moreover, they are gradually relocating the current Bike Trail so that it will be closer to Lake Marion. The lake breezes will be very welcome in summertime.

Besides the very pleasant picnic area on the shore of Lake Marion, the east end of the park features a swimming area, open only in summer. To walk from the eastern end of the Bike Trail to the Limestone Trail, turn left on the paved road; the trailhead for the Limestone Trail is 100 to 200 feet away, and clearly marked. To drive here, turn right at the park entrance, stopping at the fee station if it is operating, and proceed to a fork. Take the left (east) fork and look for the trail sign on the right, just before the tennis courts.

The Limestone Nature Trail is a real surprise. Scenic, cool, and winding, this is like the mountains. A heavily wooded trail around the park's swimming lake, it provides a very pleasant 0.8-mile walk (round trip). The only fly in the ointment is the bridge that crosses the upper end of the swimming lake. Though rickety, it is also short, and sturdy enough to cross. The terrain is hilly and interesting, good for wildflowers and wildlife. The trail is blazed white, irregularly. Although it is short, this is a super trail.

The Sinkhole Nature Trail (0.4 mile round trip) is also in the eastern end of the park, but take the right fork after the fee station. Look on the right for a small parking area. There is no sign, but a sinkhole right next to the parking area provides an identifying marker of sorts. This is an interpretive trail, with a very interesting sign explaining the formation of sinkholes. The wonderful scent of wax myrtle pervades the area. For such a short trail, it passes through a dizzying array of habitats, from very dry pine forest, to wetter areas around the sinkhole pond, to near-desert conditions around the dry sinkholes. The pond is intermittent. Sometimes, there is no pond, sometimes there appear to be two or more ponds, and sometimes the trail is completely inundated with water. The high grass here should be good for birds during migrations.

Santee State Park offers another opportunity to get close to nature beside hiking. Fisheagle Tours leads nature-based boat tours of Lake Marion daily from the park's tackle shop.

Santee State Park

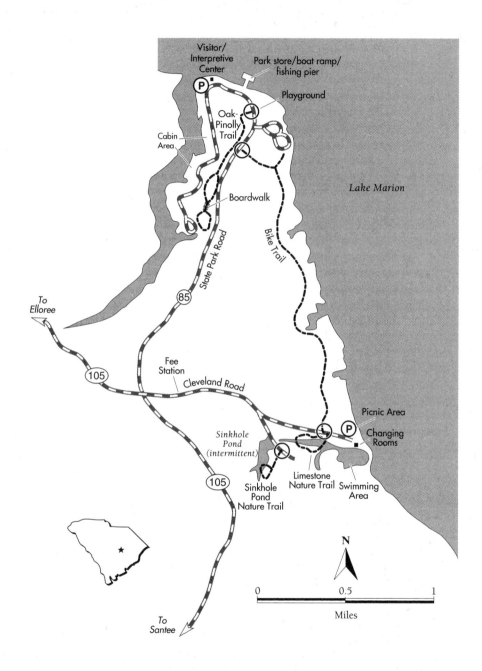

Visitor/ Interpretive Center

Park store/boat ramp/ fishing pier

Playground

Oak-Pinolly Trail

Cabin Area

Boardwalk

Lake Marion

Bike Trail

State Park Road

To Elloree

85

Fee Station

Cleveland Road

105

Sinkhole Pond (intermittent)

Picnic Area

P

Changing Rooms

Limestone Nature Trail

Swimming Area

Sinkhole Pond Nature Trail

105

N

0   0.5   1

Miles

To Santee

Facilities: Water, rest rooms. Santee State Park also offers a restaurant and park store.

Lodging and amenities: The park has 174 campsites and 30 cabins. The larger of the two Santee Cooper lakes, Lake Marion is a world-renowned fishing destination, so campgrounds, motels, and restaurants are plentiful, particularly in Santee and at other exits along I-95.

For more information: Santee State Park; Fisheagle Tours. See Appendix A: For More Information.

38 Congaree Swamp

General description:	A variety of hikes through one of the last unlogged bottomland swamps in the United States, offering huge trees and plentiful wildlife viewing opportunities.
General location:	South of Columbia, in the center of the state.
Distance:	Varies.
Difficulty:	Easy.
Trail conditions:	Conditions are good to poor. Traffic is light to heavy.
Best time to go:	Fall, winter, and spring.
Maps:	Congaree Swamp National Monument map; Gadsden and Wateree USGS quads. See Appendix A: For More Information.
Fees:	None.

Finding the trailhead: Congaree Swamp National Monument is about 20 miles southeast of Columbia. From Columbia, take South Carolina Highway 48 (Bluff Road) southeast, following signs toward the national monument. After 12 miles, Old Bluff Road forks off to the right (southwest). Follow it another 6 miles, then turn right (west) onto the monument entrance road. After 5:30 P.M., the park gate is closed and locked, so you may consider parking outside the gate. There are parking lots inside the gate, one by the ranger station and another farther down the park road.

The southern trailhead for the Kingsnake Trail is on South Cedar Creek Road (Secondary Road 1288). To reach it, continue on Old Bluff Road past Caroline Sims Road until Old Bluff Road ends at South Cedar Creek Road. Turn right (south). The trailhead is 1.8 miles south of this junction. Or, from Columbia, continue on SC 48 (Bluff Road) 6.2 miles past the Old Bluff Road turnoff, then turn right onto South Cedar Creek Road. The Kingsnake Trailhead is 2 miles south of Bluff Road.

The hikes: Congaree Swamp National Monument, in the heart of the Congaree River floodplain, is the largest stand of old-growth riverbottom hardwood forest in the United States. In 1983, it was named an International Biosphere Reserve. Hit hard by Hurricane Hugo and other powerful windstorms in recent years, Congaree Swamp has lost many of its record-size trees, but a host of impressive trees still remain.

Before you visit call the ranger station to check the mosquito forecast and trail conditions. The swamp floods about ten times a year, making many trails impassable. Because of this periodic inundation, the national monument has constructed a 2-mile boardwalk loop. The boardwalk combines with the more than 18 miles of dirt trails that run through the 22,000-acre preserve to make Congaree Swamp the most popular hiking destination in the Midlands.

While the individual trails are relatively short, their distances do add up. Plan on taking several days to enjoy the rich rewards of Congaree Swamp. Botanists have identified more than 320 plant species within the monument's boundaries.

White-tailed deer, feral hogs, and opossums are often seen, while bobcats are present but secretive. The plentiful bird life includes barred and great horned owls, great blue herons, all eight of the state's woodpecker species (the pileated woodpecker is the most often encountered), great crested flycatchers, Acadian flycatchers, northern parulas, and many other warblers.

Another element of interest at Congaree Swamp is Cedar Creek, which, with the Congaree River, offers an 21-mile canoe trail from where Cedar Creek crosses Bluff Road to the U.S. Highway 601 bridge over the Congaree River.

The monument is open daily from dawn to dusk; the gates are open from 8:30 A.M. to 5:30 P.M.

Wild azaleas are found along the trail. YVONNE MICHEL PHOTO

Congaree Swamp

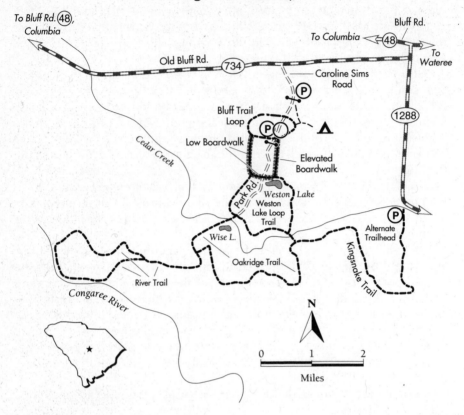

To reach either the low or the elevated boardwalk, follow a bit of the Bluff Trail (1.4 miles, blazed blue), which runs along a bluff overlooking the swamp. This is one of the higher, drier parts of the park and offers a very pleasant walk through the woods. Interpretive signs on the section of trail leading to the low boardwalk educate you about the flora and fauna you are likely to see.

The elevated boardwalk (0.7 mile) runs down to Weston Lake, where there is a lovely overlook. Along the way, you pass dwarf palmetto, loblolly pine, sweet bay, and baldcypress. At Weston Lake, the elevated boardwalk links with the low boardwalk (1.1 miles). Here, the cypresses are quite impressive.

The Weston Lake Loop Trail (2.8 miles, blazed yellow) is a wondrous trail. It starts at Weston Lake, at the end of the elevated boardwalk. Weston Lake is an oxbow lake (part of an old river channel left over when the river changed course). The loop runs alongside the lake for only a very short distance, but it seems to have water and cypresses adjacent to it for practically its entire length. Much of the trail runs beside beautiful Cedar Creek, and scenic vistas are frequent. As it circles back to the low boardwalk, the loop passes an abandoned hunting lodge next to Wise Lake.

The Oakridge Trail (3.7 miles, blazed red) is also a loop. To reach it, take the low boardwalk from the Bluff Trail, but go straight (southeast) on Weston Lake Loop when the boardwalk turns off to the left. At Wise Lake, cross Cedar Creek onto the Oakridge Trail. This trail is perhaps the best place to see very big trees. Loblollies, swamp chestnut oaks, and even hollies can be huge. The trail crosses a number of small watercourses, so there are plenty of baldcypresses and tupelos as well. The Oakridge Trail meets the western end of the Kingsnake Trail. Where these two trails meet, cross Cedar Creek, and take the Weston Lake Loop Trail back to the elevated boardwalk.

The River Trail (6.5 miles, blazed white) takes you to the banks of the Congaree River. You see little of the river itself, but a sign provides directions to a sandbar which is the best viewing place. You have a good chance of seeing animal tracks, particularly deer tracks, here. This area was once logged, so there are fewer substantial trees here than elsewhere in the monument. Still, the understory is interesting, with many daisies and other wildflowers. To reach the River Trail, start the Oakridge Trail at Wise Lake, but turn right (southwest) after 0.7 mile onto the River Trail. Follow a linear trail for 1.2 miles, then circle clockwise on the 4.1-mile loop at the end, returning to the linear trail, which you follow back the way you came.

The Kingsnake Trail (3.7 miles, blazed orange) is by far the most rustic of Congaree Swamp's trails. It receives little use, and maintenance is spotty. For this reason, you are likely to encounter numerous spider webs. The trail

Baldcypress trees. JOHN DANTZLER PHOTO

Author John Clark on Bluff Trail. Yvonne Michel photo

passes beneath many huge trees, particularly cherrybark oaks. It crosses many baldcypress sloughs, and in the last 1 mile runs parallel to Cedar Creek. Wildlife viewing opportunities are very good here; chances are you will spot at least one deer. The best way to hike this trail is to use two vehicles and begin at the trailhead on South Cedar Creek Road. Traverse the Kingsnake Trail, then turn right (north) onto the Weston Lake Loop Trail to emerge at the main parking area at the ranger station.

Facilities: Rest rooms, water fountain, and soft-drink machine at the ranger station.

Lodging and amenities: There is a small primitive campground just inside Congaree Swamp National Monument. The Columbia area offers all services and the picturesque town of St. Matthews is also nearby.

For more information: Congaree Swamp National Monument. See Appendix A: For More Information.

39 Poinsett State Park

General description:	Half a day's hike along three connected trails through hilly and wonderfully diverse terrain with an interesting mix of mountain and coastal plain flora.
General location:	West of Sumter, in the east-central part of the state.
Distance:	Trails total about 8 miles.
Difficulty:	Moderate.
Trail conditions:	Conditions are generally excellent. Traffic is light.
Best time to go:	Year-round.
Maps:	Park brochure; Poinsett State Park USGS quad. See Appendix A: For More Information.
Fees:	$2 per vehicle seasonal parking fee.

Finding the trailhead: From Columbia, take U.S. Highway 76/378 east 29 miles to South Carolina Highway 261 (6.1 miles past the Wateree River bridge). From Sumter take US 76/378 west 11 miles (2 miles past Shaw Air Force Base) to the same point. Go 10.2 miles south on SC 261 and turn right (west) onto Secondary Road 63 (Poinsett Park Road). The park is 1.9 miles down this road. The trailhead is at the end of the road, beside the park office next to Old Levi Mill Pond.

The hike: Poinsett State Park (open from 9 A.M. to 9 P.M., April through October, and 9 A.M. to 6 P.M., November through March) is a unique and exciting place. It features 1,000 acres of hilly terrain adjacent to and partly incorporating Wateree Swamp. The hills here, growing incongruously as

Poinsett State Park

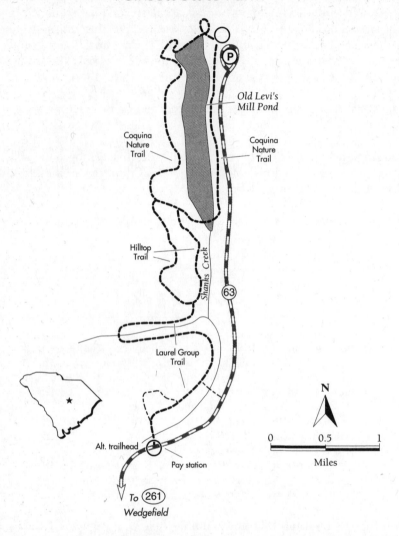

Old Levi's Mill Pond

Coquina Nature Trail

Coquina Nature Trail

Hilltop Trail

Shanks Creek

63

Laurel Group Trail

Alt. trailhead

Pay station

To 261
Wedgefield

N

0   0.5   1

Miles

they do out of the swamp, are a bit of a surprise. These are the High Hills of Santee, an area famous for producing political and military leaders. But there is another reason to treasure the High Hills: The juxtaposition of mountain habitat on coastal plain produces marvelous hiking, a spectacular variety of plant life, and a number of different habitats to delight the wildlife watcher.

Surveys have identified 337 species of flowering plants in the park. Wildflowers put on an impressive show in the early spring. You may encounter pokeweed, goldenrod, broom sedge, aster, prickly pear cactus, sweet pepper-bush, blue-eyed grass, partridgeberry, wild ginger, strawberry bush (hearts-a-bursting), fairy wand, elephant's foot, lupine, smilax, violet, and galax.

Naturalists have also identified 65 species of trees and shrubs in the park, including loblolly pine; American holly; sweet gum; 16 varieties of oaks, including water, black, and white; sourwood; mountain laurel; sassafras; dogwood; American beech; tulip poplar; sweet bay; tupelo; and baldcypress.

Wildlife includes 40 species of snakes (6 of which are venomous), alligator, eastern fence lizard, bullfrog, southern leopard frog, squirrels (fox, flying, gray), and white-tailed deer.

In the near future, the Palmetto Trail (see the Introduction) will pass through Poinsett State Park on its way from the mountains to the sea.

The hike described here explores both the hills and the swamp, taking you on a loop that incorporates each of the park's three trails. The hike starts by the Old Levi Mill Pond on the Coquina Nature Trail. This interpretive trail features numbered interpretive markers keyed to a brochure available at the park office. The trail is named after coquina, a naturally occurring limestone made up of broken sea shells. Coquina is abundant in the park, reflecting the fact that this area was, in prehistoric times, underneath the sea. Many of the park's structures are built with coquina, including the two spillways that drain Old Levi Mill Pond, which was actually built in the 18th century as a freshwater reserve for rice fields, being used only later as a mill pond.

The ruins of Singleton's Mill can be seen just to the right of the trailhead. The mill was an important meeting place during the American Revolution. British Lieutenant Colonel Banastre Tarleton met with Loyalists here in 1780 to devise a warning system to protect British communications along the King's Highway from Charleston to Camden.

This is not your ordinary walk around a state park lake. This trail requires some climbing. After a 0.5-mile ascent, you reach a trailside shelter, roughly 100 feet directly above the lake.

The aptly named Hilltop Trail forks right after another 0.8 mile. It continues the climbing tone set by the Coquina Trail. The Hilltop Trail makes a 1-mile loop, connecting back to the Coquina Trail. Midway along the Hilltop Trail loop, the trail descends to intersect with the Laurel Group Trail, a linear trail onto which you should turn right (south).

During summertime, butterfly peas decorate both the Hilltop and Laurel Group trails. Both of these trails require a good amount of climbing, share a nice winding character, and pass through pleasantly rolling terrain. The Laurel Group Trail runs mostly alongside and above Shanks Creek, which feeds Old Levi Mill Pond. A spur trail to the left heads to the park's cabin lodgings. About 0.8 mile from the Hilltop Trail intersection, a switchback leads away from the more level main trail, an indication of interesting things to come.

The level part of the trail leads to the park road, emerging just outside the gates, about 0.2 mile from this point. Ascend the switchback and keep climbing. At the top is an unusual sight: tall trees festooned with weeping beards of Spanish moss—at the top of a mountain! Granted, it is not a very high mountain, but it makes for an unusual experience nevertheless. This is a sort of loop spur of the Laurel Group Trail; keep going, and after 0.5 mile you climb back down to the main trail. Retrace your steps to the Hilltop Trail and follow it to its second intersection with the Coquina Trail.

At this point, you can turn left (northwest) on the Coquina Trail to see the part of the trail you missed by taking the Hilltop Trail. This also entails a moderate climb. An interesting feature found along this trail is fuller's earth, a highly absorbent clay. Once used by fullers (cloth processors) to remove grease from wool, it now serves as a base ingredient in a number of cosmetics and lubricants.

From the second junction of the Coquina and Hilltop trails, the Coquina Trail circles back around to Old Levi Mill Pond and the park's swimming area. It passes first through a swamp, where you may get a glimpse of an alligator. The rest of the trail runs beside Old Levi Mill Pond, in the shade of baldcypresses and tupelos, and is pleasant and level.

Facilities: Rest rooms, water, soft-drink machine.

Lodging and amenities: The park features 4 cabins and 50 campsites. All other services are available at Sumter.

For more information: Poinsett State Park. See Appendix A: For More Information.

40 Carolina Sandhills National Wildlife Refuge

General description:	Two short hikes in a restored woodland with attractive opportunities for wildlife viewing, especially of waterfowl on lakes and ponds.
General location:	Northwest of Florence, in the north-central part of the state.
Distance:	Varies.
Difficulty:	Easy.
Trail conditions:	Conditions are good. Traffic is light.
Best time to go:	Winter for waterfowl, spring for wildflowers.
Maps:	Middendorf and Angelus USGS quads. See Appendix A: For More Information.
Fees:	None.

Finding the trailhead: From Interstate 95, take Exit 164 at Florence. Travel 8 miles north on U.S. Highway 52 to Darlington, then turn west on South Carolina Highway 151 and drive 26 miles to McBee. Here, turn right (northeast) onto US 1 and drive 2 miles before turning left (north) onto SC 145. Continue for 3 miles, turning left (west) into Lake Bee Recreation Area, a part of the Refuge.

Carolina Sandhills National Wildlife Refuge

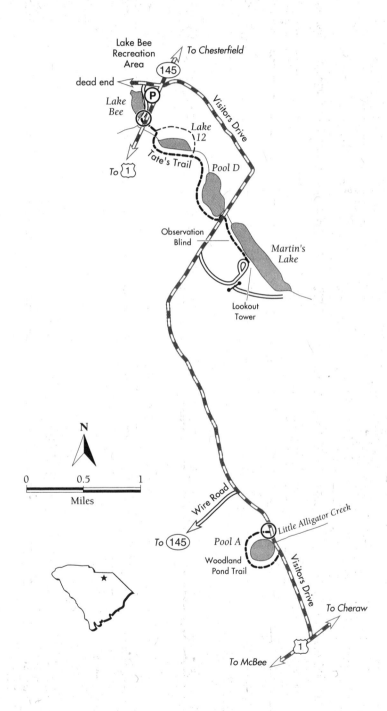

Lake Bee Recreation Area

To Chesterfield

145

dead end

Lake Bee

P

Lake 12

Visitors Drive

Tate's Trail

Pool D

To 1

Observation Blind

Martin's Lake

Lookout Tower

N

0   0.5   1
Miles

Wire Road

Little Alligator Creek

To 145

Pool A

Woodland Pond Trail

Visitors Drive

To Cheraw

To McBee

1

To approach the refuge from Columbia, take I-20 east 30 miles to Exit 92, south of Camden. Take Exit 92 and follow US 601 north 2 miles to where it merges with US 1, headed north through Camden. Follow US 1 for 29 miles to its intersection with SC 145, then turn left (north) and follow SC 145 for 3 miles to the Lake Bee Recreation Area entrance on the left (west).

Upon entering the recreation area, turn left (south) again almost immediately into the picnic area, where the trailhead for Tate's Trail is located.

The other end of Tate's Trail lies on the other side of SC 145 from Lake Bee Recreation Area. At the turnoff for Lake Bee Recreation Area on SC 145, turn right onto Carolina Sandhills National Wildlife Refuge's Visitors Drive. Follow the road for about 1 mile, at which point it makes a hard turn to the right, and continue for another 1 mile before turning left (east) onto a rough, unpaved road. Follow signs for Martin's Lake, turning left again after 0.4 mile. Park at the end of the road; the trail runs downhill to the observation tower on Martin's Lake.

The Woodland Pond Trailhead is a small parking area on the west side of Visitors Drive, 2.5 miles past the turnoff for Martin's Lake.

The hike: Located in the upper part of the Sandhills belt that was South Carolina's coastline millions of years ago, the Carolina Sandhills National Wildlife Refuge was established in 1939 on 46,000 acres of land exhausted and eroded by farming. Through careful management, it has been restored to a rich, varied environment for many kinds of wildlife.

Traversing the property is historic Wire Road, a route used by Civil War general William Tecumseh Sherman's army on its rampaging northward march through South Carolina.

Although the refuge is in the Sandhills, the two trails here pass mainly through wet areas, impoundments established to help wildlife populations, particularly water birds. The refuge has been an important inland stopover for migratory water birds, although the traffic has diminished in recent years due to improved availability of wintertime food in the birds' home regions. Wood ducks and Canada geese are found here year-round. The refuge also provides habitat for the endangered red-cockaded woodpecker, and there are more of them here than at any other national wildlife refuge. Trees housing nests of red-cockadeds are identified by white rings painted around the trunks.

The wildflowers really go wild in the spring. Look for trailing arbutus, orange milkwort, yellow jessamine, sweet pepper-bush, woolly mullein, sensitive brier, lizard's tail, prickly pear, mountain laurel, Saint John's wort, and blueberry.

The trails are marked by white, keyhole-shaped blazes. Tate's Trail starts at one of the larger impoundments, Lake Bee, and runs past delightful Lake 12 and Pool D (making a loop around the former) before ending at Martin's Lake. The latter has both a photo blind and an observation tower. In winter, Martin's Lake is a special place for observing migratory water birds. The wildlife food plots on the other side of the lake create additional opportunities for wildlife viewing.

The loop around Lake 12 features a short boardwalk; watch for signs of beaver activity here. Between impoundments, the terrain is very sandy. The trail is somewhat overgrown for a 0.25-mile stretch by Pool D, but the wildflowers and butterflies provide compensation. There are a couple of lengthy boardwalks running through the baldcypresses and briers beside Martin's Lake.

The Woodland Pond Trail is a 1-mile loop around the refuge's Pool A. Ferns are everywhere along the trail, and wildflowers are numerous as well. Keep an eye out for beavers. The trail stays near the impoundment and is cool, wet, and delightful. It circles back to Visitors Drive, which you follow back to the parking area.

Although the Tate's and Woodland Pond trails are the official hiking trails here, the refuge is crisscrossed by nearly 100 miles of dirt roads open to hikers, bikers, and vehicles. Nearby Sandhills State Forest also offers a plethora of hiking opportunities, including popular Sugar Loaf Mountain.

Facilities: Picnic facilities and rest rooms at Lake Bee Recreation Area.

Lodging and amenities: Most services, including motel and bed-and-breakfast accommodations, are available at the attractive towns of Cheraw, Bennettsville, and Hartsville. Camping is available at Cheraw and Lee state parks.

For more information: Carolina Sandhills National Wildlife Refuge. See Appendix A: For More Information.

41 Cheraw State Park

General description:	A pleasant half-day walk that passes through pine forest and red-cockaded woodpecker habitat, climaxing with baldcypresses at the head of the park's lake.
General location:	North of Florence, in the northeastern part of the state.
Distance:	4.5 miles, loop.
Difficulty:	Easy.
Trail conditions:	Conditions are good. Traffic is light.
Elevation changes:	Negligible.
Best time to go:	Year-round.
Maps:	Cheraw and Cash USGS quads. See Appendix A: For More Information.
Fees:	None.

Finding the trailhead: The entrance to Cheraw State Park is 4 miles south of Cheraw on U.S. Highway 52. From Interstate 95 at Florence, it is 37 miles

Cheraw State Park

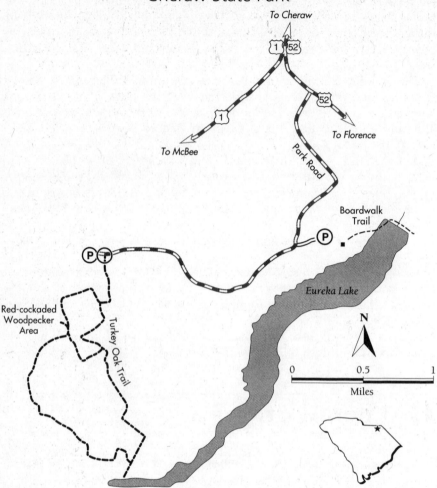

To Cheraw

1 52

52

To Florence

To McBee

1

Park Road

Boardwalk Trail

P

P

Red-cockaded Woodpecker Area

Turkey Oak Trail

Eureka Lake

N

0   0.5   1

Miles

north on US 52 (Exit 64). From the first stop sign within the park, turn right (west). The trailhead is 1 mile past the golf clubhouse.

The hike: Longleaf pine, blackjack oak, turkey oak, and hickory dominate the wooded areas of Cheraw State Park. Here in the Sandhills, visitors frequently encounter speedy lizards, particularly the aptly named six-lined racerunner. You may or may not meet the red-cockaded woodpecker, but you will certainly hear the raucous call of its pileated cousin. On the lake expect to see Canada goose, wood duck, coot, great egret, and pied-billed grebe. In the wintertime, a wide variety of ducks visit.

While you are at Cheraw State Park, be sure to take the boardwalk along the northwest edge of the lake, adjacent to the swimming and picnic areas.

It is a wonderful, unique experience, and a great opportunity to watch diving pond turtles and other aquatic life. At the far end of the boardwalk, a short trail crosses the park dam. You can, with care, go downstream some distance below the dam on old trails. (The suds in the water, which sometimes form what look like snowdrifts across the stream, are not the result of too much laundry detergent, but rather are a natural soap formed by the decay of leaves).

The park is open from 7 A.M. to 9 P.M., April through October, and from 8 A.M. to 6 P.M., November through March, Cheraw State Park is South Carolina's oldest state park, but features one of its newest nature trails, the Turkey Oak Trail. This trail offers opportunities to see the rare red-cockaded woodpecker close at hand, as well as the lovely headwaters of the park's lake, which is shaded by abundant baldcypress trees. The Turkey Oak Trail is a 4.5-mile loop. For visitors not wanting to walk so great a distance, a shorter loop offers a pleasant 1.5-mile alternative.

The first segment passes through cool, shady woods. Then the trail takes a 90-degree turn to begin its big loop. Within the first 1 mile (mileage markers are conveniently provided every half mile), a short spur departs to see the red-cockaded woodpecker nesting area, which features interesting interpretive signs.

Within a few hundred feet after you return to the main trail, the shorter loop, blazed red, turns off to the left (southwest). If you go this way, pay attention to the signs and trail blazes, as there is a 90-degree turn from one abandoned road (or perhaps "firebreak" would be a better word) to another, marked only by a sign that faces away from you. The short loop then intersects again with the longer loop; turn left to return to the trailhead.

The longer loop trail intermittently follows old, unpaved country roads. After 2 miles, the terrain becomes increasingly interesting, with many rolls and turns. At a bench, turn right to find the lake and the marvelous, spooky baldcypresses. If you decide to take the short loop, consider coming here first and doubling back after seeing this wonderful place and pausing to smell the sweet scent of the titi here. From here, continue the loop until you return to where you started, and return to the parking area the way you came.

Facilities: None at trailhead. The main area of Cheraw State Park features rest rooms, water, and a drink machine.

Lodging and amenities: There are 17 campsites and 8 cabins at Cheraw State Park, which also features an 18-hole golf course. Other amenities, including quaint bed-and-breakfast accommodations, can be found at the gracious, historic towns of Cheraw and Bennettsville.

For more information: Cheraw State Park. See Appendix A: For More Information.

Coastal Plain

The Coastal Plain offers the state's easiest hiking, in terms of steepness of terrain. The greatest challenges in this area come from the heat and insects during warm weather and the difficulty of crossing wetland areas after periods of heavy rain.

The majority of the hikes in this region traverse former rice plantations, and the habitats they offer reflect their conversion two to three centuries ago from baldcypress swamps to rice fields.

From colonial days until the end of the 19th century, rice was one of coastal South Carolina's most lucrative exports. Carolina Gold rice was so called both for its fine color and for the fortunes that were built upon it. The legacy of rice cultivation is evident far and wide. Because rice crops require frequent flooding, the crop was grown in the vicinity of all the state's tidal rivers. Swamps were drained and canals were built, separated by dikes.

After rice cultivation moved on to Louisiana and Texas in the decades following the Civil War, wealthy northern interests bought many of the former plantations and maintained the manmade wetlands as habitat for water birds, especially ducks, for their hunt clubs. Many of these lands are so maintained to this day, some in public ownership, and some still in private hands. They offer wonderful hiking.

Fortunately for natural diversity, the rice culture only cleared a portion of the state's vast acreage of baldcypress swamps, and much swampland remains for the needs of wildlife and the pleasure of hikers. The swamps are places of peace, beauty, and tranquillity. Even though swamps are by definition wet places, there is frequently enough high ground to allow the construction of trails. Elevated boardwalks have also been built unobtrusively into several of the swamps featured in this book.

Baldcypress swamps are dominated, of course, by baldcypress trees, usually accompanied by tupelo trees. Birds abound in baldcypress swamps. Some of the more charismatic include prothonotary warblers, pileated woodpeckers, barred owls, great blue herons, wood ducks, and wood storks. White-tailed deer are frequently encountered bounding through the shallow water. Snakes and alligators are also abundant, but are virtually never problematic for hikers on trails and boardwalks.

An interesting feature of a few of our coastal hikes is the presence of shell middens, remnants of the earliest days of human habitation of this region. Shell middens are in essence garbage heaps of antiquity, built up over centuries, primarily from the remains of shellfish eaten by our Native American predecessors. Archeologists have dated some middens at thousands of years old. Three centuries of coastal development by European settlers has destroyed most shell middens, but middens may still be viewed at a few places, including along the Sewee Shell Mound, Magnolia Gardens, Edisto Beach State Park, and Sea Pines Forest Preserve hikes.

The Coastal Plain is a magical place. The ghosts of Georgetown and Pawleys Island have inspired numerous stories and a cottage industry of ghost-related sightseeing. Edgar Allen Poe wrote *The Gold Bug* on Sullivan's Island, and all of Pat Conroy's novels (*The Great Santini, Lords of Discipline, Prince of Tides,* and *Beach Music*), as well as his great nonfiction work, *The Water is Wide,* are set in the coastal area stretching from Charleston in the north to Daufuskie Island, adjacent to Hilton Head Island, in the south.

All hikes in the Coastal Plain are reasonably accessible from Interstate 95, but the best roadway from which to reach most of the trails is U.S. Highway 17, which runs along the coast from the North Carolina border above Myrtle Beach all the way to the Georgia border, just northwest of Beaufort and Hilton Head Island. The road bulges in the middle of its course through the state, separating into US 17 and US 17A between Georgetown, south of Huntington Beach State Park (Hike 42), and Pocotaligo, just south of the Combahee Unit of the ACE Basin National Wildlife Refuge (Hike 58).

Accommodations in the coastal area are numerous, including the beach destinations of Myrtle Beach and the Grand Strand and Hilton Head Island, historic Charleston and vicinity, charming Georgetown and Beaufort, and the many facilities along I-95. For something different, try the bed-and-breakfast establishments at the "arrogantly shabby" beach community of Pawleys Island, the quaint fishing village of McClellanville, one of the live oak-shrouded plantations near Moncks Corner, or one of the laid-back creekside houses on Edisto Island.

The food, especially the seafood, is great at all the aforementioned locations, as well as at Murrells Inlet, a village with wall-to-wall seafood restaurants, and at Bowens Island Restaurant (on the road from Charleston to Folly Beach), a marshland establishment that offers great roasted oysters and an ambiance that gives new meaning to the term "rustic."

The names people use for South Carolina's coastal plain can be a bit confusing. Many South Carolinians refer to this entire area as the Lowcountry (also written Low Country, low country and lowcountry), but the boundaries of the Lowcountry are open to question. Some refer to the southernmost counties of the state as the Lowcountry, and some to the historic plantation area around Charleston. Others use the term to refer to all of the area formerly dominated by river plantations from the Waccamaw River wetlands above Georgetown all the way to Beaufort.

The Coastal Plain is noted for wetlands. Development is constantly shrinking these important habitats throughout the Southeast. South Carolina is fortunate to have many of its remaining wetlands protected as national wildlife refuges, state parks, wildlife management areas, as private property with irrevocable conservation easements, and as state-managed heritage preserves.

The ACE Basin along the lower coast is a special wetland treasure. ACE is an acronym for the Ashepoo, Combahee, and Edisto Rivers, which flow to the ocean between Charleston and Beaufort. The Combahee and Edisto form the borders on the west and east, respectively, while the Ashepoo bisects the basin. The ACE Basin, at 350,000 acres, is one of the largest remaining undeveloped wetlands in the country. Although undeveloped, the region has not been left unchanged by humankind. However, the changes made to the landscape by the rice planters of the 18th and 19th centuries created highly attractive habitat for wildlife, particularly for migratory birds. A large proportion of the ACE Basin is under permanent protection from development, due to the conservation arrangements of private landholders in cooperation with the state and federal governments.

The Coastal Plain hikes in this guide range from hikes through the old rice fields of the coast, to inland swamps, to woodland paths, to sandy ocean beachfront, to cultivated plantation gardens. The major points of departure for these hikes are Myrtle Beach, Georgetown, Moncks Corner, Charleston, Beaufort, and Hilton Head Island.

42 Huntington Beach State Park

General description:	A day hike through freshwater and saltwater marshes, pristine sandy beaches, and maritime forests in one of the state's most generous bird habitats.
General location:	South of Myrtle Beach, along the state's upper coast.
Distance:	8.7 miles, loop.
Difficulty:	Easy.
Trail conditions:	Sandpiper Pond Nature Trail is soggy after rains. Traffic is light to moderate.
Best time to go:	Year-round.
Maps:	Brochure available at entrance station. Brookgreen and Magnolia Beach USGS quads. See Appendix A: For More Information.
Fees:	$4 per person, $2 per child age 6–12.

Finding the trailhead: Huntington Beach State Park is 3 miles south of Murrells Inlet on U.S. Highway 17, midway between Myrtle Beach and Georgetown. The entrance is directly across the highway from the fighting stallion sculpture which marks the entrance to Brookgreen Gardens. After entering the park and crossing the causeway between the saltwater and freshwater marshes, bear north at the fork and look immediately on the left for the parking lot at the saltwater marsh boardwalk. The Sandpiper Pond Trailhead is across the road.

The hike: Huntington Beach State Park is a relatively secluded and well-preserved 2,500-acre jewel tucked into South Carolina's otherwise highly developed Grand Strand coastal area. It is the largest expanse of undeveloped beach with easy public access along the state's upper coast.

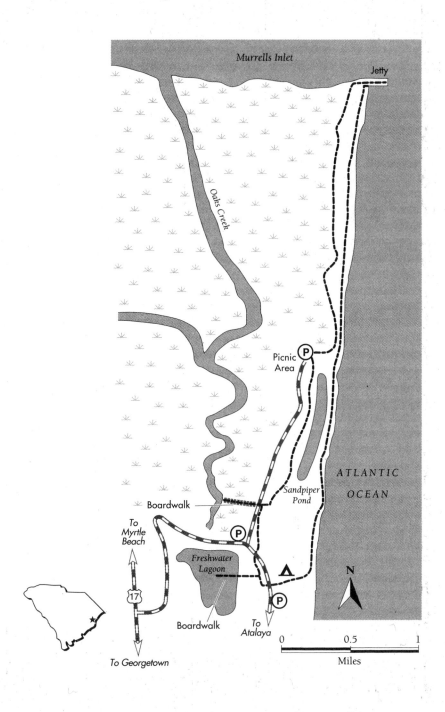

Murrells Inlet

Jetty

Oaks Creek

ATLANTIC OCEAN

Picnic Area

Sandpiper Pond

Boardwalk

To Myrtle Beach

Freshwater Lagoon

Boardwalk

To Atalaya

17

To Georgetown

N

0   0.5   1

Miles

The salt water marsh boardwalk. Yvonne Michel photo

Named after noted American sculptor Anna Hyatt Huntington and her husband, Archer Milton Huntington, Huntington Beach was opened to the public in the 1960s, after many years of private use by the Huntington family. Park hours are 6 A.M. to 6 P.M., September through April; 6 A.M. to 9 P.M., May through August.

The Sandpiper Pond Trail provides you with a pleasant journey through layers of coastal ecosystems. From the parking lot for the salt marsh boardwalk, begin by strolling out on the boardwalk, over spartina grass and black pluffmud laced with oysters, to an observation deck midway along, and then beyond to the pier abutting Oaks Creek.

After returning from the salt marsh, cross the road and begin the 1.2-mile Sandpiper Pond Nature Trail, which takes you through forest and thicket smothered with live and laurel oaks, loblolly pines, redcedars, palmettos, wax myrtles, and numerous creeping vines. As the trail winds behind a saltwater pond, you pass observation towers for viewing herons, gulls, ospreys, hawks, and numerous other birds.

The trail emerges at the north end parking lot. Follow the boardwalk through the large, vegetated sand dunes to the beach. Sandspur, beach pea, primrose, pennywort, prickly pear cactus, and sea oats are abundant. Though all these plants help, the roots of the sea oats are especially important in anchoring the dunes and preventing them from being blown away by the wind or washed away by ocean waves. Cutting or uprooting beach vegetation is illegal.

Turn north and walk toward the Murrells Inlet Jetty, a double row of large stones that project into the sea 2.9 miles from the end of the Sandpiper

Nature Trail. Observe the tidal coves behind the white dunes, the seabirds and the sandcrabs of the Carolina coast, and, sometimes, dolphins playing in the surf. Sandpipers abound. Walk the smooth asphalt surface of the jetty to its end, feel the bracing salt breeze, and watch the parade of fishing boats entering and exiting the Murrells Inlet harbor.

Keep an eye out for collectible shells as you turn around and head south along the strand all the way to the entrance to the campground at the south end of the park 4 miles away. Cross the dunes at the designated walkway and follow the road 0.6 mile back to the starting point, pausing for a stroll along the boardwalk over the cattail-rimmed freshwater lagoon to observe ducks and perhaps an alligator or two.

The white structure at the south end of the beach is Atalaya, a mansion built between 1931 and 1933 as a winter home for the Huntingtons and as a studio for Anna Huntington's sculpture. *Atalaya* is a Spanish term meaning watchtower. Archer Huntington, a noted authority on Spanish history, designed the house in the style of the Moorish architecture along the Spanish Mediterranean coast.

Atalaya is open to the public. The outer walls form a square 200 feet on each side, with the front facing the ocean. Within the walled one-story structure there is a large, open inner court with a small entry court in the rear. The dominant tree in the courtyard is the Carolina palmetto, South Carolina's state tree. The living quarters consist of 30 rooms around three sides of the perimeter, with stables and other utilitarian areas on the back side.

Facilities: Rest rooms, drinking water, bathhouses, and picnic areas at both

The salt water marsh boardwalk. YVONNE MICHEL PHOTO

the north and south end parking lots. Refreshments are available at a well-stocked store at the south end.

Lodging and amenities: There is a 186-site campground at the south end of the Huntington Beach State Park. There are also campsites at Myrtle Beach State Park and a large number of commercial camping facilities in the Myrtle Beach area. Numerous services and amenities are available along the stretch of US 17 from Myrtle Beach to Georgetown. Murrells Inlet is famous for its many seafood restaurants, Pawleys Island prides itself on being "arrogantly shabby," and the old section of Georgetown offers charm without glitter.

For more information: Huntington Beach State Park. See Appendix A: For More Information.

43 Santee Coastal Reserve

General description:	Half a day's walk through a delightful mix of freshwater and saltwater ecosystems.
General location:	South of Georgetown, along the state's central coast.
Distance:	7.8 miles.
Difficulty:	Easy.
Trail conditions:	Conditions are good. Traffic is light to moderate.
Best time to go:	Late winter, early spring.
Maps:	Map posted on bulletin board at trailhead, and free maps sometimes available in a box there. Minim Island and Cape Romain USGS quads. See Appendix A: For More Information.
Fees:	None.

Finding the trailhead: From Charleston, follow U.S. Highway 17 north 45 miles. About 3 miles past McClellanville, turn right (northeast) on Santee Road (Secondary Road 857). The entrance to Santee Coastal Reserve is 2 miles farther, at Lillypond Mission Baptist Church (7245 Santee Road). Turn right (east) at the church onto Santee Gun Club Road. The trailhead is 3 miles down Santee Gun Club Road.

From Georgetown, travel south on US 17 for 15 miles. One mile past the South Santee River bridge, turn left (southeast) onto Santee Road and go 1 mile before turning left (east) onto Santee Gun Club Road at Lillypond Mission Baptist Church.

The hike: The 24,000-acre Santee Coastal Reserve, located on the south side of the huge Santee River Delta, offers maritime forest, great expanses of rice field wetlands, and paths bordering the Intracoastal Waterway and

Santee Coastal Reserve

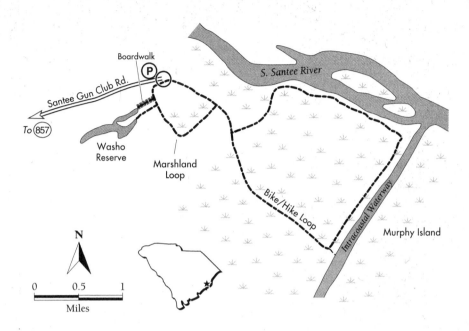

the South Santee River. Santee Coastal Reserve is a former rice plantation, used during much of this century as a hunt club and acquired in 1974 by The Nature Conservancy. With the exception of the Washo Reserve area, The Nature Conservancy has turned over the property to the South Carolina Department of Natural Resources, which manages it as a wildlife management area. Hunting is allowed at specified times. The Reserve is closed to the general public from November 1 through January 31. Hours are 8 A.M. to 5 P.M. Mondays through Saturdays and 1 P.M. to 5 P.M. on Sundays, March 1 through October 31. In February, the Reserve is open from 1 P.M. to 5 P.M., seven days a week.

Santee Coastal Reserve is a birder's paradise—almost 300 avian species have been spotted here. The reserve provides great wintering ground for several duck species and serves as a permanent residence for brown pelicans, mottled ducks, wood ducks, black-bellied plovers, pine and yellow-throated warblers, Carolina and marsh wrens, coots, and many birds of prey, including bald eagles and a large concentration of ospreys. Shorebirds, swallow-tailed kites, herons, egrets and ibis are plentiful. Large turkey buzzards haunt the trees bordering the marshlands.

But birds are not the only wildlife here. Alligators prowl the waters, and white-tailed deer, feral hogs, and many small mammals frequent the woodlands and marshes.

The Washo Reserve, the pristine 1,040-acre enclave retained by The Nature Conservancy after its purchase of the property, offers an 800-foot boardwalk through a swamp and to the edge of a baldcypress–rimmed pond teeming with aquatic vegetation and wetland wildlife.

From the bulletin board at the trailhead, proceed counterclockwise along the Marshland Trail. Walk a short distance through hardwoods and turn right (west) onto the 800-foot boardwalk that extends into the Washo Reserve swamp. The boardwalk ends at a pristine pond which once served as the source of fresh water for the rice crops on the diked marshland along the Santee River. The pond is laced with floating water lily and bladderwort.

The Marshland Loop Trail winds on through forest and along dikes surrounded by wetlands. In spring, blue flag iris is abundant, as are lizard's tail, butterweed, swamp dogwood, cattail, and water willow. The maritime forested areas include live oak draped in Spanish moss, resurrection fern, holly, bull-bay, sweet gum, and sparkleberry.

At the junction at 1.4 miles, turn right (southeast) and walk 0.3 mile to the beginning of the Bike/Hike Trail.

Tall cordgrass, black needle rush, water lilies, cattail, and bullrush dominate the vista along the dikes comprising the Bike/Hike Trail, a 5.1-mile loop which takes you through open rice fields, up the Intracoastal Waterway past islands of scrub trees in marshland seas, along the South Santee River, and through a maritime forest back to the beginning of the loop.

At the end of the Bike/Hike Trail, turn right (southwest) and walk 1 mile back to the trailhead.

Additional hiking is available on the 1.1-mile Woodland Trail loop located on the north side of Santee Gun Club Road, 2 miles past the Reserve entrance. This trail winds through a highland stand of old-growth mixed pine and hardwoods, where bright green ferns carpeting the forest floor add a magical air. For most of the way, the trail follows deer-hunting and firebreak tracks, but is beautifully shaded as it cuts through a full canopy of stately green. Bachman's sparrows, red-cockaded woodpeckers and warblers are among the attractions in this prime deer habitat. This short hike is a worthwhile contrast to the marshland a short distance away.

Facilities: Rudimentary rest rooms are available a few feet north of the trailhead.

Lodging and amenities: Camping is allowed in the Santee Coastal Reserve with permit from the reserve's headquarters. Buck Hall Campground in Francis Marion National Forest near McClellanville has full amenities. All services are available in and around Charleston. Georgetown, half an hour north, is a historic port city with all services, including interesting riverfront restaurants and comfortable bed-and-breakfast accommodations. Bed-and-breakfast lodging and some services are available at McClellanville, a quaint fishing village just to the south of the reserve.

For more information: Santee Coastal Reserve. See Appendix A: For More Information.

44 Bull Island

General description:	A day's hike through forests and wetlands and along beaches on a barrier island. Expect alligators and an infinite variety of birds.
General location:	Northeast of Charleston, along the state's central coast.
Distance:	2 miles, loop. There are 16 miles of trails on the island.
Difficulty:	Easy.
Trail conditions:	Conditions are generally excellent. Traffic is light.
Best time to go:	Late fall, winter, early spring.
Maps:	Available at Sewee Visitor and Environmental Education Center and from Coastal Expeditions (ferry operator); Sewee Bay and Bull Island USGS quads. See Appendix A: For More Information.
Fees:	Ferry fee is $20 per person.

Finding the trailhead: Bull Island is in Bull's Bay, off the coast of the community of Awendaw. From Charleston, follow U.S. Highway 17 north 15 miles. Turn right (northeast) on Secondary Road 584 (Sewee Road). Continue 3.5 miles, then turn right (east) on SR 1170, which ends after 1.5 miles at Moore's Landing, site of the ferry to Bull Island. Be sure to call in advance to make sure the ferry is running on the day you plan to visit (843-881-4582). From March to November the ferry operates four days a week (Tuesday, Thursday, Friday, and Saturday); for the rest of the year it operates on Saturdays only.

Once on the island, follow the road from the dock to the visitor contact station, which is the trailhead.

The hike: Bull Island is a major component of the Cape Romain National Wildlife Refuge. Accessible only by boat, it is remote and permanently sheltered from development. It is not sheltered from the elements, however. The storm surge from Hurricane Hugo in 1989 washed completely over the island. Nature will need centuries to repair the damage to the island's glorious maritime forest of loblolly pine and live oak. And nature will get the chance, because refuge managers have decided to let the island recover at its own pace.

Hugo largely destroyed the forest; fortunately, what remains is great wildlife habitat. Bull Island is a mecca for birders, particularly during winter. Nearly 350 bird species have been seen at Cape Romain National Wildlife Refuge, most of them at Bull Island. About half of all the American oystercatchers on the East Coast winter here, making for a spectacular sight.

Loggerhead turtles nest on the beach in early summer. Fox squirrels scamper among the trees, and alligators are quite plentiful at the island's freshwater

Bull Island

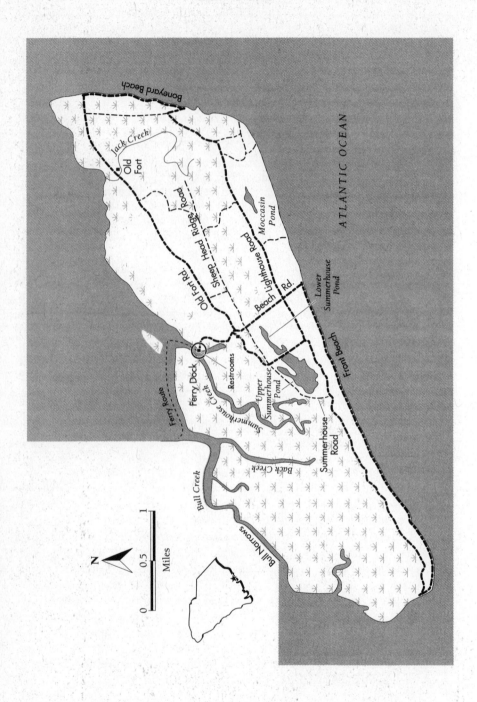

habitats. Red wolves have been introduced in hopes of reestablishing them on this and other islands.

Many old roads and trails crisscross this barrier island. Hiking opportunities are limited only by the time available to you before the ferry returns to the mainland.

The main trail, a 2-mile loop, starts from the visitor contact station. The trail runs near the island's lookout tower, crosses Sheep Head Ridge Road, and mounts a dike between Upper Summerhouse Pond and Lower Summerhouse Pond. This is a great place to see both birds and alligators. On the other side of the ponds, the trail makes a sharp left (east) turn.

Here you may choose a much longer alternate route. If instead of turning left (northeast), you turn right (southwest), you can walk all the way to the end of the island, 3 miles away. Along this route you can see a splendid heron and ibis rookery at one of the freshwater pools. At the end of the island, gaze across Price Creek to Capers Island, another protected barrier island.

Walk back along Front Beach, where you will find a bonanza if you are a seashell hunter. Summer visitors also find this an especially attractive route, because the island's large, aggressive flies seldom venture onto the beach.

Past the left turn on the main trail 0.5 mile is Beach Road, a great place for blackberries in season. (Beach Road, as the name implies, runs all the way to the beach. If you took the previous detour to the southern end of the island, after 3 miles of beachcombing, you reach Beach Road. Turn left and pick up the main trail again.) Big Pond, off to the right, offers more birding opportunities. Turn left (north) on Beach Road to return to the visitor contact station, about 0.75 mile away. A right (south) turn will take you to the beach, about 0.3 mile away.

Another long alternate route takes you straight (east) across Beach Road onto Lighthouse Road, instead of turning on Beach Road. This loop route adds at least 6.5 miles to the trip (depending how far you walk on Boneyard Beach). After 2 miles on Lighthouse Road, you reach a right (southeast) turnoff leading to famous Boneyard Beach at the eastern end of the island. This is perhaps the wildest, most beautiful seashore on the South Carolina coast. You pass through a ravaged post-Hugo landscape of dead trees (which gives the beach its name), and cover is scarce. However, there is an alluring wild beauty here that makes the trip worthwhile.

Walk 1.5 miles north on Boneyard Beach, then turn left (west) onto Old Fort Road, which leads back to the trailhead. At Jack Creek you come across the few remains of the Old Fort, little more than a short tabby wall. Although the origin of the Old Fort is unknown, the best guess is that it was built as a defense against pirates.

Facilities: Rest room, water fountain, picnic tables.

Lodging and amenities: No camping is allowed on Bull Island, but Buck Hall Campground in the Francis Marion National Forest offers full service

Bull Island trail. SUSAN NELLE PHOTO

campsites. McClellanville offers food and limited services, and the Charleston area offers all services. The Sewee Restaurant on US 17 offers good food and a down-home atmosphere.

For more information: Cape Romain National Wildlife Refuge; Sewee Visitor and Environmental Education Center; Coastal Expeditions for ferry information. See Appendix A: For More Information.

45 Sewee Shell Mound

General description:	A short walk through coastal woodland to ancient Native American shell mounds.
General location:	North of Charleston, along the state's central coast.
Distance:	1 mile loop.
Difficulty:	Easy.
Best time to go:	Year-round.
Maps:	Available at Sewee Visitor and Environmental Education Center; Sewee Bay USGS quad. See Appendix A: For More Information.
Fees:	None.

Finding the trailhead: From Charleston, drive north about 18 miles on U.S. Highway 17, turning right (northeast) at Secondary Road 432 (Doar Road). Continue 2.5 miles to gravel Salt Pond Road (Forest Service Road 243). Turn right (east) on Salt Pond Road and drive 0.5 mile to the trailhead, which is marked by a sign on the right. Park on the side of the road. (Salt Pond Road is a one-lane road with a turning loop at its terminus, a short distance farther on.)

The hike: The Sewee Shell Ring, about 4,000 years old and on the National Register of Historic Places, is a type of archeological site unique to the Atlantic coast from South Carolina to northern Florida.

At the trailhead stands an information board with a map and a brief description of the area. A loop with two spurs, the Sewee Mound Interpretive Trail is marked with directional signs and takes you along a small tidal creek which empties into the Intracoastal Waterway just beyond the marsh bank. At several places, interpretive markers provide brief explanations of the viewing points.

This area was devastated by Hurricane Hugo in 1989; the eye of the storm came ashore right about here. The forest suffered from an intense fire two years afterward. What once was a stand of large oaks and mature pines is now predominately brush and scrub standing about head high. Tall, blackened trunks, the only remains of the mature trees, loom over the green of the recent growth. This landscape is stark, but not lifeless. You may see at

Sewee Shell Mound

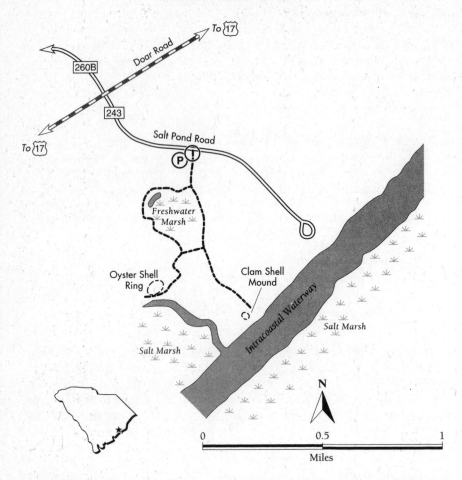

close range an osprey perched at the top of a 60-foot tree trunk, woodpeckers reclaiming their habitat, a cluster of blue flag iris growing wild in the wetlands, or chinaback fiddler crabs numbering in the hundreds running at the edges of the shell mounds.

The trail emerges from a dense stand of young pines and takes you through a large field. In this open place, you can observe swallowtail butterflies, the low lying yellow five-finger, the bright red flowering coral bean, and the trumpet honeysuckle.

Turn left (east) on the first spur and head toward the creek, where stunted live oaks, Carolina palmettos, and southern redcedars survived the storm and were spared by the fire. At the end sits a mound of discarded clam shells made by Native Americans who obviously were mainly consumers of shellfish. Walking around the mound, you reach the sandy start of the marsh that lines the creek and waterway. Fiddler crabs and their burrows dot the intertidal zone from marsh edge to the low-water mark. The interpretive sign tells about the eagles, hawks, ospreys, and gulls that frequent this place. American oystercatchers are present year-round, and marbled godwits can be seen in winter and early spring.

Retrace your steps, returning to the loop, and turn left (west) to follow the trail along the creek until you reach the spur that leads to the oyster shell ring. The ring is quite visible from the boardwalk that takes you to the sandy creek edge.

The ring of oyster shells is an ancient trash pile accumulated over several centuries. Native Americans lived in huts arranged in a circle and discarded oyster shells and other refuse in the center to form the ring. The open interior of the ring may have served some communal purpose; possibly it was used for ceremonies. This ring is the best preserved of a number of such shell rings found along the Atlantic coast from South Carolina to northern Florida.

A comfortable bench on the boardwalk allows you to rest and enjoy stimulating salt breezes and the open view of the creek and the marshlands stretching to the Intracoastal Waterway and Bull's Bay beyond.

The return portion of the loop takes you through more scrub forest. On the way you pass a freshwater pond brimming with cattails and pickerelweeds.

Facilities: None at trailhead, but rest rooms and drinking water are available at Sewee Visitor and Environmental Education Center, on U.S. Highway 17.

Lodging and amenities: Buck Hall Campground, in Francis Marion National Forest just off U.S. Highway 17 south of McClellanville, offers full camping facilities. The Charleston area provides many lodging, eating, and entertainment options. Seewee Restaurant, a converted gas station on US 17, provides a unique atmosphere for she-crab soup and other foods of the Coastal Plain.

For more information: Sewee Visitor and Environmental Education Center. See Appendix A: For More Information.

46 I'on Swamp

General description:	A walk along dikes through a swamp full of bird life, alligators, and beautiful baldcypresses.
General location:	Northeast of Charleston, along the state's central coast.
Distance:	2 miles, loop.
Difficulty:	Easy.
Trail conditions:	Conditions good except after heavy rains. Traffic is light.
Best time to go:	Fall and spring.
Maps:	Trail map available from Francis Marion National Forest office and at Sewee Visitor and Environmental Education Center; Ocean Bay USGS quad. See Appendix A: For More Information.
Fees:	None.

Finding the trailhead: From Charleston, take U.S. Highway 17 northeast about 15 miles. I'on Swamp Road (Forest Service Road 228) is on the left (west) side and unpaved. (Sewee Visitor and Environmental Education Center is about 100 yards farther up US 17, on the right.) Proceed 2 miles on I'on Swamp Road to a parking area on the left (south) side of the road. The I'on Swamp Trail begins on a short boardwalk leading from the parking area.

The hike: I'on Swamp Trail loops along a gridwork of dikes on what was once part of Witheywood Plantation, a rice-growing estate.

From the parking area, you enter a tangle of young trees, heavy vines, and thick brush. A short boardwalk takes you across water-soaked ground to an old roadbed. The roadbed gives way to a footpath running along the top of an earthen dike which is the only high ground in sight as you move through the quiet and still wetlands. To your right the piped wellhead of a natural artesian well splashes sparkling clear water in the black swamp. On the left is open water, home, in season, to impressive alligators and water lilies.

I'on Swamp is famous among birders for its wide variety of species, particularly during fall and spring migrations. It is a great spot for warblers; the popular prothonotary warbler is often seen. The most elusive bird in North America, Bachman's warbler, has been sighted here, although not in recent years. Deer are common in the swamp, and turtles are sufficiently plentiful to keep the abundant alligators well fed.

After 0.5 mile, the trail forks at an intersection with another dike which borders the remains of Witheywood Canal. The left fork begins the trail loop and the right fork ends it. This first 1 mile of the trail features seven interpretive markers that describe I'on Swamp and its inhabitants.

Turn left (southwest) at the canal. The trail follows the crest of a dike, and hugs the canal closely. The canal waters are black, but frequently punctuated

I'on Swamp

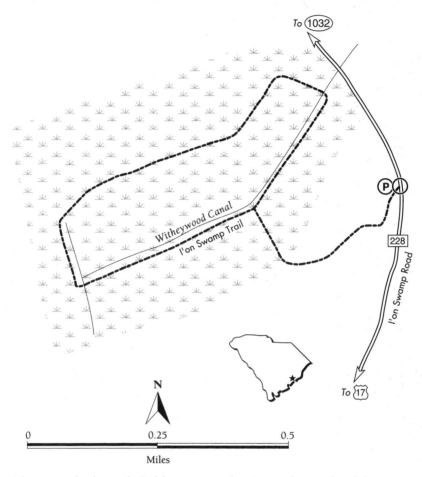

To (1032)

P

228

I'on Swamp Road

Witheywood Canal

I'on Swamp Trail

N

To ⑰

0   0.25   0.5

Miles

with green duckweed. Baldcypresses dominate the wetland forest on the left. As you progress you notice that as the terrain on this side of the trail becomes progressively wetter, the likelihood of spotting alligators also grows progressively.

After about 0.5 mile along the dike, the trail crosses a larger canal or pond on a bridge and turns right (northwest). At times, this pond fills to the brim with alligators. Herons and turtles are also present in good numbers. Here, the trail leaves the shade for a while, and sun-loving blackberries and other briers spring up. After perhaps 0.1 mile, bear right (northeast) and return to shady swamp habitat.

This 1-mile-long backstretch of the trail weaves through more wondrous wetlands. The footpath is uneven along this stretch and undulates considerably

Baldcypress tree. JOHN CLARK PHOTO

as it passes through the broad, murky swampland along remnants of rice field dikes. At the end of the mile, the trail bends sharply to the right (southeast), back toward Witheywood Canal, which it crosses on a culvert.

After the culvert, bear right (southwest). The trail sticks close to Witheywood Canal for the remainder of the hike until you reach the path leading from I'on Swamp Road after about 0.5 mile, where you turn left (south) to return to the parking area.

Facilities: None at the trail, but rest rooms, drinking water, and refreshments are available at the Sewee Visitor and Environmental Education Center, nearby on U.S. Highway 17.

Lodging and amenities: Public campsites are available at Buck Hall Campground in Francis Marion National Forest on U.S. Highway 17. Primitive camping with water availability is available at Halfway Creek Campground on Halfway Creek Road (Secondary Road 100). There are commercial camping facilities in the Charleston area, as well as all other services. McClellanville offers limited services.

For more information: Sewee Visitor and Environmental Education Center. See Appendix A: For More Information.

---

47 Swamp Fox Trail

General description:	A long, level, three- or four-day backpack through typical coastal pine forest and swampy wetlands.
General location:	Northeast of Charleston, along the state's central coast.
Distance:	42 miles one way.
Difficulty:	Easy, except after heavy rains.
Trail conditions:	Generally good conditions degenerate after heavy rains. Traffic is light to moderate.
Best time to go:	Late fall, winter and early spring. Take care during fall hunting season.
Maps:	Francis Marion National Forest maps; Palmetto Trail maps; Bonneau, Cordesville, Bethera, Huger, Ocean Bay, and Awendaw USGS quads. See Appendix A: For More Information.
Fees:	None.

Finding the trailhead: To reach the southeastern trailhead, travel 25 miles north from Charleston on U.S. Highway 17 to the community of Awendaw. The trailhead is on the left (west) side of US 17, a few yards past the intersection of US 17 and Steed Creek Road (Secondary Road 133). It is easy to miss when approaching from the south because a curve in the wide highway turns your view in another direction.

The middle trailhead is at the Witherbee Ranger Station. From the Awendaw Trailhead, go to the intersection of US 17 and Steed Creek Road. Follow Steed Creek Road north for 12 miles to the crossroads at Huger, where you should bear left onto South Carolina Highway 402. (From Charleston, go north on US 17 for 9 miles, turn left onto SC 41 and travel 17 miles to the intersection with SC 402 and Steed Creek Road in Huger.) After 3 miles on SC 402, turn right (north) onto Copperhead Road (SC 125) and travel 2 miles to Witherbee Road. Turn right (northeast) onto Witherbee Road and travel 0.5 mile to the ranger station and parking area on the right. (From Moncks Corner, follow US 52 north across the Tailrace Canal, then

Swamp Fox Trail

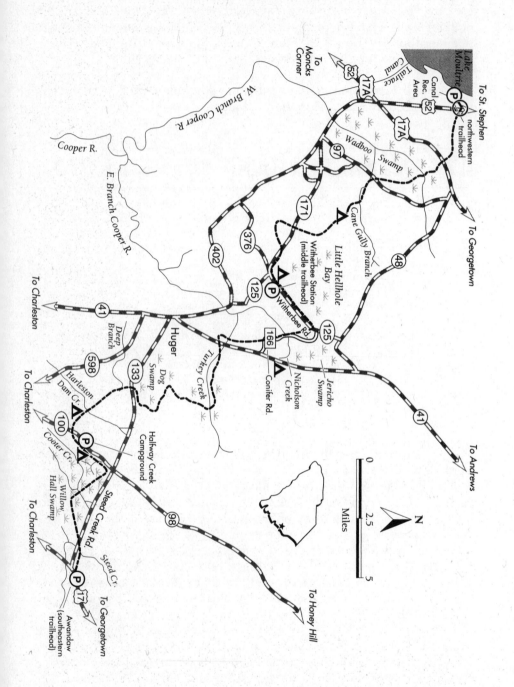

turn right on SC 402 and drive 3 miles to Witherbee Road. Turn left and travel 7 miles to the ranger station and parking lot on the right.)

The northwestern trailhead is at Canal Recreation Area, on US 52, 6 miles north of Moncks Corner. It is on the left (west) side of the road, 3.6 miles from the point at which US 17A forks east, away from US 52.

The hike: The Francis Marion National Forest and the Swamp Fox Trail are both named for General Francis Marion, a local Revolutionary War hero who was a genius at guerrilla warfare. Evading counterattack and capture by the British, he continually faded into the myriad swamps throughout the South Carolina coastal plain. Marion became known by friend and foe alike as the "Swamp Fox."

The Swamp Fox Trail, whose southeasternmost 27 miles are designated a National Recreation Trail, also serves as the Swamp Fox Passage of the Palmetto Trail (see Introduction). At present, the Swamp Fox Trail begins at Awendaw, near the coast, and wends through 42 miles of forest to the Canal Recreation Area near Lake Moultrie, where the Swamp Fox Trail links with the 28-mile Lake Moultrie Passage to form the state's longest unbroken hiking opportunity outside the mountains.

Originally built by Boy Scouts in 1968, the Swamp Fox Trail is still maintained, in part, by the efforts of local troops. Hikers share the trail with mountain bikers. Until the Jericho Horse Trail is fully relocated, several miles of the Swamp Fox Trail between Dog Swamp and the Witherbee Ranger Station will be temporarily shared with horseback riders.

With a variety of hardwoods scattered through a forest largely made up of longleaf pines, the Swamp Fox Trail offers attractive fall foliage, good

A boardwalk through Dog Swamp wetlands. YVONNE MICHEL PHOTO

views of wintering birds, and a beautiful array of springtime wild flowers. Flowers and other attractive foliage and wildlife are also present throughout the summer months, but heat, humidity, redbugs, ticks, and mosquitoes make the trail somewhat less appealing from May through September.

In general, the trail is well marked and the surface makes for easy walking. Most of the Swamp Fox Trail is grassy or covered with pine straw, although the trail occasionally passes along old dirt logging roadbeds. At times, the grass can become rather high, and the trail can be difficult after heavy rains, when paths through low-lying areas become submerged or quite muddy. Passage through wet areas is, however, facilitated by numerous footbridges, boardwalks, and mounted split plank logs.

Most of the pine forest is relatively young. The eye of Hurricane Hugo came ashore at Awendaw, and the storm passed through this area in full fury. You will see plenty of pines snapped off at heights of 15 to 20 feet by Hugo's roaring winds. Scattered areas throughout the forest show the aftermath of large-scale clearcutting. The effects of Hugo and clearcutting are uneven, resulting in a trail that is generally blessed with good shade, but has frequent stretches of sparse canopy. In a pine forest, the sparse canopy keeps you warm in winter, but it is uncomfortable in the heat of summer.

Although it is generally easy walking, the entire 42-mile hike requires the better part of three or four days, especially during the recommended cooler seasons, when daylight hours are fewer. The trail makes numerous crossings of both paved and dirt roads, so it is easy to enjoy in segments suitable to almost any preference, especially if you use two vehicles so that there is no need to double back. Road crossings are marked with signs which are small but detectable, allowing you to access the trail at a large number of points along its route.

Departing from the Awendaw (southeastern) trailhead, you journey about 1 mile before crossing a sturdy footbridge over the foreboding black waters of Steed Creek, then another 1 mile to cross Steed Creek Road. From Steed Creek Road, the trail plunges through wetlands along an old railbed with an array of pitcher plants on either side, through mixed hardwood and pine forest, and through pinelands which have been logged by humans and flattened by Hugo. After 4 miles past Steed Creek Road, soon after crossing an ample Boy Scout–constructed bridge over Cooter Creek, you reach Halfway Creek Campground. This grassy primitive camping area is located off Halfway Creek Road (SC 98), 0.5 mile south of its intersection with Steed Creek Road. A hand-pumped well here dispenses potable water.

From Halfway Creek Campground, traverse pine forest for 2 miles, cross Halfway Creek Road, and walk a 4-mile stretch to the next crossing of Steed Creek Road. The highlights of this section are the wetlands of Harleston Dam Creek and Deep Branch.

The 8 miles between the second crossing of Steed Creek Road and the trail crossing at SC 41 is perhaps the most diverse segment of the trail. Circling the eastern perimeter of Dog Swamp, the trail moves through grassy savanna heavy with broom straw, many different stages of pine growth, scattered wetlands, and across Turkey Creek and its accompanying swamp. This section has many low-lying stretches and is difficult to traverse after heavy rains. After Turkey Creek, the hiking trail joins the Jericho Horse Trail and continues to the SC 41 crossing.

On the other side of SC 41, the combined hiking and equestrian trail follows an extremely straight railbed for the next 4.5 miles, the highlights of which are dark and placid Nicholson Creek and the wetlands beyond, which form the western edge of Jericho Swamp. Just beyond the Nicholson Creek bridge is a very primitive campsite.

After the combined trail completes its railbed traverse of Jericho Swamp, the Swamp Fox Trail veers left, away from the horse trail, and crosses Witherbee Road (SC 125) near its intersection with Conifer Road (Forest Service Road 166, unpaved). The trail then heads southwest for 2.5 miles to the middle trailhead, located at the Witherbee Ranger Station parking lot. This section, which parallels and is often in sight of Witherbee Road, winds through young pines and scrub oaks to complete the 27-mile section of the Swamp Fox Trail designated as a National Recreation Trail.

The last 15 miles, between Witherbee Ranger Station and Canal Recreation Area, is the newest section of the Swamp Fox Trail. This low-lying route passes through Wadboo Swamp and other wetlands, and should be avoided after heavy rains.

From the Witherbee Trailhead, the trail circles the western fringe of Little Hellhole Bay, crossing SR 171 a couple of times, then heads across relatively high ground before descending into the wetlands of Cane Gully Branch and crossing the newly constructed bridge over the main channel of the creek, about 9 miles from Witherbee Ranger Station.

Next, you cross SR 97, then slog through formidable Wadboo Swamp, a passage made possible only recently by the construction of the Henry Brown Bridge over the main body of Wadboo Creek. The Henry Brown Bridge is 3 miles from the Cane Gully Branch crossing. Wadboo Swamp is prime fishing territory for bass, bream, and catfish; deer, otters, and alligators prowl the baldcypress–forested wetlands.

After emerging from the swamp, cross US 17A and move through higher and drier pine forest to cover the final 3 miles to Canal Recreation Area, on the west side of US 52.

Facilities: No rest rooms or drinking water at Awendaw trailhead. Witherbee Ranger Station has rest rooms and water during office hours, 8 A.M. to 4 P.M., Monday through Friday. Rudimentary rest rooms and drinking water are available at the Canal Recreation Area trailhead, and there are full facilities at the Sewee Visitor and Environmental Education Center, on U.S. Highway 17 just south of the Awendaw trailhead. Additionally, a hand-pumped well dispenses potable water at the Halfway Creek Campground, 6 miles along the trail from the Awendaw trailhead.

Lodging and amenities: Primitive camping is available at Halfway Creek

Campground and at several other designated sites along the trail. Buck Hall Campground, located in Francis Marion National Forest near McClellanville, offers campsites. Commercial campgrounds and numerous lodging and eating options are available throughout the Charleston area and at Moncks Corner and in the Lake Moultrie vicinity.

For more information: Sewee Visitor and Environmental Education Center; Witherbee Ranger District of Francis Marion National Forest; Palmetto Trails. See Appendix A: For More Information.

48 Lake Moultrie Passage

General description:	A two- to three-day backpack around the eastern side of Lake Moultrie that offers panoramic views of Lake Moultrie, cypress-filled wetlands, and plentiful waterfowl habitat.
General location:	North of Charleston, in the state's central coastal plain.
Distance:	28.4 miles one way.
Difficulty:	Easy to moderate.
Trail conditions:	Conditions are excellent. Traffic varies from light to heavy.
Best time to go:	Early spring, late fall, and winter. Take care during hunting seasons.
Maps:	Brochures available at southern trailhead, and from the Santee Cooper Property Management Division or Palmetto Trails; Bonneau, St. Stephen, and Pineville USGS quads. See Appendix A: For More Information.
Fees:	None.

Finding the trailhead: The southern trailhead is located at Francis Marion National Forest's Canal Recreation Area, 6 miles north of Moncks Corner on the west side of U.S. Highway 52.

The northern trailhead is on the Diversion Canal. From Interstate 26, take the Pinopolis-Jedburg exit and head east toward Pinopolis. Follow Secondary Road 16 for 18 miles to South Carolina Highway 6. Follow SC 6 north to the community of Cross and the intersection with SC 45. Take SC 45 east toward St. Stephen. After 5 miles, SC 45 crosses the Diversion Canal. Take the first dirt road (Eadie Lane) to the right (south) and follow it to the parking area beside the Canal. From the Santee exit on I-95, follow SC 6 for 30 miles south to the community of Cross, where SC 45 forks east toward St. Stephen. Continue on to the parking lot as directed above.

The hike: Lake Moultrie was constructed between 1939 and 1941 as part of the Santee Cooper Hydroelectric and Navigation Project, a massive federal effort to provide electricity to rural South Carolina. The lake and dam system originally diverted a large volume of water from the Santee River, which empties into the ocean south of Georgetown, and into the Cooper River, the major river feeding into Charleston Harbor. Now, the Rediversion Canal, which the trail crosses, diverts much of the water back into the Santee River.

The Pinopolis Dam just north of Moncks Corner generates hydroelectric power. A huge lock at the Pinopolis Dam allows boaters to pass from Lake Moultrie into the Tail Race Canal and on down the Cooper River to Charleston. Hikers can see the stacks of coal-fired power plants beside the Pinopolis Dam on the south side of the lake's perimeter and adjacent to the Diversion Canal on the north side.

The Lake Moultrie Passage is a major segment of the Palmetto Trail. It is a joint venture of the Palmetto Trails Organization and Santee Cooper, the state-owned electric utility that owns most of the property and maintains the trail.

Although much of the Lake Moultrie Passage takes you over service roads on top of the lake's dike system, the scenery is quite varied. The trail winds along the eastern edge of Lake Moultrie, passing through lush wetlands, regrowth forests, open loblolly pine savannas, and dense lowland forests. White-tailed deer, wild turkeys, red-tailed hawks, and hundreds of other species abound. Wildflowers bloom year-round.

At the Canal Recreation Area (southern) Trailhead, a covered kiosk with trail brochures and precautionary instructions is located just across a small brook fed by spillage from the lake. The trail begins with a 0.5-mile walk west through a generously green stand of young pines, across a railroad track, and up a stairway made of railway ties to the top of the large, earthen Pinopolis East Dike. The view of the lake from this point is spectacular, particularly at sunset. The sinking sun sets the forest on fire, and the drama is played out doubly over the expanse of the reflective lake.

The trail continues north 3.5 miles along the top of the dike to the community of Bonneau Beach. On the lake side of the walkway, stone and gravel reinforce the dike and the waters rise to about 20 feet from the top of the embankment. On the land side, the 40-foot drop to the adjacent wetlands is quite steep. Fragrant water lilies and floating hearts greet you as you descend the dike and enter Bonneau Beach.

The trail's 2.2-mile temporary section over the paved commercial and residential streets of rustic Bonneau Beach is the least appealing portion of the Lake Moultrie Passage. You proceed west briefly along Black Oak Drive (SR 42) past the Black Oak Motel and L and M's Grocery, then turn north on Butter Road (SR 470). From Butter Road, turn east on Barn Road, then north on Pauline Drive, then east on General Moultrie Road, which leads to the reemergence of the dike at the intersection with Martin Lane in General Moultrie Subdivision Section II.

Along this and remaining sections, the dike is entirely earthen on both sides. The lake below sports bays and backwaters, islands, marshy patches, and wading baldcypress trees. These quiet waters are home to pickerelweeds,

Lake Moultrie Passage

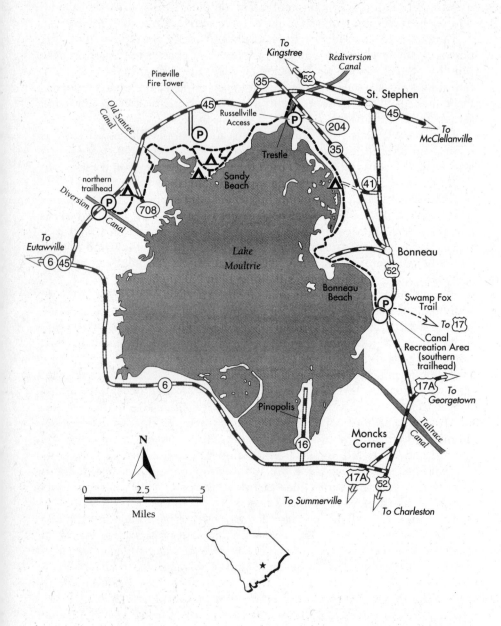

fragrant water lilies, floating hearts, and handsome cattails. On the land side mixed tracts of pine and hardwoods are interspersed with cultivated fields in power-line rights of way. The dike itself has a bounty of wildflowers, including common dandelions, strikingly beautiful passionflowers, daisies, and spike lobelias.

A dirt extension of SR 41 ends at the dike 1.8 miles north of Bonneau Beach. Near this intersection there is a designated camping site, located about 0.3 mile from the trail, inside the dike.

The trail continues 3.9 miles on the dike to a boat landing on the Rediversion Canal (not to be confused with the Diversion Canal) near the community of Russellville.

Here the trail follows the canal inland 1 mile, crosses the canal on SR 35, a paved road, and returns 1 mile along the west side of the canal to pick up the dike again. A railroad trestle crosses the canal at the Russellville boat landing, and hikers may eventually be able to avoid this 2-mile detour if arrangements are ever made to allow foot traffic across the trestle.

The next section of the dike is bordered by wetlands and wetland forest on the lake side and by more elevated forests and cultivated power-line rights of way on the land side.

Another campsite nestles in a handsome stand of straw pine 0.2 mile on the lake side of the dike, along a turn-off 3.6 miles from the Rediversion Canal. At this point, optional loop trails veer off through the Sandy Beach Wildlife Management Area, rejoining the Lake Moultrie Passage on the dike about 1.5 miles west. The 4.5-mile loops adds 3 miles to the journey, but are well worth it. The wildlife management area is open to the public from March 2 to November 15.

The Sandy Beach Trail (actually a series of wildlife management access roads) follows lowland forest, then emerges into open controlled wetlands, with glimpses of the main body of Lake Moultrie to the south. The wetlands support numerous waterfowl and other bird species, as well as deer, raccoons, opossums, frogs, turtles, snakes, and alligators. A few baldcypress trees shade the plentiful water lilies. In the shrubs that sometimes line the trail, brilliant red trumpet honeysuckles bloom on long vines. In shallow pools and ditches, pickerelweeds produce their lovely violet flower spikes.

A short spur leads to Sandy Beach, a baldcypress–framed area that offers primitive camping facilities, a sandy lake floor ideal for frolicking, a reasonably close-up view of a bald eagle nest, and a panoramic view of Lake Moultrie to the south.

Return to the main loop trail and continue through wetlands past a broad, shallow pond (on the left) where deer enjoy grazing. The best time to appreciate the field of fragrant water lilies here—or anywhere else—is before noon, when the flowers are in full bloom. After midday, the large white flowers close and sink, allowing just the tip to show above the water.

On the right, a small canal borders grassy fields and new-growth forest. Red-winged blackbirds, sparrows, and eastern kingbirds are visible, but the songs and voices of many other birds surround you as well. Along the road

221

grow daisy-like mayweeds and white-topped sedges, with their long, drooping bracts.

At the edge of the wildlife management area, a drivable dirt road returns you to the dike and a parking area. (The parking area can be reached from SC 45 by following dirt Sandy Beach Road south from the Pineville Fire Tower, 8 miles east of the Diversion Canal.) (If you do not take the Sandy Beach Loop, you walk 1.5 miles along the dike from the campground turn off to the Sandy Beach Road junction.)

Continue on the dike trail, now decorated with fleabane, dandelions, and deep purple bull thistles, for 1.1 miles to its end at the Old Santee Canal. Here, you cross the canal on a railroad trestle, which offers a pleasing view of the dark waters of the old canal, then proceed southeast on the woods road which parallels the quiet canal waters. Fragrant water lilies and white water buttercups flourish in the canal's calmer spots, and baldcypress trees rise from the dark surface. On the right is new-growth forest with only occasional tall pines. The damage wrought by Hurricane Hugo in 1989 is still in evidence.

About 0.4 mile beyond the canal crossing, the trail turns southwest onto a grassy abandoned service road through a mature forest of mixed hardwoods and pine. This part of the trail, filled with the calls of birds, has a deep woods quality about it and is quite inviting. The trail, aided by boardwalks in the wettest places, winds for 1.4 miles, where it crosses Quattlebaum's Canal on a narrow footbridge.

Beyond the footbridge, a narrow trail weaves 1.3 miles through shrub forest, marshy bottoms, and young pines. The trail crosses railroad tracks and moves to higher ground along a dirt road occasionally fringed by flowering lizard's tails, ending at paved SR 708. Turn right (northwest) and proceed 0.4 mile to another unpaved forest road, on the left. There is a primitive campsite 0.3 mile along this road.

The road continues past the campsite another 1.5 miles to the parking area alongside the Diversion Canal, a major boating thoroughfare connecting Lakes Moultrie and Marion. The very last portion of the Lake Moultrie Passage passes hill-sized, kudzu-covered mounds of earth, remnants of the dredging of the Diversion Canal.

Facilities: Rest rooms and water are available at the Canal Recreation Area. There are no facilities at the northern trailhead.

Lodging and amenities: There are four primitive campsites along the trail. Motels, restaurants, and other services are available in the Moncks Corner and Bonneau Beach areas. Fish camps in the community of Cross, near the Diversion Canal trailhead, offer cabins and full-service camping.

For more information: Santee Cooper Property Management Division; Palmetto Trails. See Appendix A: For More Information.

222

49 Old Santee Canal State Historic Site

General description:	A pleasant walk along the shores of Biggin Creek and the Old Santee Canal where you can enjoy steep limestone bluffs overlooking swamps and a blackwater stream.
General location:	North of Charleston, in the state's central coastal plain.
Distance:	2.4 miles.
Difficulty:	Easy.
Trail conditions:	Conditions are excellent. Traffic is moderate.
Best time to go:	Year-round.
Maps:	See Appendix A: For More Information.
Fees:	$3 per vehicle.

Finding the trailhead: From Charleston, follow U.S. Highway 52 north to Moncks Corner. At the south end of town, the highway forks into US 52 Business and US 52 Bypass. Take the bypass (northeast) for 1 mile. Stony Landing Road and Old Santee Canal State Park are on the right (east). Access the trails through the interpretive center north of the parking lot.

The hike: Old Santee Canal State Historic Site preserves the portion of the defunct Old Santee Canal at its southern terminus, where the canal brought the waters of the Santee River to Biggin Creek, which flows into the Cooper River.

The Santee River, a giant watershed for much of the state, empties into the Atlantic at a relatively unpopulated area between Charleston and Georgetown. The canal brought the commercial activity of this watershed to the much shorter Cooper River and the Port of Charleston. The canal's economic usefulness withered away in the 1840s when railway lines were completed to Columbia and Camden.

Old Santee Canal State Historic Site is open from 9 A.M. to 6 P.M., Monday through Friday, and 9 A.M. to 7 P.M., Saturday and Sunday, April through October; and from 9 A.M. to 5 P.M. daily, November through March.

Walks in the park begin at the historical and natural interpretive visitor center. The natural beauty of the canal's location shows in the wildlife displays and the 30-foot replica of a live oak that towers to the center's ceiling.

Outside, the trail winds and crisscrosses along Biggin Creek, Old Santee Canal, and the currently active Tail Race Canal, which carries water and boats from Lake Moultrie and the Santee Cooper hydroelectric facility to the Cooper River.

The trees in the park typify the swampland of the Coastal Plain. Giant baldcypress is the king, but it is attended by quite a court, including sweet gum, laurel oak, live oak, red maple, dogwood, and magnolia. The stars of the bird set are the ospreys perched high in their nests, but they have plenty

Old Santee Canal State Historic Site

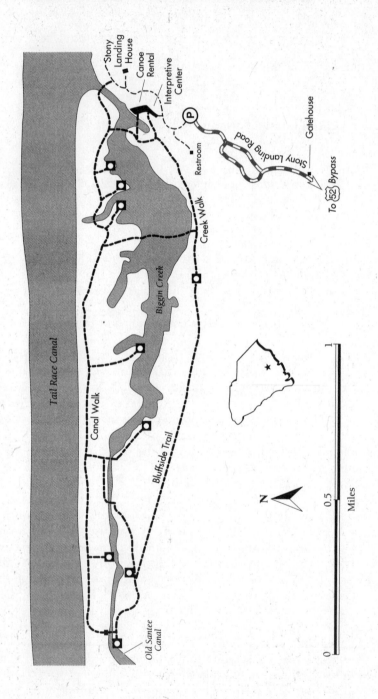

Stony Landing House
Canoe Rental
Interpretive Center
Restroom
P
Creek Walk
Biggin Creek
Tail Race Canal
Canal Walk
Bluffside Trail
Old Santee Canal
Stony Landing Road
Gatehouse
To 52 Bypass

N

0   0.5   1
Miles

of company, including red-winged blackbirds and red-shouldered hawks. Alligators lazily police the waterways, in the company of a variety of frogs and turtles, and white-tailed deer and wild turkeys roam the woodlands.

Start by exiting the visitor center and heading right (north) over a short bridge over Biggin Creek. At this point, the creek resembles a large, swampy pond. Head east to circle the wide expanse of creek in a clockwise fashion. Observation Points 1,2, and 3, at the end of spurs on the left (south), provide views of this portion of the baldcypress-fringed waterway.

Continue east and then turn left (south) on a long boardwalk bridge heading back across a wide expanse of Biggin Creek to complete a 0.4-mile semi-circle route from the visitor center. The bridge provides a good opportunity to spot an osprey nest downstream.

Turn right (west) when you reach the south bank and follow a path along the base of a steep bluff on the left (south), with Biggin Creek on the right. The bluff is composed of limestone rock known as Cooper marl, formed from tiny ocean organisms left behind by the sea millions of years ago. High levels of calcium in the marl make the soils of the bluff alkaline, allowing calcium-loving plants to prosper here.

After walking to the observation overlook a few hundred feet up the bluff, continue west along the bluff on a 1-mile hiking trail, which takes you to Observation Point 7, a platform overlooking the beginning of the Old Santee Canal.

Head west and cross the mouth of the canal to head east along the strip of land between Old Santee Canal and Biggin Creek on the right (south) and Tail Race Canal on the left. A spur on the right leads 0.25 mile to Observation Point 6, a water-level view of Old Santee Canal from opposite Observation Point 7 on the limestone bluff.

From here, continue east another 0.25 mile to the spur carrying you to Observation Point 4, which offers views of heron and osprey nests. Return to the path that parallels Tail Race Canal and continue east, turning right (south) at the junction with the boardwalk bridge across Biggin Creek. Retrace your steps across the bridge, then turn left (east) and return to the visitor center, a distance of 0.5 mile from Observation Point 4.

A few hundred feet northeast of the visitor center is the Stony Landing House, built around 1840, and a dock extending into the Cooper River. You may also choose to explore the Berkeley County Historical Society Museum, located at the entrance to the park.

Facilities: Old Santee Canal State Historic Site has drinking water, rest rooms, and a great interpretive center. Canoes can be rented at the interpretive center.

Lodging and amenities: Camping is available in the Francis Marion National Forest and at commercial sites in the community of Cross. Moncks Corner has motels and restaurants, and all services are available in the Charleston area.

For more information: Old Santee Canal State Historic Site. See Appendix A: For More Information.

50 Cypress Gardens

General description:	Half a day's walk through cultivated gardens and natural areas in a cypress-tupelo blackwater swamp.
General location:	North of Charleston, in the state's central coastal plain.
Distance:	3.8 miles (suggested route).
Difficulty:	Easy.
Trail conditions:	Conditions are good. Traffic varies with season and weather.
Best time to go:	Year-round.
Maps:	Cypress Gardens Visitor Information and Map; Kittredge USGS quad. See Appendix A: For More Information.
Fees:	$6 for adults and $2 for children aged 6 to 12.

Finding the trailhead: From downtown Charleston, take Interstate 26 northwest 12 miles to the U.S. Highway 52 exit toward Moncks Corner. Follow US 52 north 12 miles to Old Highway 52 (Secondary Road 791) on the right (northeast). Drive 2.1 miles on Old Highway 52 and turn right (east) on SR 9 (Cypress Gardens Road). Proceed 4 miles to the entrance to Cypress Gardens, on the right.

From Moncks Corner, follow Old Highway 52 south 5 miles and turn left (east) on SR 9. Proceed 4 miles to the entrance to Cypress Gardens, on the right.

The hike: Cypress Gardens is a 163-acre blend of natural and exotic vegetation in the heart of Dean Hall Plantation. The centerpiece of Cypress Gardens is a shallow blackwater wetland with a rich history dating back to the early 1700s. Early colonial rice agriculture cleared vast acres of marshes and riverine forests. The natural beauty of this cypress swamp was spared the plow and the saw because of its ability to collect and to retain rainwater, which made it a natural reservoir of fresh water, needed to flood the cleared fields for rice cultivation.

After the Civil War, labor-intensive rice growing on the plantation became unprofitable. The property experienced many years of disuse before Benjamin Kittredge purchased the plantation in the early 1900s to serve as his winter retreat.

The gardens are an eye-popping wonder of blazing azaleas, flowering dogwoods, colorful daffodils, scented wisteria, and numerous other blooming specimens that double their beauty through their perfect reflections in the dark, quiet waters. The flowers are in peak bloom in March and April, but the gardens are beautiful at any time of year. The natural beauty of Cypress Gardens has not gone unnoticed by Hollywood, and a number of movies have been filmed here, including *The Yearling*, *North and South*, and *Rear View Mirror*.

Cypress Gardens

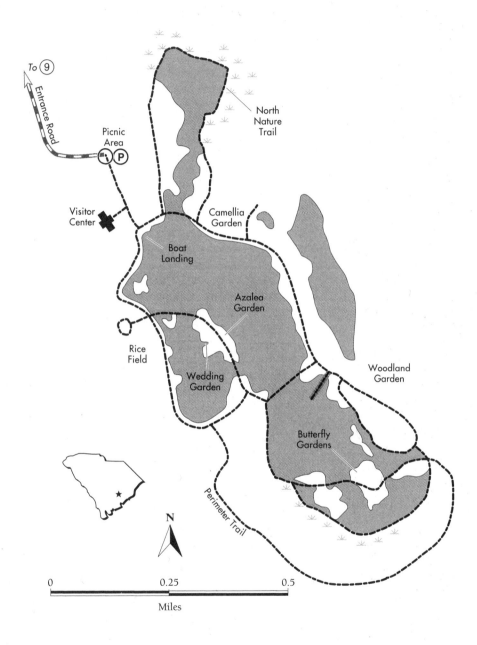

To ⑨

Entrance Road

Picnic Area

Visitor Center

North Nature Trail

Camellia Garden

Boat Landing

Azalea Garden

Rice Field

Wedding Garden

Woodland Garden

Butterfly Gardens

Perimeter Trail

N

0   0.25   0.5

Miles

Cypress Gardens is open from 9 A.M. to 5 P.M., except for the month of January, when it is closed.

From the entrance, follow the sandy walking path which loops around and through the cypress swamp and surrounding lowland oak forest. Turning right (southwest) at the boat dock, the trail hugs the edge of the swamp pond. The first view of the stately baldcypresses standing deep in the tannin-colored waters is impressive. At 0.3 mile from the entrance, the trail passes a small, inland rice field on the right (west). Bearing right (south), you skirt the swamp on the left (east) with the oak forest on the right (west). The sandy paths are dry even during the rainiest of seasons.

At the next trail intersection 0.4 mile from the rice field, bear right (south) again and take the Perimeter Trail through the nature preserve. Hurricane Hugo in 1989 caused considerable damage to the oak forest in this area. Although many magnificent trees were lost, this natural disaster presents an opportunity, welcomed by the garden managers, to nurture the regrowth of the forest to its native state of wild habitat and natural diversity. The trail is grassy and can be wet and muddy following heavy rains.

The Perimeter Trail rejoins the garden walkway after 1.2 miles. This is the only section of the property that demonstrates any elevation changes. From this point on the trail, you have a long, downward view of the cypress swamp and its flower-covered banks. Continue 0.3 mile to the right (north) and pass the Kittredge Gravesite, where a massive cross guards the grounds. The trail returns to the water's edge and zero feet of elevation at the Boardwalk. An interesting, moss-covered bird-viewing blind gives visitors an unusual perspective.

At the next trail intersection, continue to the right (north). The next 0.4 mile path section crosses the swamp and passes both the Garden of Memories and the Camellia Garden on the right.

Just past the Camellia Garden take the right (north-tending) path, which loops 1 mile around a section of swamp with large, multi-kneed baldcypress trees. One small island on the left (west) seems to be made up almost entirely of cypress knees, the knobby projections which appear randomly around the bases of baldcypress trees.

The path returns you to the boat dock and the visitor center, where you are asked to complete a log of your wildlife sightings. At the end of the day, the sighting log is a very impressive listing. Cypress Gardens is a great bird viewing area. Residents and visitors include high-flying bald eagles, ospreys, red-shouldered and red-tailed hawks, and dozens of other species.

Facilities: Rest rooms, drinking water, and refreshments are available at the visitor center.

Lodging and amenities: The nearest public campgrounds are at Francis Marion National Forest, Givhans Ferry State Park, and James Island County Park near Charleston. There are commercial campgrounds in the Charleston area and around Lakes Moultrie and Marion. Lodging, restaurants, and other services are available in the Moncks Corner, Summerville, and Charleston areas.

For more information: Cypress Gardens. See Appendix A: For More Information.

51 Marrington Plantation

General description:	A short nature trail through the wetlands of the Back River.
General location:	Northeast of Charleston, in the state's central coastal plain.
Distance:	4.2 miles loop.
Difficulty:	Easy.
Trail conditions:	Conditions are excellent. Traffic is light.
Best time to go:	Fall, winter, and spring.
Maps:	Trail guide available from box along trail; North Charleston USGS quad. See Appendix A: For More Information.
Fees:	None.

Finding the trailhead: From Charleston, travel north on Interstate 26 West for 9 miles. Take Exit 212 to I-526 East, heading toward Mount Pleasant. Travel 2 miles and take Exit 19 to Brown (formerly North Rhett) Avenue. Turn north on Brown Avenue and drive 5.7 miles to Redbank Road. Turn right (east) on Redbank and continue 2.7 miles past the entrance to the Naval Weapons Station to the entrance to Marrington Plantation, on the left (north). Travel a few yards on the gravel drive and stop at the first parking area on the right (east) side. We recommend this trailhead though the official trailhead is 0.3 mile farther up the drive, just across the road from the entrance to the horse stable.

The hike: The hiking experience at Marrington Plantation consists of a 1.1-mile-long interpretative trail, with associated boardwalks, piers, and towers, along with more than 3 miles of additional hiking options through forests and across rice-field dikes. As is the case with all walks in the wetlands of South Carolina's coastal plain, it is necessary to prepare for insects in warm weather, and advisable to stay on delineated trails to avoid snakes.

The plantation property is a diverse system of freshwater wetlands and lowland forest bordering the Back River and its tributary, Foster Creek. The plantation's trails meander along and across rice fields and swamp forest.

The trail begins as a pleasant 0.7-mile walk through a lowland forest of mostly oaks, hickories, sweet gums, red maples, ironwoods, and dogwoods.

Marrington Plantation

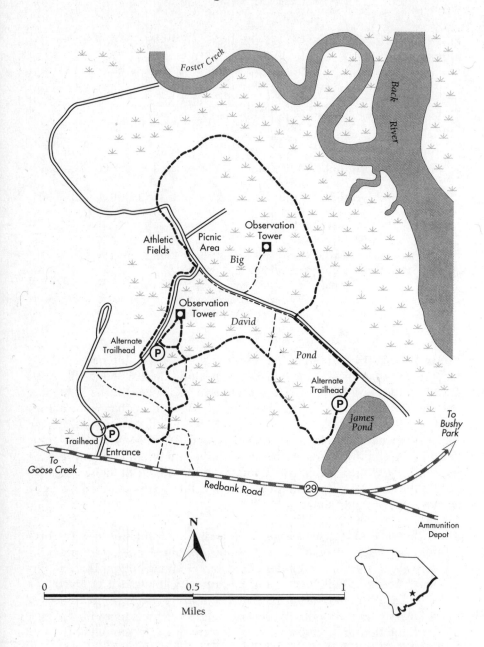

Foster Creek

Back River

Athletic Fields

Picnic Area

Observation Tower

Big

Observation Tower

David

Pond

Alternate Trailhead

Alternate Trailhead

James Pond

Trailhead

Entrance

To Goose Creek

Redbank Road

29

To Bushy Park

Ammunition Depot

N

0   0.5   1

Miles

The trail generally follows marshland on the left (north), then crosses the marsh on a footbridge and separates into three spurs. The rightmost (western) path takes you across a small peninsula, across another wetland and to a parking lot. The 1.1-mile interpretative portion of the trail begins on the north side of this parking lot, and there is a black mailbox containing trail guides a few yards farther along the trail.

The trail guide provides written descriptions of areas along the trail marked by numbered posts. Continuing along the interpretive trail, you soon reach an observation tower with a great view of Big David Pond, a wetland filled with fragrant water lily and yellow-flowering water primrose. This is a great spot for viewing birds of prey and waterfowl in cool-weather months.

The trail follows the marsh, advancing over a bridge and the tip of a small peninsula before crossing a long stretch of boardwalk over a watery area that allows a close-up view that would normally be available only over the side of a boat.

Walk the interpretative trail along the edge of marshland, crossing over fingers of lily-filled water, sometimes encountering the beautiful blue flag iris in spring. At the end of a dike, the trail comes to James Pond, and the interpretative portion of the walk ends at a wide, wooden observation deck. Sit down and enjoy a handsome view of a relatively open section of the pond. Extending from this deck are a number of access points for fishing.

To continue the hike, follow the dirt road out to a circular parking area and walk 0.1 mile on to the gravel road. Turn left (northwest) on the gravel road. After about 0.2 mile, you have two options. Just before a large culvert under the road, you can follow a trail to the right which goes through forestland and across a long dike before curving back to the gravel road after about 1 mile. After reaching the gravel road, turn left (southeast) and follow the road 0.2 mile to the picnic area.

A shorter option is to continue 0.1 mile across the culvert to a parking area just before a causeway and follow the next trail to the right (northeast). This trail leads 0.1 mile to an observation tower overlooking another area of the Big David Pond wetlands. From the tower, return to the gravel road and continue 0.1 mile across the causeway to the picnic area.

From the picnic area, follow an intersecting causeway southwest. There are athletic fields on the right (west) side, but look east for more great views of the rice-field wetlands.

Leave the causeway and walk past the parking lot (0.3 mile from the picnic area) that begins the interpretive trail on the left (east) side. Continue to the pathway on the left (east) that is a few yards past the parking lot. Turn onto this pathway and proceed 0.6 mile south and east through forest and marshland back to the trailhead.

Facilities: There are rest rooms at the picnic area.

Lodging and amenities: Camping and cabins are available at the Navy's Short Stay facility for retired military personnel and personnel on active

A view of Big David Pond from the observation tower. John Clark photo

duty. All services are available throughout the Charleston area. The nearest public campsites are at James Island and Folly Beach county parks.

For more information: Naval Weapons Station. See Appendix A: For More Information.

---

52 Magnolia Gardens

General description:	Half a day's hike through 300-year-old plantation garden, a 125-acre waterfowl refuge, and a 60-acre blackwater swamp garden.
General location:	Just northwest of Charleston, in the state's central coastal plain.
Distance:	Recommended route is about 4 miles.
Difficulty:	Easy.
Trail conditions:	Excellent. Traffic is heavy to moderate.
Best time to go:	Year-round.
Maps:	Provided with admission to each of the gardens; Ladson and Johns Island USGS quads. See Appendix A: For More Information.
Fees:	(Age-dependent admission fees) $5 to $10 for Magnolia Gardens; $3 to $5 for Audubon Swamp Garden.

Finding the trailhead: From downtown Charleston, travel west on U.S. Highway 17 South, cross the Ashley River Bridge, then turn right immediately onto South Carolina Highway 61 (Ashley River Road). Magnolia Plantation is 10 miles north on SC 61, on the right (east) side of the road.

The hike: Magnolia Plantation is the centuries-old home of the Draytons, one of the original families of South Carolina's colonial aristocracy. The plantation and its gardens were begun around 1676 by the Drayton and Fox families, who had immigrated from the overcrowded Caribbean island of Barbados.

Although considerably smaller than it was in its majestic antebellum days, Magnolia Plantation is today a wildlife sanctuary of 500 beautiful acres. This is one of the best birding sites in the state, and more than 240 species have been identified here. Nature trails for hikers and mountain bikers wind through its woodlands. The nearby Audubon Swamp Garden provides a taste of the inland wetlands typical of South Carolina's coastal plain.

The plantation is open from 8 A.M. until dusk every day of the year. While plants are in their most riotous bloom in March and April, the garden is planted to offer maximum color throughout the year.

Begin at the entrance to the formal gardens and explore the maze of graveled paths through some of the most beautiful flora in the world. A map, available at the entrance, provides an interpretive loop route around the formal gardens. The high, dense, green foliage bordering the walkways sometimes gives the feeling of an enclosed emerald corridor. Crowned by stately live oaks and lovely magnolia trees, the 50 acres of formal lawns and gardens along the banks of the Ashley River and around three small lakes contain more than 250 varieties of azaleas and 900 varieties of camellias.

The Ashley River. YVONNE MICHEL PHOTO

Magnolia Gardens

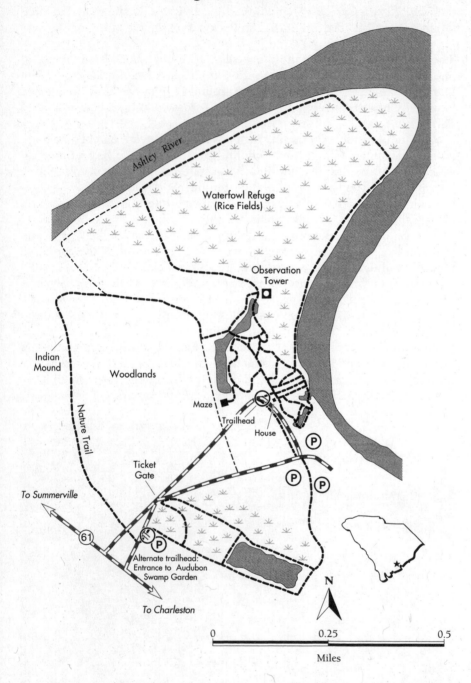

Ashley River

Waterfowl Refuge
(Rice Fields)

Observation
Tower

Indian
Mound

Woodlands

Nature Trail

Maze

Trailhead

House

P

P

P

Ticket
Gate

To Summerville

61

P

Alternate trailhead:
Entrance to Audubon
Swamp Garden

To Charleston

N

0   0.25   0.5

Miles

On the south side of the formal gardens are three small specialty gardens. The Biblical Garden represents an effort to interpret Biblical descriptions of plants and display those plants. The Herb Garden replicates 17th century functional plantation gardens which grew herbs for their own medicinal and culinary use. The indoor Barbados Tropical Garden, a tribute to the ancestral homeland of the founders of Magnolia Plantation, is filled with exotic plants; colorful finches, doves, and parakeets make their tiny nests in trees.

After exploring the formal gardens, walk upstream along the Ashley River. Turn right at the canoe area and enter the 125-acre Waterfowl Refuge on the northeast side of the plantation. The trail proceeds along a dike between the Ashley River, on the right, and old plantation rice fields, on the left. The refuge is set in a gentle bend in the river, which means that although you are walking a loop, the river continues to be on your right for most of the way.

At the end of the loop, climb the observation tower at the corner of the rice field. It is a great place for bird viewing and gaining a wider geographic perspective on the plantation. The rice field is a favorite of ducks, herons, egrets, white and glossy ibises, ospreys, rails, and bitterns. Alligators nest here, and yellow-bellied pond slider turtles sun themselves.

Next, circle the woodlands on the nature trail, passing an ancient Indian mound and continuing on toward the swamp garden. Along the way, listen and watch for the many birds common to the forests and wetlands of Magnolia Plantation.

At the end of the trail around the woodlands, cross the entrance road to reach the Audubon Swamp Garden. Once a freshwater reservoir for Magnolia Plantation's rice fields, the wetlands of the 60-acre Audubon Swamp Garden have become fertile ground for water oaks, black cypresses, red maples, and tupelos. The swamp includes both indigenous and imported species.

The boardwalks, bridges, and dikes that compose the Audubon Swamp Garden trail have been constructed to provide the utmost privacy to the native wildlife, which includes alligators, frogs, turtles, otters, marsh rabbits, and an array of birds. The benches are screened with palmetto fronds to allow discreet observation and photography. At the far (southern) end of the swamp loop, hikers may turn left (north) on the paved tram path and return directly to the parking area at the entrance to the formal gardens.

Facilities: All facilities available on the grounds, including a picnic area and an excellent snack shop. Rest rooms are also available at the entrance to the Audubon Swamp Garden.

Lodging and amenities: All services are available in the Charleston area. The nearest public campgrounds are at James Island and Folly Beach county parks, and north up SC 61 at Givhans Ferry and Colleton state parks.

For more information: Magnolia Plantation and its Gardens. See Appendix A: For More Information.

53 Francis Beidler Forest

General description: A boardwalk loop through a wetland wonderland containing the largest remaining baldcypress-tupelo swamp in the world.

General location: Northwest of Charleston, in the state's central coastal plain.

Distance: 1.5 miles, loop.

Trail conditions: Conditions are excellent. Traffic is light to moderate.

Difficulty: Easy.

Best time to go: Year-round.

Maps: Harleyville USGS quad. See Appendix A: For More Information.

Fees: $5 for adults, $2.50 for children age 6 to 18, free for children under 6.

Finding the trailhead: Take Interstate 26 northwest from Charleston to Exit 187. Take the exit and turn left (south) at the interchange onto SC 27. Go 1 mile and turn right (west) onto US 78. When the road splits, take the right fork (northwest) onto US 178. After 0.8 mile, turn right (north) onto SR 28, proceeding 7 miles to the sanctuary entrance on the right as described above. Access the boardwalk through the visitor center.

From the Charleston/Summerville area, take I-26 northwest to Exit 187. Turn left (south) on SC 27. Go 1 mile and turn right (north) on SR 28, proceeding 7 miles to the sanctuary entrance on the right as described above. Access the boardwalk at the Visitor Center.

The hike: The Francis Beidler Forest, located in Four Holes Swamp, is quite unique. The largest remaining tract of virgin baldcypress–tupelo swamp in the world, this place was preserved by a visionary 19th-century lumberman named Francis Beidler. During the Revolutionary War, both General Francis Marion, the "Swamp Fox," and General Nathanael Greene conducted guerrilla operations against the occupying British forces from Four Holes Swamp. The 10,728-acre sanctuary here, now managed by the National Audubon Society, revolves around 1,800 acres of ancient trees, some of which have evaded the ax and the saw for more than 1,000 years. Francis Beidler Forest is closed Mondays and on major holidays. Regular daily hours are 9 A.M. to 5 P.M.

Wildflowers are not something most people would expect to find in a swamp, but cardinal flowers, greenfly orchids, butterweed, swamp azalea, and atamasco lily are present, and the sanctuary is home to South Carolina's only known population of the rare Carolina trillium.

The wildlife here is abundant and tremendously varied. At least 44 mammal species have been identified, including deer, mink, flying squirrel, red fox, bobcat, river otter, and numerous varieties of bats. There are 50 reptile species, including alligator, water moccasin as well as many nonvenomous

Francis Beidler Forest

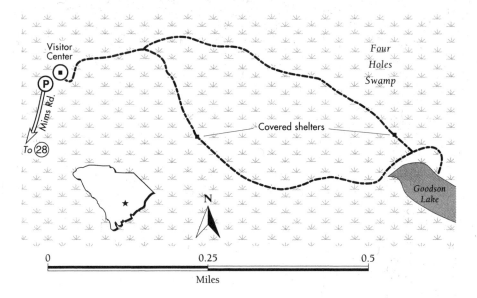

snakes, and a wide variety of turtles. Naturalists also have identified 140 species of birds here. Warblers are particularly common during spring migration, especially northern parulas and prothonotaries. The trail runs entirely along an elevated boardwalk, offering a great opportunity to see an important ecosystem safely and comfortably. After about 0.1 mile, the board-walk forks. Go left (northeast).

Along the way rest stops with benches allow you to contemplate the quiet beauty of nature. Two are covered and offer protection in event of rain. Four Holes Swamp is mainly rain-fed, meaning that water levels fluc-tuate seasonally. The water is generally higher in the cooler months and lower in the warmer months. The wildlife you encounter will vary depend-ing on water levels, but you are sure to be fascinated by what you see.

Huge baldcypresses—including one that is 1,500 years old—dominate the canopy. Tupelos which, like cypresses, have buttressed trunks but which, unlike cypresses, do not have knees, are the other major tree species. On slightly higher ground, dwarf palmettos nudge in.

Beidler Forest took a direct hit from Hurricane Hugo in 1989. Many of the forest's pines fell, but few of the well-buttressed cypresses toppled. Nearly half of the boardwalk was destroyed or suffered significant damage, but it has since been rebuilt. The boardwalk's farthest point is Goodson Lake, a permanent pond at the eastern end of the walkway. This is the best place to see wildlife under low-water conditions.

Upon leaving the lake overlook, take the left (southwest) fork to return to the visitor center via slightly higher ground peppered with dwarf palmettos and black gum trees.

Facilities: The visitor center has rest rooms, drinking water, and educational materials.

Lodging and amenities: Some facilities, including accommodations, at St. George. Camping is available at Givhans Ferry State Park and at Colleton State Park. All services are available at Summerville and Charleston.

For more information: Francis Beidler Forest. See Appendix A: For More Information.

54 Edisto Beach State Park

General description:	Half a day's walk through a maritime forest to an ancient mound of seashells.
General location:	South of Charleston, along the state's southern coast.
Distance:	3.8 miles round trip.
Difficulty:	Easy.
Trail conditions	Conditions are good. Traffic is light to moderate.
Best time to go:	Year-round.
Maps:	Edisto Beach State Park brochure; Edisto Beach USGS quad. See Appendix A: For More Information.
Fees:	Beach access is $3 per vehicle.

Finding the trailhead: From Charleston, go south 12 miles on U.S. Highway 17 South. Turn left onto South Carolina Highway 162. Follow SC 162 for 13 miles, then turn left onto SC 174 and drive 23 miles to Edisto Beach State Park. Turn right (west) onto State Cabin Road (which is 0.25 mile before the main park entrance and beach access area, both on the left). The trailhead is on the right (north) side of State Cabin Road, 0.2 mile west of SC 174.

The hike: Edisto Island, named after a local tribe, was inhabited by Native Americans for at least 4,000 years and was developed by Europeans as a fertile plantation island beginning around 1690. Occupied by federal troops during most of the Civil War, it was once famous for its high-quality and financially-lucrative Sea Island cotton. The state park's 1,255 acres comprise a dense live oak forest, an expansive salt marsh, and a 1.5- mile stretch of beach bordered by some of the state's tallest palmetto trees.

The Indian Mound Trail begins under a cool canopy of stately live oaks, then moves through a maritime forest dominated by live oaks and Carolina palmettos. Other species include loblolly pines, sweet gums, water oaks, willow oaks, and redcedars.

The trail forks after 0.4 mile. This fork and a fork at 1 mile form a loop in the forest portion of the trail, allowing you some variety in your trip to and

Edisto Beach State Park

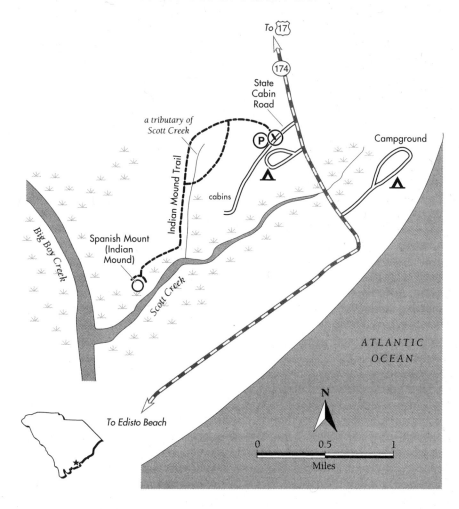

from the shell mound. At both intersections, take the left (southeastern) fork going out to the mound, and the left (northwestern) fork on the return.

After the first intersection, the trail continues through forest, then proceeds along the edge of a marsh, at 0.9 mile crossing a tidal creek highlighted by spartina grass. The trail then plunges into dense vegetation and follows Scott Creek before reaching, at 1.8 miles, Spanish Mount, a 15-foot-high, 40-foot-wide mound of broken shells and pottery fragments.

Thousands of years ago, the mound formed the centerpiece of a Native American shell ring. These rings were created by Native Americans all along the southern Atlantic coast, for reasons not yet fully understood by archeologists. Please respect our cultural heritage by staying on the pathway and not removing any material.

The mound is a great place from which to view bird life over the open salt marsh expanses of Big Bay Creek and its tributaries. From the edge of the marsh, you may see terns, gulls, barn swallows, pelicans, and herons.

To return, retrace your steps 0.8 mile along Scott Creek to the southern-most intersection, then take the left (north) fork to follow the northwestern side of the loop back to the trailhead.

Facilities: Rest rooms in the beach parking area.

Lodging and amenities: Edisto Beach State Park has 103 full-service camp-sites and five cabins, plus a large primitive camping area for organized groups. The town of Edisto Beach has lodging and restaurant facilities, and bed-and-breakfast accommodations are available on Edisto Island.

For more information: Edisto Beach State Park. See Appendix A: For More Information.

55 Edisto Nature Trail

General description:	A short nature walk through an extremely diverse forest. The trail features the historic King's Highway and an old phosphate operation.
General location:	In the Edisto River wetlands of the ACE (Ashepoo, Combahee, and Edisto rivers) Basin, just east of the village of Jacksonboro, between Charleston and Beaufort.
Distance:	1 mile, loop.
Difficulty:	Easy.
Trail conditions:	Conditions are excellent. Traffic is light to moderate.
Best time to go:	Year-round.
Maps:	Edisto Nature Trail brochure available at trailhead and from Westvaco Corporation; Jacksonboro USGS quad. See Appendix A: For More Information.
Fees:	None.

Finding the trailhead: From Charleston, drive 29 miles south on U.S. Highway 17 toward Beaufort. The trailhead is on the right (north) side of the road, just after the bridge over the Edisto River and just before the Jacksonboro town limits.

The hike: This excellently marked, well-maintained trail is provided by Westvaco, a paper and packaging manufacturer with large forest holdings in South Carolina's coastal plain. Extensive interpretive signs identify veg-etation species and other items of interest, and guide pamphlets available

Edisto Nature Trail

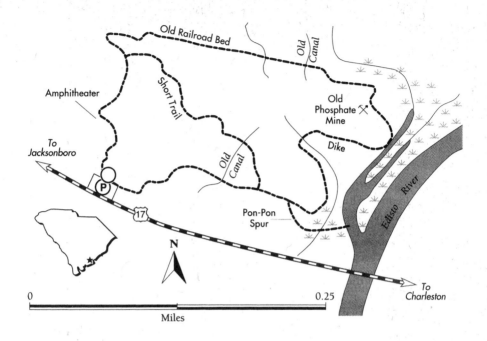

from a mailbox at the trailhead provide detailed descriptions and background information for the walk.

The trail meanders through forest typical of South Carolina's coastal plain. The land here was once heavily farmed, logged, and mined, but nature has long since reclaimed it. Boardwalks and footbridges in low-lying areas facilitate passage for visitors.

Begin in a mixed forest amid hardwoods and pines. Walk along the bed of an old roadway that once led to Charleston, following the trail counterclockwise as it crosses an old canal and an abandoned agricultural field filled with slash pines. A boardwalk spur leads to a cypress-swamp pond. The main trail continues over brooks, through a phosphate mining area, along the remnants of a barge canal, and past sites of buildings once used for phosphate and lumber processing. It then moves along an old railbed that once carried timber and over dikes past old rice fields. A small amphitheater is located near the end of the loop, a short distance from the trailhead and parking area.

More than 50 varieties of vegetation are identified by labels along the trail. White-tailed deer, raccoons, squirrels, and rabbits inhabit these woods, along with a variety of birds.

Facilities: No rest rooms or drinking water.

Lodging and amenities: Full-service camping is available at Edisto Beach State Park, at Colleton State Park, and at commercial campgrounds along Interstate 95. Limited services are available at Jacksonboro, and all amenities are available at Charleston, Beaufort, and Walterboro.

For more information: Westvaco Corporation. See Appendix A: For More Information.

---

56 Bear Island Wildlife Management Area

General description:	Up to three days' worth of hiking along old dikes in waterfowl-rich coastal marshes and through adjoining woodlands.
General location:	South of Charleston, near the state's southern coast.
Distance:	Suggested hike 2.75 miles, with an additional 2-mile round-trip spur option. Bear Island WMA has more than 20 miles of trails.
Difficulty:	Easy.
Trail conditions:	Conditions are good. Traffic is light.
Best time to go:	October through early spring.
Maps:	Department of Natural Resources Bear Island Wildlife Management Area map (available at Titi Road entrance); Bennetts Point USGS quad. See Appendix A: For More Information.
Fees:	None.

Finding the trailhead: From Charleston, follow U.S. Highway 17 south 36 miles. Turn left (south) onto Bennetts Point Road (Secondary Road 26), which is 7 miles past Jacksonboro. After 10 miles, Bennetts Point Road crosses a major bridge over the Ashepoo River. The trail begins at a small parking area 0.1 mile south of this bridge, on the left (east) side of Bennetts Point Road.

The main entrance to Bear Island Wildlife Management Area, which offers many other hiking opportunities, is 2 miles farther at unpaved Titi Road, on the left (east) side. An information kiosk is just past the entrance to Titi Road.

The hike: Bear Island Wildlife Management Area features the state's largest expanse of publicly owned and easily accessible marshland in the state. The hiking areas are closed from November 1 through January 20, and on Sundays year-round.

The many miles of dikes, woodland paths, and dirt roads in Bear Island Wildlife Management Area offer you many choices. Maps showing all of

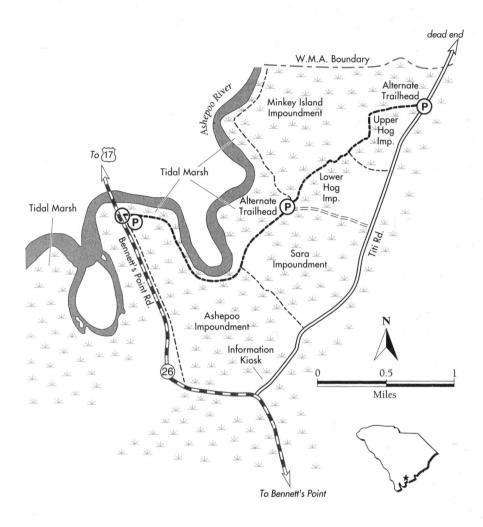

these opportunities are available at the information kiosk, and can also be obtained from the Department of Natural Resources. The dike trails are the primary attraction for hikers.

We recommend a pleasant 4.75-mile outing along dikes from Bennetts Point Road near the Ashepoo River bridge to Titi Road between the Minkey Island and Upper Hog impoundments (reservoirs). From the parking area on Bennetts Point Road, the dike stretches south along the highway and east along the river. You should proceed east, with salt marsh on the left (north) and the brackish Ashepoo Impoundment on the right (south). The Ashepoo River comes into view on the left (north) after about 0.5 mile, and you continue alongside the river another 0.5 mile to a hammock island shaded by palmettos, oaks, and other hardwoods.

(From here, you can choose to loop back to the parking lot by following the intersecting dike on the right (southeast) 0.5 mile to Titi Road, then following Titi Road and Bennetts Point Road west 1 mile to a trail paralleling Bennetts Point Road, then following this trail through woods and along a dike another 1.25 miles to the trailhead and parking lot.)

After passing straight across the island, continue northeast on the dike, with the Sara Impoundment on the right (southeast) and saltwater marsh on the left (northwest). The area around the next hammock island, 0.5 mile farther on, is a locally popular fishing area. This area makes a good alternative trailhead and can be reached by car from Titi Road along the 0.5-mile dike on the right (east) that separates Sara and Lower Hog impoundments. The small forest is cool and inviting, with cardinal birds in the trees and cardinal flowers on the ground.

Here, you can take a woodland spur trail to the left (northwest). Emerging from the forest after 100 feet, the path follows a dike for a 1-mile walk to the Ashepoo River. The path here is heavily lined with blackberry bushes and shows evidence of a large population of raccoons. Return along the same route to the woodland area.

If you continue straight past the alternative trailhead, you emerge from this second hammock island and follow a dike surrounded by two more brackish impoundments, Minkey Island on the left (northwest) and Lower Hog on the right (southeast). A 0.5-mile walk takes you to the next island area, this one planted with crops intended to attract and sustain wildlife. A dike on the right (east) leads 0.25 mile to Titi Road. Past this dike is Upper

Rice trunk. JOHN CLARK PHOTO

The Ashepoo River. JOHN CLARK PHOTO

Hog Impoundment. The dike between Upper Hog and Minkey Island impoundments continues for 0.75 mile until it intersects with Titi Road.

Turn around and retrace your steps back to the trailhead on Bennetts Point Road.

Along the dikes, giant cordgrass, blackberries, and a variety of wildflowers grow abundantly. Thick stands of cattails inhabit the shallows. Black needle rush and sawgrass are evident throughout the brackish wetlands, and hammock islands sprout small forests of oaks, palmettos, pines, and wax myrtles.

Bear Island is managed for waterfowl, other migratory birds, and terrestrial wildlife. Alligators are plentiful and frequently seen, and the woodlands teem with white-tailed deer, raccoons, gray squirrels, and bobcats.

Facilities: No drinking water or rest room facilities.

Lodging and amenities: Campsites are available at Wood Brothers Store, on U.S. Highway 17 in Green Pond, and at Edisto Beach State Park. Limited services are available at Jacksonboro, and all amenities are available at Charleston, Beaufort, and Walterboro.

For more information: Bear Island Wildlife Management Area. See Appendix A: For More Information.

245

57 Donnelley Wildlife Management Area

General description:	A walk along Boynton Nature Trail through forest and along dikes in the old rice fields of the former Mary's Island Plantation. Donnelly teems with natural attractions, including waterfowl, wildflowers, wild turkeys, white-tail deer, and alligators.
General location:	South of Charleston, near the state's southern coast.
Distance:	2.2 miles, loop.
Difficulty:	Easy.
Trail conditions:	Conditions are good. Traffic is light to moderate.
Best time to go:	Late winter and early spring, before the waterfowl fly north.
Maps:	Maps available outside management area office; Green Pond USGS quad. See Appendix A: For More Information.
Fees:	None.

Finding the trailhead: From Charleston, follow U.S. Highway 17 south 29 miles to Jacksonboro and continue on. The entrance to Donnelley Wildlife Management Area is on the left (south side), 10 miles south of Jacksonboro. Follow the unpaved road 0.5 mile to the office on the left, then continue 2 miles to the green "Nature Trail" sign, which shows an arrow pointing right (west). Turn right at the sign and continue a few hundred yards to the Boynton Trailhead, which is at a parking area beside an abandoned house.

The hike: Donnelley Wildlife Management Area is in the heart of South Carolina's 350,000-acre ACE (Ashepoo, Combahee, and Edisto rivers) Basin, one of the East Coast's largest undeveloped areas of estuaries and associated wetlands. Donnelley is a wildlife management area owned and operated by the South Carolina Department of Natural Resources. Hunting is allowed during specified periods, mainly autumn. Boynton Nature Trail is closed from November 1 to January 21, and at some other times for special hunts. Otherwise, the trail is open from 8 A.M. to 5 P.M., Mondays through Saturdays. Free maps of the Donnelley Wildlife Management Area, as well as bird guides, are available in a box at the covered bulletin board near the entrance to the preserve, outside the wildlife management area office.

A few yards after the Boynton Nature Trail begins, take a right (west) turn to enjoy a 0.1-mile spur path to the edge of a dense backwater tupelo swamp, a dark wetland habitat favored by wood ducks.

Return to the main trail and turn right (southwest). Cross a narrow canal and emerge on Mail Route Road, a grassy earthen dike fringed with tallow trees (also known as popcorn trees) that stretches between watery rice fields.

246

Donnelley Wildlife Management Area

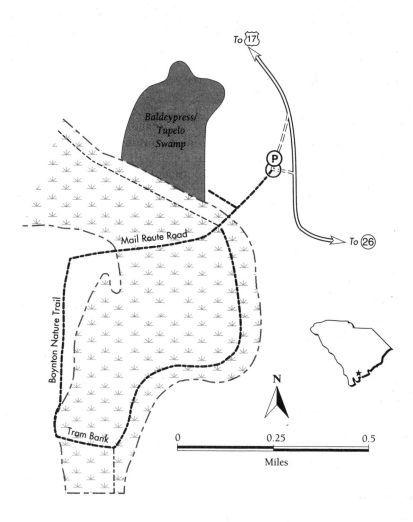

On the far (western) side of the wildlife-rich rice fields, 0.5 mile from the trailhead, the trail winds 0.5 mile through uplands alive with songbirds and forested with live oaks, magnolias, hickories, redbays, dogwoods, pines, holly, honeysuckle, yellow jasmine, wild azaleas, resurrection ferns, and dwarf palmetto.

Recross the rice fields via the 0.3 mile Tram Bank dike and enjoy expansive views over the open wetlands. Turn north along a narrower dike that borders a forest-fringed canal. After 0.7 mile, you reach a junction with Mail Route Road dike. Turn right and return to the parking area.

Bald eagles, turkey vultures, ospreys, wood storks, gallinules, coots, cor-

Rice trunk and wetlands. JOHN CLARK PHOTO

morants, eastern kingbirds, red-winged blackbirds, anhingas, and varieties of geese, grebes, loons, terns, vireos, ducks, sparrows, wrens, mergansers, warblers, hawks, herons, and many others make Donnelly WMA a mother lode of birds. Alligators, turtles, frogs, and otters populate the waterways; and the woods are filled with white-tailed deer, raccoons, wild turkeys, and foxes.

You may also wish to experience Backwater Trail, a 1.4-mile loop, located on the Donnelley property between U.S. Highway 17 and the office gate. Because it is outside the gate, this trail is accessible during hours the remainder of the wildlife management area is closed. The trail winds through mixed pines and hardwoods, affording attractive vistas of rice fields and their accompanying wildlife.

In addition to the two nature trails, Donnelly WMA offers several miles of viewing points along unpaved roads. An especially good place for alligator viewing is along the dike road leading in from the southwest entrance to Donnelly, off Secondary Road 26.

Facilities: No rest rooms or drinking water at the trailhead, but there are rest rooms at the management area's check station.

Lodging and amenities: Campsites are available at Wood Brothers Store, on U.S. Highway 17 in Green Pond, and at Edisto Beach State Park. Limited services are available at Jacksonboro, and all amenities are available at Charleston, Beaufort, and Walterboro.

For more information: Donnelley Wildlife Management Area. See Appendix A: For More Information.

58 Combahee Unit, ACE Basin National Wildlife Refuge

General description: Half a day's walk through the wetlands of the Combahee River basin, in the Combahee Unit of the ACE Basin National Wildlife Refuge.
General location: North of Beaufort, near the state's southern coast.
Distance: 3 miles, loop.
Difficulty: Easy.
Trail conditions: Trail conditions are excellent. Traffic is light.
Best time to go: Fall, winter, spring.
Maps: ACE Basin National Wildlife Refuge brochure; Yemassee and Sheldon USGS quads. See Appendix A: For More Information.
Fees: None.

Finding the trailhead: From Charleston, follow U.S. Highway 17 south 45 miles and, 1.5 miles after crossing the Beaufort County line at the bridge over the Combahee River, turn right (north) on Secondary Road 33 (River Road). Drive 2 miles on SR 33 and look for parking on the left (southwest) after the pedestrian crossing sign, almost directly across the highway from a large white plantation house. The trail begins at the parking lot.

The hike: The Combahee Unit of the ACE Basin National Wildlife Refuge is divided into two sections; the main trail is in the southern section. (ACE is an acronym for the Ashepoo, Combahee, and Edisto rivers).

This is a good trail for viewing waterfowl of all kinds. The trail runs on dikes among canals left over from the region's rice-growing days. Beginning at the parking area, it first passes between green, duckweed-covered ponds, but quickly reaches a lovely canal. Cross the canal on a wooden bridge and turn left (southeast) onto the dike path. The tea-black waters of the canal on the left beautifully set off the white spider lilies overhanging it.

After 0.5 mile, the dike takes a 90-degree turn to the right when another canal cuts across its path. Follow the dike path to the right (south). (A second wooden bridge, this one in poorer condition, crosses the first canal to the left (north), and the path on the other side leads back to SR 33.)

You proceed along the dike with woodlands to your left and acres of old rice-field wetlands to your right. After 0.25 mile, you reach a fork at a rice trunk, a wooden structure for regulating water levels. Go left (south) and follow the water on both sides of the trail. The trail here is shady and pleasant. Saw palmettos, cypresses, and Spanish moss decorate the way.

After another 0.25 mile, you reach a second fork at a second rice trunk. Bear right (west). The left fork leads to the refuge's southern boundary, about 0.1 mile away. There is a lot of open water on both sides of the trail along the left fork; we recommend it as a side trip during waterfowl migration periods.

Combahee Unit, ACE Basin National Wildlife Refuge

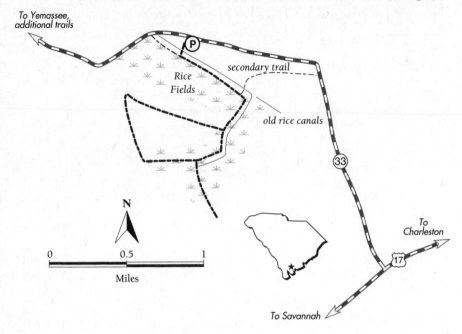

Farther on 0.25 mile, the trail turns right (north) onto a dirt road follow-ing a power line, passing through a wooded area of mostly young pines, with some scattered hardwoods. After 0.3 mile, the trail turns right (east) sharply to return to the first rice trunk and fork. From the rice trunk, return the way you came by turning left (north) and returning to the parking lot.

On the east side of SR 33, the ACE Basin National Wildlife Refuge contin-ues on substantial parcels of land lining both banks of the Combahee River. These lands are crisscrossed with old dikes and offer excellent hiking op-portunities. From the parking area, continue south on SR 33 for 0.2 mile. You will see a small ACE Basin NWR/Ducks Unlimited sign on the left. An unpaved gated road leads onto the property. Park beside it, taking care not to block the gate. Official trails in these sections are still in the planning stage, but hikers are welcome in the areas with direct access from SR 33. (Public access to the refuge parcel on the eastern side of the Combahee River is not likely in the near future, because the only road to this property passes through private land.)

Three short trails run from SR 33 (River Road) into the northern section of the Combahee Unit, just south of Yemassee. To reach them, drive north on SR 33. After 6 miles, Auldbrass Plantation, the Frank Lloyd Wright–designed estate of Hollywood producer Joel Silver, is on the right. The sec-ond dirt road on the right (east) side after Auldbrass Plantation is the first trail. The second and third trails are another 0.6 mile and 1.1 mile from this point, respectively. Both are also on the right (east) side of the road.

All three of these trails are former logging roads that pass through property once owned by a paper company. The terrain is dominated by young pines, so shade is at a premium. Each trail is 0.5 mile long—1 mile round trip—and leads to a backwater of the Combahee River. Bobwhites, turkeys, and mourning doves may be encountered along the way. The destinations, overlooked by baldcypresses and bordered by their knees, are worth the trip.

There are two other short trails in the refuge. To reach them, continue to Yemassee, where River Road (SR 33) ends at Railroad Avenue. Turn left (west), then turn right (north) when Railroad Avenue ends after 0.2 mile. At the flashing light, bear right (east) onto US 17A. After 2 miles, turn left (north) onto a dirt road just before the highway bridge over the Combahee River. The two trails are 0.3 and 0.4 mile up the road, respectively. Both are on the left (west) side and are former logging roads. Both are also shady and 0.5 mile long (1 mile round trip).

The first trail features a pretty pond, on the right after 0.25 mile, where water birds such as the great blue heron will likely be found. The second trail features a lovely swampy portion dominated by baldcypresses. This trail ends at power lines shading heavy undergrowth. The fearless who bushwhack to the other side will find a small pond that is sometimes inhabited by large alligators. Both trails are good spots to meet wildlife, including large deer; you will sometimes find them browsing in the middle of the trail. Both trails are also good spots to view the southern blue flag iris.

Facilities: None.

Lodging and amenities: Yemassee has limited services. There are commercial campgrounds and motels nearby along I-95. Restaurants, motels, and bed-and-breakfast accommodations can be found at lovely Beaufort, about 25 miles to the south.

For more information: ACE Basin National Wildlife Refuge. See Appendix A: For More Information.

59 Webb Wildlife Center

General description:	Half a day's walk in lush wetlands along the mighty Savannah River, with majestic cypresses and abundant wildflowers.
General location:	North of Savannah, Georgia, in the southwest corner of the state.
Distance:	4 miles round trip.
Difficulty:	Easy.
Trail conditions:	Conditions are average to poor. Traffic is light.
Best time to go:	Winter and spring. Take care during spring and fall hunting seasons.
Maps:	Department of Natural Resources Lower Coastal Region Wildlife Management Area map; Department of Natural Resources Webb Center Wildlife Management Area/Tillman Sand Ridge Wildlife Management Area brochure; Brighton USGS quad. See Appendix A: For More Information.
Fees:	None.

Finding the trailhead: From Estill, take U.S. Highway 321 south 10 miles to Garnett. Turn right (northwest) onto Secondary Road 20 and proceed 3 miles to the entrance, on the left (southwest) side of the road. Continue past the headquarters to the trailhead at Bluff Lake, at the end of the entrance road.

The hike: Webb Wildlife Center comprises 5,866 acres of wilderness. All the roads here are unpaved, but well maintained. The land is almost evenly divided between pine and hardwood forest, with wetter areas along the Savannah River floodplain, through which the trail passes.

Bluff Lake, where the trail begins, was once part of the riverbed, but it was cut off from the Savannah River by shifts in the channel. It is surrounded by a baldcypress–tupelo swamp forest. Fragrant water lilies float tranquilly on its surface.

On the trail, lizard's tail plants form miniature forests (nearly covering the trail in one place). Other wildflowers present include trumpet creepers, water willows, aquatic milkweeds, and bull nettles. Apart from cypresses and elms, a variety of water-loving oaks are present.

Birds in the area include egrets, great blue herons, barred owls, wood ducks, Acadian flycatchers, and yellow-throated warblers. Red-cockaded woodpeckers nest in pines on either side of the entrance road. White-tailed deer prance and big tortoises lumber through the area. Although this is a hunting preserve, fox squirrels are afforded special protection.

The trail is often heavily overgrown, but usually easy to discern. It runs alongside Bluff Lake for the first 0.3 mile. It passes through mature hardwood bottomland and bottomland swamp forest. Blue arrows on trees mark the trail.

Webb Wildlife Center

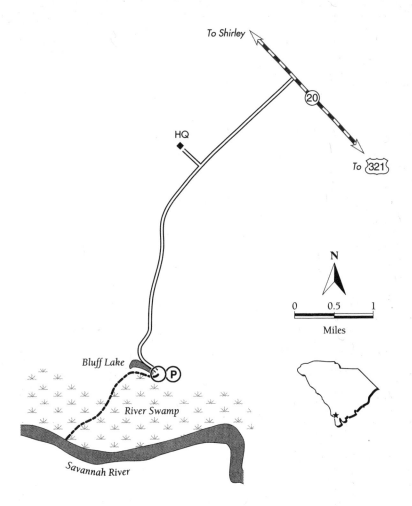

A creek ripples off to the left of the trail, about 1 mile from the trailhead decorated with some astounding baldcypress knees. One of these forms an arch above the water, with another knee growing through it. Fascinating forms are the norm in this intriguing place.

The Savannah River almost sneaks up on you, as the river banks are quite low along the floodplain. The river, too, is lined with a profusion of baldcypresses and their knees. The wide river channel is one of the few places where sunlight reaches the trail in this dark, mysterious place.

Turn around and retrace your path to the trailhead.

Facilities: Rest rooms and drinking water available at Webb Wildlife Center office.

Lodging and amenities: Lodging, food, and basic services are available at Estill and along I-95. Camping is available at Rivers Bridge State Park and at commercial sites along I-95.

For more information: Webb Wildlife Center. See Appendix A: For More Information.

60 Savannah National Wildlife Refuge

General description:	Half a day's hike through beautiful marshes. Magnificent alligators and a great variety of bird life add spice.
General location:	At the southern tip of the state, north of Savannah, Georgia, in the southwest corner of the state.
Distance:	8 miles, loop.
Difficulty:	Easy.
Trail conditions:	Conditions are good. Traffic is light.
Best time to go:	Autumn and spring.
Maps:	Savannah NWR brochure; Limehouse and Savannah USGS quads. See Appendix A: For More Information.
Fees:	None.

Canal bordered by rice fields. JOHN DANTZLER PHOTO

Savannah National Wildlife Refuge

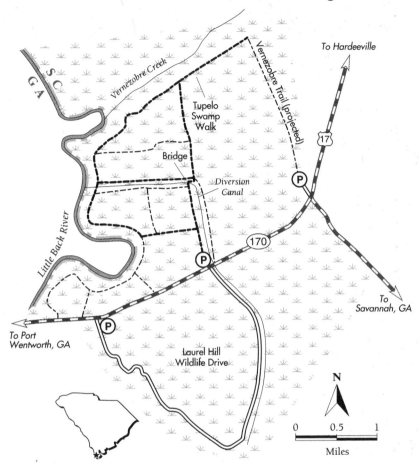

Finding the trailhead: From Exit 5 on Interstate 95 at Hardeeville, take U.S. Highway 17 south 6.5 miles, at which point the highway forks. Take the right (southwest) fork, which is South Carolina 170. After 1 mile, you see the end of one-way Laurel Hill Wildlife Drive to your left (south). To the right (north), directly across the highway, is a gated road, closed to vehicles. Park here, being sure not to block the gate. The trail begins beyond the gate.

The hike: Savannah National Wildlife Refuge is an example of dikes and ponds built for rice culture in the 18th and 19th centuries finding a new career as special wetlands habitat for animals, especially marsh and water birds. This is one of the largest continuous stretches of tidal freshwater marsh in South Carolina. The entire refuge area north of SC 170 is closed from December 1 to February 28 to protect breeding birds. Between these dates, hiking is still permitted on the dikes encircled by Laurel Hill Wildlife Drive.

The dikes crisscrossing the ponds, pools, and marshes make for especially lovely—and easy—hiking. Begin on the road leading north from the eastern end of Laurel Hill Wildlife Drive.

The trail connects numerous hardwood hammocks. There is a good chance of encountering great horned owls here at any time. During migration periods, warblers are seen in great numbers and in great variety. On the refuge, rice birds like bobolinks and red-winged blackbirds are very numerous, as is the boat-tailed grackle. Cormorants, anhingas, herons, egrets, and common moorhens are often seen; purple gallinules and least bitterns are seen often here in summer, but seldom elsewhere in South Carolina.

The stars of the show, however, are the alligators. They range from small fellows of a foot or two in length to big guys more than 10 feet long. They are quite numerous.

The first section of the trail runs remarkably straight. The trail runs north from SC 170 along the refuge's diversion canal, which is to your right. This is where the largest numbers, and largest sizes, of alligators congregate. If you can take your eyes off the reptiles, you will see that gorgeous wild irises decorate the way. On the left-hand side of the dike is a huge impoundment filled with an infinite number of water lilies.

After 1 mile, you reach a bridge. It crosses the diversion canal, which now heads due west. Cross the bridge and continue north. This section of dike is grassier and more pleasant; also, it is lower and therefore nearer to the water. About 0.75 mile after the bridge, you enter a wooded area or hammock. The pleasant shade afforded by the trees continues almost uninterrupted for 0.5 mile, right up to the Tupelo Trail.

At the end of the north-south-tending dike you have been walking on all the way from SC 170, turn right (northeast) for Tupelo Trail, which provides the rare opportunity to walk through a coastal baldcypress–tupelo swamp. Elsewhere in the refuge, dikes have been built up higher and wider than they stood during the rice culture era. The Tupelo Trail allows a glimpse of what they looked like centuries ago. In addition to baldcypresses and tupelos, saw palmettos grow in profusion. To the north of the Tupelo Trail a tributary of Vernezobre Creek flows alongside. To the south is another great wetland filled with trees, mostly oaks. When you reach a big live oak growing right in the middle of the trail, start paying attention. Even bigger live oaks are just ahead. Refuge managers estimate that some of these trees are more than 150 years old.

After 1 mile, Tupelo Trail ends at the refuge's boundary. Turn around and return the way you came. At the point where you started the Tupelo Trail, continue straight ahead. The dike becomes a road, grassy and shady. The tree cover to the right (north) is almost unbroken, but the Vernezobre Creek's tributary can still be seen periodically through the trees. Spanish moss and (in season) honeysuckle are recurring themes. After 1.5 miles, follow a bend to the left (south), paralleling Little Back River, a channel of the Savannah River. Stay on this dike passing one dike to the left (east), and then turn left (east) onto the second intersecting dike. This dike runs alongside the diversion

Spanish moss–hung final view of Vernezobre Creek. JOHN DANTZLER PHOTO

canal; if you have not seen alligators yet, you will most likely see them here. This path returns you to the main trail after about 1.3 miles; turn right (south) and cross the bridge again to return to the trailhead.

Exciting changes are in store at Savannah National Wildlife Refuge. A new parking area has been laid out on US 17, on the west side of the refuge, roughly 6 miles south of Hardeeville. A new trail, Vernezobre Trail, will lead from this parking lot and connect with the Tupelo Trail.

When the new trail is ready, our recommended trail will change somewhat. Starting from the new trailhead, take the new trail to the Tupelo Trail. Follow the Tupelo Trail dike to the refuge's western boundary, then circle back along Little Back River, just as described above. However, when you reach the present trail's main north-south dike at a point about 0.5 mile north of SC 170, turn left (north) to return to the Tupelo Trail instead of turning right to go to SC 170. At the Tupelo Trail, turn left to return to the new Vernezobre Trailhead. This hike should be about 9 miles long and take five to seven hours.

Facilities: Rest rooms at Laurel Hill Wildlife Drive.

Lodging and amenities: The entire range of visitor services, including commercial campgrounds, is available at Hilton Head Island, along I-95 near Hardeeville, and at Savannah. The nearest South Carolina state park that offers public camping is Hunting Island. Skidaway Island State Park in Georgia, 6 miles southeast of Savannah, also has a campground.

For more information: Savannah Coastal Refuges. See Appendix A: For More Information.

61 Pinckney Island National Wildlife Refuge

General description:	A day hike on a coastal island surrounded by salt marshes where large alligators loll and dolphins play offshore.
General location:	West of Hilton Head Island, along the state's southern coast.
Distance:	7 miles round trip.
Difficulty:	Easy.
Trail conditions:	Conditions are good. Traffic is moderate.
Best time to go:	Fall, winter, spring.
Maps:	Pinckney Island National Wildlife Refuge brochure; Bluffton, Spring Island, and Parris Island USGS quads. See Appendix A: For More Information.
Fees:	None.

Pinckney Island National Wildlife Refuge

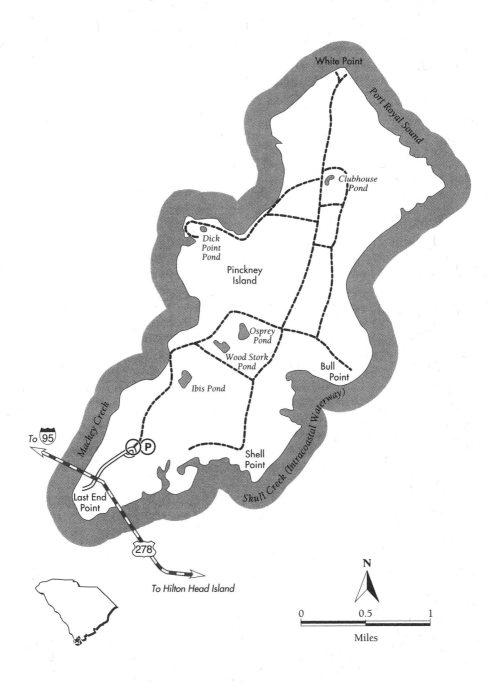

White Point

Port Royal Sound

Clubhouse Pond

Dick Point Pond

Pinckney Island

Osprey Pond

Wood Stork Pond

Bull Point

Ibis Pond

Mackey Creek

To 95

P

Shell Point

Skull Creek (Intracoastal Waterway)

Last End Point

278

To Hilton Head Island

N

0   0.5   1

Miles

Finding the trailhead: From Interstate 95, take U.S. Highway 278 toward Hilton Head Island. Go 4.7 miles past the turnoff for South Carolina Highway 46 and Bluffton. The entrance to Pinckney Island National Wildlife Refuge lies on the left (northeast) side, between the two bridges leading onto Hilton Head Island. If you approach from the north, make sure you are in the left lane. The trailhead is at the parking area.

The hike: Although it is unpopulated now, Pinckney Island has a long history of human activity. The island shows evidence of Native American settlement dating back 10,000 years. Europeans were living here by 1715. In 1734, the island passed to the Pinckneys, a prominent Charleston family. Charles Cotesworth Pinckney, a signer of the United States Constitution, established a Sea Island cotton plantation that thrived here until the Civil War, when Union forces occupied the area.

Two-thirds of Pinckney Island's 4,000 acres are made up of salt marsh. Higher ground at the refuge is popular with breeding wading birds. The refuge features all three of South Carolina's palmetto species and longleaf, slash, and loblolly pines. Other trees include live oaks, sweet gums, red maples, sycamores, and hickories.

In spring, Pinckney Island National Wildlife Refuge may be the best-smelling place on earth. The scent is something like roses, something like honeysuckle, and something like magnolia.

The parking area greets you with a picturesque display of majestic live oaks festooned with Spanish moss. The graveled main trail leads north from here, bisecting almost the entire island. Numerous well-marked grassy paths (generally as wide as roads) branch off periodically. The gravel path is largely devoid of canopy; a hat is a good idea in all seasons.

About 0.8 mile along the way is a sign for Ibis Pond, on the right (east) side. Opposite the sign, a tiny trail leads past a bench to a magnificent live oak on Mackay Creek. If you want to achieve a view of Ibis Pond, you have to do a little bushwhacking through high grass. The pond has supported a rookery for egrets and ibises.

The grass path to Osprey Pond 0.7 mile up the main gravel trail from Ibis Pond, is well marked. In mating season, this pond provides a rookery for a wide variety of birds, in astonishing numbers. Thousands of egrets and ibises have been observed roosting or nesting at Osprey Pond during the summer months. Expect to see snowy and cattle egrets, ibises, and little blue herons.

The graveled main trail continues 2 miles east then north to Clubhouse Pond. Alligators are sometimes encountered around this pond. Beyond Clubhouse Pond, a grass trail continues north for the last 0.5 mile to White Point, the northern tip of the island. This is a first-rate spot for watching dolphins at play in Port Royal Sound.

Return to Clubhouse Pond and proceed east and south toward Bull Point and back westward toward Osprey Pond. When you reach the main graveled trail again, turn left (south) on a grass path, the Shell Point Trail. This is a good way to see more wildflowers and other habitat types. You can go all the way to Shell Point, but unless you have a great deal of time and energy, it is best to take the first trail to the right (west), which is a branch of the Shell Point Trail, back to the gravel main road. Turn left to return to the trailhead.

Facilities: None.

Lodging and amenities: Abundant food and lodging facilities can be found at Hilton Head Island, as well as at charming nearby Bluffton. Commercial campgrounds are available along I-95 and at Bluffton and Hilton Head Island. South Carolina's nearest public campground with facilities is at Hunting Island State Park.

For more information: Savannah Coastal Refuges. See Appendix A: For More Information.

62 Sea Pines Forest Preserve

General description:	A short walk through maritime forest and marshlands in a well-protected preserve.
General location:	On Hilton Head Island, along the state's southern coast.
Distance:	3.7 miles, loop.
Difficulty:	Easy.
Trail conditions:	Excellent. Traffic is mderate.
Best time to go:	Year-round.
Maps:	Sea Pines Forest Preserve map, available at trailheads; Tybee Island North USGS quad. See Appendix A: For More Information.
Fees:	Sea Pines Plantation entry fee of $5 per vehicle.

Finding the trailhead: Reach Hilton Head Island by following U.S. Highway 278 south from Interstate 95. About 2.5 miles after crossing the bridge onto Hilton Head Island, take the Cross Island Parkway ($1 toll) 4 miles to its end at Palmetto Bay Road, then follow Palmetto Bay Road south (left) 1.5 miles to Sea Pines Circle. Alternatively, continue past the Cross Island Parkway entrance for an additional 11 miles on US 278 (William Hilton Parkway) to reach Sea Pines Circle. From Sea Pines Circle, follow Greenwood Drive 0.2 mile to the Sea Pines Greenwood Gate, pay the visitors fee, then continue another 1 mile to the Greenwood Entrance to the Sea Pines Forest Preserve, on the left.

Reach the Lawton Entrance and Fish Island alternate trailheads by taking Pope Avenue southeast from Sea Pines Circle, then turning right on

Sea Pines Forest Preserve

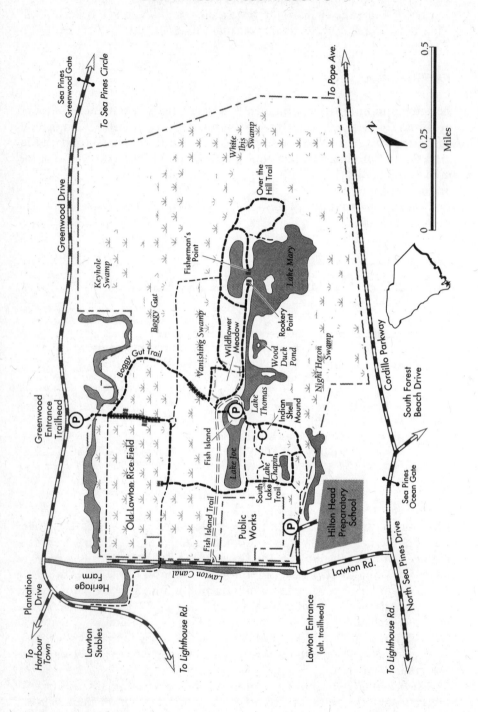

Cordillo Parkway. Follow Cordillo Parkway to the Sea Pines Ocean Gate. After the gate, follow North Sea Pines Drive, then take the first right, onto Lawton Road. Follow signs to the Lawton Entrance (at the rear of Hilton Head Preparatory School), or to Fish Island, which is reached via Lawton Road and Fish Island Trail, a dirt road.

The hike: Hilton Head Island is a barrier island, 11 miles long and 3 miles wide, on South Carolina's southernmost coast. Evidence of Native American habitation dates back 4,000 years. The first European settlers came here in the 18th century to grow rice, indigo, and cotton. The island was occupied by Union troops for nearly all of the Civil War, after which the plantation economy fell to ruin.

In 1956, a public bridge was constructed to connect the island to the mainland, leading the way for increased tourism, and Hilton Head Island now sees 1.6 million visitors a year. Developers have set aside protected habitats at Sea Pines Plantation, the oldest development on the island. The 605-acre Sea Pines Forest Preserve is just inside the community's gates.

The preserve has three entrances and trailheads, and a 6-mile maze of variously named trails that provide numerous hiking options. This narrative recommends a 3.7-mile course that begins at the Greenwood Entrance, the major pedestrian entrance. The route can easily be altered to suit your needs and preferences.

From the Greenwood Entrance, a parking lot off Greenwood Drive shaded by live oaks laden with Spanish moss, walk past the turnoff for the Rice Dike Trail on the right (southwest). At 0.1 mile from the trailhead, reach the

A view of Rookery Island. JOHN DANTZLER PHOTO

Lake Thomas and Wildflower Meadow. JOHN DANTZLER PHOTO

intersection of the Rice Field Boardwalk and Boggy Gut Trail. Bear right (south) onto the boardwalk, which offers great views of the Old Lawton Rice Field on the right (southwest) and the Boggy Gut marshland on the left (northeast). The rice field dates from antebellum plantation days. Observation points with benches line both sides of the boardwalk.

Omnipresent large turtles offer themselves as tasty meals for the alligators lurking in the dark waters and dense undergrowth. In evenings, especially after summer rains, the sound of frogs chirruping fills the air. Waterfowl are numerous, and red-winged blackbirds frolic about. Willow trees, cattails, sawgrass, southern bayberries, and the green surface scum known as duckweed are the primary plants around the water, which has been stained coffee-brown by the tannic acid of fallen leaves.

At the end of the 0.2-mile boardwalk, follow the signs pointing toward the observation deck to the right (southwest). Walk 0.2 mile along the path between Vanishing Swamp and Old Lawton Rice Field to the sign indicating the observation deck on the right (northwest). Watch for a stately old magnolia tree on the right and marsh rabbits scurrying across the path through the maritime forest of pines, live oaks, red bays, and other vegetation able to tolerate the salt air. Climb to the top of the elevated observation deck, which has benches for those with tired feet, and enjoy a panoramic view of the rice field and its denizens, including egrets and herons.

After descending from the observation deck, follow the trail southeast through Vanishing Swamp toward Lake Joe 0.2 mile away. The rope-like scuppernong grape vine coils to the top of host hardwood trees in this moist setting, which is a good area to watch and listen for warblers and the multitudes of other forest birds that flock to the preserve. Deer and raccoons also make their home in and around the swamp and adjacent woodlands.

Emerging from the swamp, cross the dirt road (Fish Island Trail) and continue straight 0.1 mile on Lake Joe Trail, with Lake Joe on the left (northeast) and a thick stand of cane on the right (southwest). After rounding the southeast corner of the lake, turn right (southeast) onto South Lake Trail, in the direction of the Lawton Entrance.

Continue 0.2 mile on South Lake Trail past the Palmetto Trail, on the left (east side) to tiny Lake Chapin, where a bench offers you an opportunity to enjoy the tranquil beauty of this relatively isolated spot.

Turn left (northeast) just past Lake Chapin and follow Lake View Trail 0.1 mile to the next intersection. Turn right (east) onto North Lake Trail, then turn left (north) onto Shell Ring Trail (a right turn here leads west to the Lawton Entrance). The next 0.2 mile is quite scenic, offering attractive views of Night Heron Swamp on the right (southeast), boardwalk crossings of a verdant wetland, and tall Carolina palmettos, until you come to the grassy Indian shell ring clearing in the forest.

On the National Register of Historic Places and one of only 20 such shell rings still in existence on the East Coast, the 150-foot-wide grass-covered ring of bones and oyster, clam, and mussel shells is about 4,000 years old. A box dispenses brochures with information on this site and the Native Americans who created the ring, and benches offer visitors a rest in this sylvan setting.

From the ring, continue 0.2 mile on Shell Ring and North Lake trails toward Fish Island, actually a peninsula between Lake Joe and Lake Thomas, where there are a parking area, rest rooms, drinking water, and picnic facilities. Lakes Joe and Thomas, as well as Lake Mary to the east, harbor ducks, other waterfowl, alligators, turtles, and a considerable quantity of bream, crappie, and bass.

From Fish Island, cross the footbridge on the north side and bear right (east) toward the signs at the south edge of the Wildflower Meadow. The signs identify almost 40 varieties of native flowers growing in the meadow.

Continue 0.4 mile on the east side of the meadow along the Overlook Trail to Rookery Point, where an elevated observation platform (with benches at ground level and on the platform) provides a great view of Lake Mary—on three sides of the point—and Rookery Island and Fisherman's Point across the water. This is another great spot for viewing waterfowl, especially ducks.

After leaving Rookery Point, walk 0.4 mile around the west side of Lake Mary along the Anhinga Trail to Fisherman's Point, where you are met with more watery vistas. Near the end of the Anhinga Trail there is a picnic area on the lake's north side. Take the Over the Hill Trail that forks to the left (east). The Over the Hill Trail, which provides a route over higher terrain through varied habitat, heads back to the west side of Lake Mary and on to the Meadow Trail, leading to an observation platform on the Wildflower

Meadow's north side, 0.8 mile from the beginning of the Over the Hill Trail.

Next, proceed 0.1 mile through the forest along the Meadow Trail, on the northwest side of the meadow, and turn right (north) onto the boardwalk, which leads 0.1 mile back through Vanishing Swamp toward Boggy Gut.

At the trail intersection on the northwest side of Vanishing Swamp, continue straight (north) onto the Boggy Gut Trail. The 0.4-mile trail through the Boggy Gut marshland offers more great birding opportunities and the possibility of spotting an alligator prowling the duckweed. Look for lily pads in the lagoon bordering Boggy Gut Trail.

After passing through Boggy Gut, you can continue a few hundred feet back to the Greenwood Entrance Trailhead. If you have stamina and time remaining, however, you may want to first bear left (southwest) and make a 0.75-mile round-trip traverse of the Rice Dike Trail, a grassy pathway that follows the length of the northwest side of the Old Lawton Rice Field. Wonderful opportunities for wildlife viewing make this detour quite worthwhile.

Facilities: No rest rooms or drinking water at Greenwood or Lawton trailheads. Rest rooms, drinking water, and a picnic area are available at Fish Island, located in the center of the preserve and accessible by vehicle as an alternate trailhead.

Lodging and amenities: Commercial camping facilities are available on Hilton Head Island and at Bluffton, as well as along I-95. The nearest public campground with facilities in South Carolina is at Hunting Island State Park. Hilton Head Island abounds in restaurants and both conventional and luxury accommodation options.

For more information: Sea Pines Forest Preserve, care of Community Services Associates, Inc. See Appendix A: For More Information.

Appendix A: For More Information

ACE Basin National Wildlife Refuge, P.O. Box 848, Hollywood, SC 29449; (843) 889-3084.

Andrew Pickens Ranger District, Sumter National Forest, 112 Andrew Pickens Circle, Mountain Rest, SC 29664; (864) 638-9568.

Anne Springs Close Greenway, P.O. Box 1209, Fort Mill, SC 29716; (803) 548-7252.

Bear Island Wildlife Management Area, 585 Donnelley Drive, Green Pond, SC 29446; (843) 844-8957.

Blue Ridge Council, Boy Scouts of America, P.O. Box 6628, Station B, Greenville, SC 29606; (864) 233-8363.

Cape Romain National Wildlife Refuge, 5801 Highway 17 North, Awendaw, SC 29429; (843) 928-3368.

Carolina Sandhills National Wildlife Refuge, U.S. Fish and Wildlife Service, Route 2, Box 100, McBee, SC 29101; (843) 335-8401.

Charleston Visitor Center, 375 Meeting Street, P.O. Box 975, Charleston, SC 29402; (843) 853-8000.

Cheraw State Park, 100 State Park Road, Cheraw, SC 29520; (843) 921-1418.

Coastal Expeditions, 514-B Mill Street, Mount Pleasant, SC 29464; (843) 881-4582.

Congaree Swamp National Monument, 200 Caroline Sims Road, Hopkins, SC 29061; (803) 776-4396.

Cypress Gardens, 3030 Cypress Gardens Road, Moncks Corner, SC 29461; (843) 553-0515.

Donnelley Wildlife Management Area, 585 Donnelley Drive, Green Pond, SC 29446; (843) 844-8957.

Duke Power Company, Lake Management, P.O. Box 1006, Charlotte, NC 28201-1006; (800) 443-5193.

Edisto Beach State Park, 8377 State Cabin Road, Edisto Island, SC 29438; (843) 869-2756 (cabins), (843) 869-2156 (camping).

Enoree/Tyger Ranger District, Sumter National Forest, 20 Work Center Road, Whitmire, SC 29178, (803) 276-4810; 3557 Whitmire Highway, Union, SC

29379, (864) 427-9858.

Fisheagle Tours, P.O. Box 1086, Santee, SC 29142; (803) 854-4005, (800) 767-7739.

Foothills Trail Conference, P.O. Box 3041, Greenville, SC 29602; (864) 467-9537.

Francis Beidler Forest, 336 Sanctuary Road, Harleyville, SC 29448; (843) 462-2150; website: www.pride-net.com/swamp/.

Harbison State Forest, P.O. Box 21707, 5500 Broad River Road, Columbia, SC 29221; (803) 896-8890.

Heritage Trust Program, Preserve Manager, South Carolina Department of Natural Resources, P.O. Box 167, Columbia, SC 29202; (803) 734-3893.

Hoyett's Grocery and Tackle, 516 Jocassee Lake Road, Salem, SC 29676; (864) 944-9016.

Huntington Beach State Park, Murrells Inlet, SC 29576; (843) 237-4440.

Keowee-Toxaway State Park, 108 Residence Drive, Sunset, SC 29685; (864) 868-2605.

Kings Mountain National Military Park, P.O. Box 40, Kings Mountain, NC 28036; (864) 936-7921.

Kings Mountain State Park, 1277 Park Road, Blacksburg, SC 29702; (803) 222-3209.

Landsford Canal State Historic Site, 2051 Park Drive, Catawba, SC 29704; (803) 789-5800.

Leave No Trace, Inc.; (800) 332-4100; website: www.lnt.org.

Long Cane Ranger District, Sumter National Forest, 810 Buncombe Street, Edgefield, SC 29824; (803) 637-5396.

Magnolia Plantation and its Gardens, Route 4, Highway 61, Charleston, SC 29414; (843) 571-1266, or (800) 367-3517; website: www.magnoliaplantation.com.

Mountain Bridge Wilderness Area, Caesars Head State Park, 8155 Geer Highway, Cleveland, SC 29635; (864) 836-6115.

Naturaland Trust, P.O. Box 728, Greenville, SC 29602.

Nature Conservancy, 2231 Devine Street, Columbia, SC 29205, (803) 254-9049

Naval Weapons Station, Morale, Wellness, and Recreation Department, 2316 Redbank Road, Suite 100, Code 15 Building 708, Goose Creek, SC 29445-8601; (843) 764-7601.

Oconee State Park, 624 State Park Road, Mountain Rest, SC 29664; (864) 638-5353.

Oconee Station State Historic Site, 500 Oconee Station Road, Walhalla, SC 29691; (864) 638-0079.

Old Santee Canal State Historic Site, 900 Stony Landing Road, Moncks Corner, SC 29461; (843) 899-5200.

Palmetto Trails, Palmetto Conservation Foundation, 1314 Lincoln Street, Suite 213, Columbia, SC 29201; (803) 771-0870.

Paris Mountain State Park, 2401 State Park Road, Greenville, SC 29609; (864) 244-5565.

Pendleton District Commission, P.O. Box 565, Pendleton, SC 29670; (864) 646-3782, (800) 862-1795; website: www.mindspring.com/~lei/pendltour.

Poinsett State Park, 6660 Poinsett Park Road, Wedgefield, SC 29168; (803) 494-8177.

Santee Coastal Reserve, P.O. Box 37, McClellanville, SC 29458; (843) 546-8665.

Santee Cooper Property Management Division, 1 Riverwood Drive, Moncks Corner, SC 29461; (843) 761-4068.

Santee State Park, 251 State Park Road, Santee, SC 29162; (803) 854-2408.

Savannah Coastal Refuges, 1000 Business Center Drive, Parkway Business Center, Suite 10, Savannah, GA 31405; (912) 652-4415.

Sea Pines Forest Preserve, c/o Community Service Associates, Inc., 175 Greenwood Drive, Hilton Head Island, SC 29928; (843) 671-6486.

Sewee Visitor and Environmental Education Center, 5821 US Highway 17 North, Awendaw, SC 29429; (843) 928-3368.

State Trails Coordinator, SC Department of Parks, Recreation, and Tourism, 1205 Pendleton Street, Columbia, SC 29201; (803) 734-0130; website: www.sctrails.net.

Table Rock State Park, 246 Table Rock State Park Road, Pickens, SC 29671; (864) 878-9813.

Wambaw Ranger District, Francis Marion National Forest, P.O. Box 788,

McClellanville, SC 29458; (843) 887-3257.

Webb Wildlife Center, Garnett, SC 29922; (803) 625-3569.

Westvaco Corporation, Southern Region, Public Affairs Department, P.O. Box 1950, Summerville, SC 29484; (843) 871-5000.

Witherbee Ranger District, Francis Marion National Forest, 2421 Witherbee Road, Cordesville, SC 29434; (843) 336-3248.

YMCA Camp Greenville, P.O. Box 390, Cedar Mountain, NC 28718; (864) 836-3291

FINDING MAPS

For USGS maps, contact the Land Resources Division, South Carolina Department of Natural Resources, 2221 Devine Street, Columbia, SC 29205; (803) 734-9108.

For detailed local road maps, contact South Carolina Department of Transportation, P.O. Box 191, Columbia, SC 29202; (803) 737-1130

South Carolina Wildlife Outdoor Guide: A County by County Atlas, published by *South Carolina Wildlife* magazine, provides detailed county maps and is the best single source for finding your way around the back roads of South Carolina.

ORGANIZATIONS OF INTEREST

SOUTH CAROLINA STATE GOVERNMENT

South Carolina Department of Parks, Recreation, and Tourism

The South Carolina Tourism Office provides a wide variety of tourist information and publishes the annual South Carolina Travel Guide. Order from SCPRT, P.O. Box 71, Columbia, SC 29202; (803) 734-0122; website: www.travelsc.com.

The Division of Park Services operates South Carolina's 48 state parks. The Division makes available brochures on each state park, and publishes the excellent Parkview, which lists all the programs and outings offered at the state parks. Contact South Carolina State Parks, 1205 Pendleton Street, Columbia, SC 29201; (803) 734-0156; website: www.southcarolinaparks.com.

The Heritage Tourism Development Office is developing South Carolina's Heritage Corridor (which runs through the Edisto River Basin from Charleston to North Augusta, then northwest up the Savannah River Valley) and promoting heritage tourism throughout our state. Contact Office of Heritage Tourism Development, 1205 Pendleton Street, Columbia, SC 29201;

(803) 734-0141.

South Carolina Department of Natural Resources

For Heritage Trust, hunting, fishing, or wildlife management area information, or to contact South Carolina Wildlife magazine, write the South Carolina Department of Natural Resources, P.O. Box 167, Columbia, SC 29202. The telephone number for hunting information is (803) 734-3833; for Heritage Trust information, (803) 734-3894; for other inquiries, (803) 734-3888.

Other State Government Sources

South Carolina Department of Transportation, P.O. Box 191, Columbia, SC 29202; (803) 737-1130. {Road information and state, county, city and town maps}.

South Carolina Forestry Commission, P.O. Box 21707, Columbia, SC 29221; (803) 896-8852. {State forests}.

South Carolina State Library, 1500 Senate Street, Columbia, SC 29201; (803) 734-8666.

South Carolina State Museum, 301 Gervais Street, Columbia, SC 29201; (803) 737-4921.

South Carolina Aquarium, 57 Hasell Street, Charleston, SC 29401; (843) 720-1990.

South Carolina Department of Archives and History, P.O. Box 11669, Columbia, SC 29211-1669; (803) 734-8577.

UNITED STATES GOVERNMENT

USDA (U.S. Department of Agriculture) Forest Service

The central office for National Forest operations throughout South Carolina is: Francis Marion and Sumter National Forests, 4931 Broad River Road, Columbia, SC 29201-4021; (803) 561-4000.

U.S. Department of Interior

National Wildlife Refuges

ACE Basin National Wildlife Refuge, P.O. Box 848, Hollywood, SC 29449; (843) 889-3084.

Carolina Sandhills National Wildlife Refuge, U.S. Fish and Wildlife Service, Route 2, Box 100, McBee, SC 29101; (843) 335-8401.

Savannah Coastal Refuges, 1000 Business Center Drive, Parkway Business Center, Suite 10, Savannah, GA 31405; (912) 652-4415.

National Park Service

Congaree Swamp National Monument, 200 Caroline Sims Road, Hopkins, SC 29061; (803) 776-4396.

Kings Mountain National Military Park, P.O. Box 40, Kings Mountain, NC 28036; (864) 936-7921.

NONGOVERNMENTAL SOURCES OF INFORMATION

Center for Carolina Living, P.O. Box 5027, Columbia, SC 29250; (803) 782-7466; website: www.carolinaliving.com. {Retirement and relocation}.

Nature Conservancy, 2231 Devine Street, Columbia, SC 29205; (803) 254-9049.

South Carolina Bed and Breakfast Association, P.O. Box 1275, Sumter, SC 29150-1275. {Publishes South Carolina Bed and Breakfast Association Member Directory.}

South Carolina Campground Owners Association, P.O. Box 1184, Irmo, SC 29063; (803) 772-5354. {Publishes a directory of campgrounds in the state.}

South Carolina Wildlife Federation, 715 Woodrow Street, Columbia, SC 29205; (803) 771-4417.

Sierra Club, South Carolina Chapter, 1314 Lincoln Street, Columbia, SC 29201; (803) 256-8487. {Organized hikes almost every weekend}. Member groups: Bachman (Greater Columbia), Bartram (Greenville-Spartanburg area), Cathcart (Hilton Head Island area), Foothills (Clemson and Walhalla areas), Henry's Knob (Rock Hill area), Lunz (Charleston area), Pee Dee (Florence area), Savannah River (North Augusta area), and Winyah (Myrtle Beach area). Outings are offered through the individual groups; call the Chapter office for up-to-date contact information on hikes and local group activities.

South Carolina Nature-Based Tourism Association, c/o Discover Upcountry Carolina Association, P.O. Box 3116, Greenville, SC 29602; (864) 233-2690. {Publishes The South Carolina Nature-Based Tourism Directory}.

South Carolina Coastal Conservation League, 456 King Street, Charleston, SC 29401; (843) 723-8035.

Palmetto Conservation Foundation, 1314 Lincoln Street, Columbia, SC 29201; (803) 771-0870. {Palmetto Trails at same location}.

SOUTH CAROLINA TOURISM REGIONS

The tourism regions provide detailed tourism information and lodging assistance for the counties in their regions.

Anderson, Oconee, Pickens, Greenville, Spartanburg, Cherokee counties

Discover Upcountry Carolina Association, P.O. Box 3116, Greenville, SC 29602; (864) 233-2690; website: www.upcountry.sc.org.

Horry and Georgetown counties

Grand Strand Tourism Region, Myrtle Beach Area Chamber of Commerce, P.O. Box 2115, Myrtle Beach, SC 29578; (843) 626-7444; website: www.myrtlebeachlive.com.

Charleston and Dorchester counties

Historic Charleston Area Tourism Region, Charleston Area Convention and Visitors Bureau, P.O. Box 975, Charleston, SC 29402; (843) 853-8000; website: www.charlestoncvb.com.

Richland, Lexington, Saluda, and Newberry counties

Lake Murray Country Tourism Region, P.O. Box 1783, Irmo, SC 29063; (803) 781-5940; website: www.lakemurraycountry.com.

Beaufort, Jasper, Hampton, and Colleton counties

Lowcountry and Resort Islands Tourism Region, P.O. Box 366, Hampton, SC 29924; (843) 943-9180.

Abbeville, Edgefield, Greenwood, Laurens, and McCormick counties

Old 96 Tourism Region, P.O. Box 448, Laurens, SC 29360; (864) 984-2233; website: www.scold 96.org.

Chester, Chesterfield, Fairfield, Kershaw, Lancaster, Union, and York counties

Olde English Tourism Region, P.O. Box 1440, Chester, SC 29706; (803) 385-6800; website: web.infoave.net/ ∼ sctravel.htm.

Florence, Williamsburg, Marion, Dillon, Marlboro, Darlington, and Lee counties

Pee Dee Tourism Region, P.O. Box 3093, Florence, SC 29502; (843) 669-0950; website: pdtourism.com.

Berkeley, Orangeburg, Calhoun, Clarendon, and Sumter counties

Santee Cooper Tourism Region, P.O. Drawer 40, Santee, SC 29142; (803) 854-2131; website: www.santeecoopercountry.org.

Aiken, Allendale, Bamburg, and Barnwell counties

Thoroughbred Country Tourism Region, Lower Savannah Council of Governments, P.O. Box 850, Aiken, SC 29802; (803) 649-7981; website: www.scescape.net/~lscog/depart/thbedco.htm.

Appendix B: Further Reading

This appendix lists some of the many excellent sources for learning about South Carolina's natural resources, trail opportunities, and other attractions.

Of particular note are: Robin Carter's *Finding Birds in South Carolina*, a comprehensive description of birding locations in all 46 counties; Richard Porcher's *Wildflowers of the Carolina Lowcountry and Lower Pee Dee* (the only shortcoming of this superb reference book is that it does not cover the entire state); *South Carolina Wildlife* magazine, an excellent bimonthly publication of the South Carolina Department of Natural Resources; and the National Audubon Society Field Guide series on flora and fauna.

South Carolina Wildlife Outdoor Guide: A County by County Atlas, published by *South Carolina Wildlife* magazine, provides detailed county maps and is the best single source for finding one's way around the back roads of South Carolina.

Gene Able's *Exploring South Carolina: Wild and Natural Places* is an exhaustive compilation of places to view the state's natural beauty. Reliable trail guides besides our own include Alan De Hart's *Hiking South Carolina Trails*, a comprehensive volume, and Phillip Manning's *Palmetto Journal: Walks in the Natural Areas of South Carolina*, which focuses on the human and natural heritage of 15 trail areas.

Of the several general travel guides to South Carolina, perhaps the most readable and informative is Henry Leifermann's *Compass American Guides: South Carolina*, released by Fodor's Travel Publications in 1995.

READING LIST:

Able, Gene. *Exploring South Carolina: Wild and Natural Places*. Rock Hill, SC: Palmetto Byways Press, 1995.

Able, Gene and Jack Horan. *Paddling South Carolina: A Guide to Palmetto State River Trails*. Columbia, SC: Palmetto Byways Press, 1986.

American Birding Association. *Regional Checklist, Southeastern United States*. Available from ABA Sales, PO Box 6599, Colorado Springs, Colo. 80934 (800-634-7736).

Baldwin, William P., III. *Lowcountry Daytrips*. Greensboro, NC: Legacy Publications, 1993.

Ballantine, Todd. *Tideland Treasure*. New Edition. Hilton Head Island, SC: Deerfield Publishing, 1991.

Barry, John M. *Natural Vegetation of South Carolina*. Columbia, SC: University of South Carolina Press, 1980.

Behler, John L., and Wayne F. King. *National Audubon Society Field Guide to North American Reptiles and Amphibians*. New York: Alfred A. Knopf, 1979.

Blagden, Tom, Jr. (photos), Jane Lareau and Richard Porcher (text). *Lowcountry: The Natural Landscape*. Greensboro, NC: Legacy Publications, 1988.

Blouin, Nichole. *Palmetto Cycling Coalition Favorite Mountain Bike Trails.* Palmetto Trails Guide Series. Columbia, SC: Palmetto Trails, 1997.

Bowen, John. *Adventuring Along the Southeast Coast.* San Francisco: Sierra Club Books, 1993.

Bull, John L. *National Audubon Society Field Guide to North American Birds, Eastern Region.* New York: Alfred A. Knopf, 1994.

Carter, Robin M. *Finding Birds in South Carolina.* Columbia, SC: University of South Carolina Press, 1993.

Carter, Robin. *Audubon Society's Favorite South Carolina Bird Walks.* Palmetto Trails Guide Series. Columbia, SC: Palmetto Trails, 1998.

Chamberlain, W. David and D. M. Forsythe. *A Birding Guide to the South Carolina Lowcountry.* Charleston, SC: Charleston Natural History Society, 1988.

Chesterman, Charles W. *National Audubon Society Field Guide to North American Rocks and Minerals.* New York: Alfred A. Knopf, 1979.

Clark, John F. and John Dantzler. *South Carolina Sierra Club Favorite Day Hikes.* Palmetto Trails Guide Series. Columbia, SC: Palmetto Trails, 1997.

Clark, Robert C. (photos) and Tom Poland (text). *South Carolina: A Timeless Journey.* Columbia, SC: University of South Carolina Press, 1994.

De Hart, Allen. *Hiking South Carolina Trails.* Third Edition. Old Saybrook, Conn.: Globe Pequot Press, 1994.

Duncan, Wilbur H. and Leonard E. Foote. *Wildflowers of the Southeastern United States.* Athens, GA: University of Georgia Press, 1975.

Federal Writers' Project. *South Carolina: The WPA Guide to the Palmetto State.* Reprint. Columbia, SC: University of South Carolina Press.

Finley, Lori. *The Mountain Biker's Guide to the Southeast.* Birmingham AL: Menasha Ridge Press; and Helena, MT: Falcon Press, 1994.

Foothills Trail Conference. *Guide to the Foothills Trail,* 2d ed. Greenville SC: The Foothills Trail Conference, 1988.

Fox, William Price. *South Carolina: Off the Beaten Path.* Old Saybrook, Conn.: Globe Pequot, 1996.

Giffen, Morrison. *South Carolina: A Guide to Backcountry Travel and Adventure.* Asheville, NC: Out There Press, 1997.

Isely, N. Jane (photos), William P. Baldwin, Jr. (text) and Agnes L. Baldwin (research). *Plantations of the Low Country: South Carolina 1697–1865.* Greensboro, NC: Legacy Publications, 1985.

Leifermann, Henry. *Compass American Guides: South Carolina.* New York: Fodor's Travel Publications, 1995.

Leland, Elizabeth. *The Vanishing Coast.* Winston-Salem, NC: John F. Blair, 1992.

Little, Elbert L. *National Audubon Society Field Guide to North American Trees, Eastern Region.* New York: Alfred A. Knopf, 1980.

Manning, Phillip. *Palmetto Journal: Walks in the Natural Areas of South Carolina.* Winston-Salem NC: John F. Blair, 1995.

McLean, Norma. *Explore South Carolina: A Guide for Families, Teachers, and Youth Groups.* Columbia, SC: MCL Publications, 1996.

Naturaland Trust. *Mountain Bridge Trails.* Greenville, SC: Naturaland Trust, 1994.

Niering, William A., and Nancy C. Olmstead. *National Audubon Society Field Guide to North American Wildflowers, Eastern Region.* New York: Alfred A. Knopf, 1979.

O'Brien, Dawn. *Down the Road in the Carolinas.* Research Triangle Park, NC: Becklyn Publishing Group, 1994.

Pitzer, Sara. *Traveling in South Carolina: A Selective Guide to Where to Go, What to See, What to Do.* Columbia, SC: University of South Carolina Press, 1993.

Porcher, Richard. *Wildflowers of the Carolina Lowcountry and Lower Pee Dee.* Columbia: University of South Carolina Press, 1995.

Rhyne, Nancy. *Touring the Coastal South Carolina Backroads.* Winston-Salem, NC: John F. Blair, 1992.

Ritz, Stacy. *Hidden Carolinas: The Adventurer's Guide.* Berkeley: Ulysses Press, 1995.

Scarbrough, Jayne E. *South Carolina Horsemen's Council Favorite Horse Trails.* Palmetto Trails Guide Series. Columbia, SC: Palmetto Trails, 1997.

Skinner, Elizabeth and Charles. *The Best Bike Rides in the South.* Old Saybrook, CT: Globe Pequot Press, 1992.

South Carolina Association of Naturalists: The First Ten Years. Columbia, SC: South Carolina Association of Naturalists, 1985.

South Carolina Highway Historical Marker Guide. Columbia, SC: South Carolina Department of Archives and History, 1992.

South Carolina Wildlife Outdoor Guide: A County by County Atlas. Columbia, SC: South Carolina Wildlife Magazine, 1995.

Thompson, Ida. *National Audubon Society Field Guide to North American Fossils.* New York: Alfred A. Knopf, 1982.

Todd, Caroline W. and Sidney Wait. *South Carolina: A Day at a Time.* Orangeburg, SC: Sandlapper Publishing, 1997.

Whitaker, John O., Jr. *National Audubon Society Field Guide to North American Mammals.* 2d ed. New York: Alfred A. Knopf, 1996.

Wilderness Society. *South Carolina's Mountain Treasures: The Unprotected Wildlands of the Andrew Pickens District of the Sumter National Forest.* Atlanta: The Wilderness Society, Southeastern Office, 1993.

Wyche, Thomas (photography) and James Kilgo (text). *The Blue Wall: Wilderness of the Carolinas and Georgia.* Englewood, Colo.: Westcliffe Publishers, 1996.

One final listing might best be described as "further listening." Peterson Field Guides (Boston: Houghton Mifflin) offers a set of three compact discs entitled *Birding by Ear (Eastern/Central): A Guide to Bird-song Identification*, by Richard K. Walton and Robert W. Lawson. It is recommended in the highest terms for anyone wanting to learn how to identify birds by their songs.

Appendix C: Hiker's Checklist

For most hikes in South Carolina, there is no need to spend a lot of money on special equipment. Keep in mind the difference between day hiking and backpacking. Day hikes are short to medium hikes for which the only absolutely essential items are sufficient food and water. Day hikers usually carry all they need in a small day pack or fanny pack. Backpacking trips, on the other hand, last for two or more days and require camping overnight along the trail. You need to be able to meet every human need, including shelter, from the pack on your back. If you take up backpacking, you need to be sure you have adequate equipment, and this can be expensive. Until then, you will probably find hiking a relatively inexpensive pursuit.

Many of the items listed below are most appropriate to backpacking. However, any of them might be useful to you at some time. Tailor this list to your own personal needs, taking into consideration such factors as the length and difficulty of the trail you are undertaking, the time of year, and the size of your party (and the ages of its members).

Clothing

- ❏ dependable rain parka
- ❏ windbreaker
- ❏ thermal underwear
- ❏ shorts
- ❏ long pants
- ❏ cap or hat, preferably a wide-brimmed hat during warm weather
- ❏ wool shirt or sweater
- ❏ warm jacket
- ❏ extra socks
- ❏ underwear
- ❏ lightweight shirts
- ❏ T-shirts
- ❏ gloves
- ❏ belt

Footwear

- ❏ comfortable hiking boots
- ❏ lightweight camp shoes
- ❏ aqua shoes or sandals

Bedding

- ❑ sleeping bag
- ❑ foam pad or air mattress
- ❑ pillow (deflating)
- ❑ ground cloth (plastic or nylon)
- ❑ dependable tent

Cooking

- ❑ 1-quart plastic water container
- ❑ 1-gallon collapsible water container for camp use
- ❑ backpack stove with extra fuel
- ❑ funnel
- ❑ aluminum foil
- ❑ cooking pot
- ❑ bowl or plate
- ❑ spoon, fork, knife, spatula
- ❑ matches in waterproof container

Food and Drink

- ❑ cereal
- ❑ bread and/or crackers
- ❑ trail mix
- ❑ margarine
- ❑ powdered soups
- ❑ salt, pepper, spices
- ❑ main course meals
- ❑ snacks
- ❑ coffee, tea, hot chocolate
- ❑ powdered milk
- ❑ drink mixes

Photographic equipment

- ❑ camera
- ❑ film
- ❑ accessories
- ❑ large plastic zipper bag

Miscellaneous

- ❑ walking stick
- ❑ maps, compasses
- ❑ toilet paper
- ❑ toothbrush
- ❑ water filter or chemical purifier
- ❑ first-aid kit
- ❑ survival kit
- ❑ pocket knife

- ❏ insect repellent
- ❏ topical antihistamine salve
- ❏ lip balm
- ❏ flashlight, with spare batteries and bulb
- ❏ candles
- ❏ small trowel or shovel
- ❏ police whistle
- ❏ extra plastic bags to pack out trash
- ❏ biodegradable soap
- ❏ towel/washcloth
- ❏ waterproof covering for pack
- ❏ binoculars
- ❏ watch
- ❏ sewing kit
- ❏ fishing gear and license
- ❏ field guides
- ❏ your FalconGuide

Appendix D: Hike Index

This index categorizes the hikes in this guide by length and degree of difficulty. Please keep in mind, however, that many of the hikes have route variations that allow you to change the length and difficulty levels to suit your needs. Some of the variations have been noted, which is why some hikes are listed in more than one category.

*Hikes recommended for children are asterisked.

(2) A linear trail requiring use of 2 vehicles if hiked entirely as described.

SHORT HIKES (LESS THAN HALF A DAY)

EASY

Hike 4	East Fork Trail (2)
Hike 6	Winding Stairs Trail (2)
Hike 9	Oconee Station State Historic Site
Hike 30	Lick Fork Lake* (Lick Fork Lake Trail loop)
Hike 33	Kings Mountain* (battlefield loop; round-trip between national and state parks)
Hike 34	Anne Springs Close Greenway (Lake Haigler Nature Trail)
Hike 35	Landsford Canal State Historic Site*
Hike 36	Harbison State Forest (Eagle Trail; Firebreak Trail; Stewardship Trail)
Hike 37	Santee State Park (Oak-Pinolly Nature Trail; Limestone Nature Trail; Sinkhole Nature Trail)
Hike 38	Congaree Swamp* (boardwalk loop; Bluff Trail loop)
Hike 40	Carolina Sandhills National Wildlife Refuge*
Hike 41	Cheraw State Park*
Hike 42	Huntington Beach State Park* (Sandpiper Pond Nature Trail and marsh boardwalks)
Hike 43	Santee Coastal Reserve* (Marshland Trail)
Hike 45	Sewee Shell Mound
Hike 46	I'on Swamp
Hike 49	Old Santee Canal State Historic Site*
Hike 50	Cypress Gardens*
Hike 51	Marrington Plantation*
Hike 52	Magnolia Plantation*
Hike 53	Francis Beidler Forest*
Hike 54	Edisto Beach State Park*
Hike 55	Edisto Nature Trail*
Hike 57	Donnelley Wildlife Management Area
Hike 58	Combahee Unit, ACE Basin National Wildlife Refuge

DAY HIKES

BACKPACKING HIKES

Appendix E: Directory of South Carolina Trails

The following is a listing of all hiking and interpretive trails in the state, as compiled by the State Trail Coordinator. Trails described in this book are denoted by asterisk; the hike number is given in place of trail length. A list of abbreviations used in this table is at the end.

Agency	Phone	Name (miles)	Length

MOUNTAINS

Greenville County

Agency	Phone	Name (miles)	Length
Asbury Hills United Methodist Church	(864) 836-3711	Blue	1.0
Asbury Hills United Methodist Church	(864) 836-3711	Asbury	5.3
Asbury Hills United Methodist Church	(864) 836-3711	Gold	1.0
Camp Greenville	(864) 836-3291	Rainbow Falls*	See Hike 21
City of Greenville Park and Recreation	(864) 467-4350	Cleveland Park	3.3
City of Greenville Park and Recreation	(864) 467-4350	Reedy River Falls	0.5
City of Greenville Park and Recreation	(864) 467-4350	Fernwood Nature	0.5
Mountain Bridge Wilderness Area	(864) 836-6115	Jones Gap NRT*	See Hike 22
Mountain Bridge Wilderness Area	(864) 836-6115	Rim of the Gap*	See Hike 23
Mountain Bridge Wilderness Area	(864) 836-6115	Coldspring Branch*	See Hike 19
Mountain Bridge Wilderness Area	(864) 836-6115	Coldspring Connector*	See Hike 19
Mountain Bridge Wilderness Area	(864) 836-6115	Tom Miller*	See Hike 22
Mountain Bridge Wilderness Area	(864) 836-6115	Hospital Rock*	See Hike 25
Mountain Bridge Wilderness Area	(864) 836-6115	Naturaland Trust*	See Hike 20
Mountain Bridge Wilderness Area	(864) 836-6115	Gum Gap*	See Hike 17
Mountain Bridge Wilderness Area	(864) 836-6115	The Dismal*	See Hike 20
Mountain Bridge Wilderness Area	(864) 836-6115	Wildcat Nature	0.8
Mountain Bridge Wilderness Area	(864) 836-6115	Cleveland Connector*	See Hike 25
Mountain Bridge Wilderness Area	(864) 836-6115	Raven Cliff Falls*	See Hike 18
Mountain Bridge Wilderness Area	(864) 836-6115	Falls Creek*	See Hike 25
Mountain Bridge Wilderness Area	(864) 836-6115	Pinnacle Pass*	See Hike 24
Mountain Bridge Wilderness Area	(864) 836-6115	John Sloan*	See Hike 24
Mountain Bridge Wilderness Area	(864) 836-6115	6 & 20 Connector*	See Hike 24
Mountain Bridge Wilderness Area	(864) 836-6115	Frank Coggins*	See Hike 20
Mountain Bridge Wilderness Area	(864) 836-6115	Bill Kimball*	See Hike 19

Paris Mountain State Park	(864) 244-5565	Brissy Ridge*	See Hike 26
Paris Mountain State Park	(864) 244-5565	Lake Placid	1.0
Paris Mountain State Park	(864) 244-5565	Sulphur Springs Loop*	See Hike26
Greer Parks and Recreation	(864) 877-9289	Tryon Park	0.2
Mauldin Parks and Recreation Department	(864) 288-3354	Mauldin Park	0.5
Pleasant Ridge County Park	(864) 836-6589	Pleasant Ridge Nature	0.7
Simpsonville Parks and Recreation	(864) 963-5958	Simpsonville Nature	0.5

Oconee County

Devils Fork State Park	(864) 944-2639	Oconee Bells Nature	1.0
Duke Power	(800) 443-5193	Lower Whitewater Falls*	See Hike 12
Duke World of Energy	(800) 771-0004	World of Energy Nature	1.4
Foothills Trail Conference	(864) 467-9537	Foothills*	See Hikes 1, 11
Lake Hartwell State Park	(864) 972-3352	Beech Ridge	1.4
Oconee County PRC	(843) 638-9585	Chau-Ram	1.0
Oconee State Park	(864) 638-5353	Hidden Falls*	See Hike 7
Oconee State Park	(864) 638-5353	Tamassee Knob*	See Hike 7
Oconee State Park	(864) 638-5353	Oconee*	See Hike 7
Oconee State Park	(864) 638-5353	Lake	0.6
Oconee State Park	(864) 638-5353	Old Water Wheel*	See Hike 7
Oconee State Park	(864) 638-5353	Foothills Trail Access*	See Hike 1
Oconee Station State Hist. Site	(864) 638-0079	Oconee Station*	See Hike 9
Pendleton District Commission	(864) 646-3782	Issaqueena Falls	0.2
Pendleton District Commission	(864) 646-3782	Blue Ridge Railroad Historical*	See Hike 8
Sumter NF - Pickens RD	(864) 638-9568	Big Bend*	See Hike 5
Sumter NF - Pickens RD	(864) 638-9568	East Fork*	See Hike 4
Sumter NF - Pickens RD	(864) 638-9568	Fall Creek	0.6
Sumter NF - Pickens RD	(864) 638-9568	Thrift's Ferry	0.4
Sumter NF - Pickens RD	(864) 638-9568	Sandy Ford	0.3
Sumter NF - Pickens RD	(864) 638-9568	Woodall Shoals	0.2
Sumter NF - Pickens RD	(864) 638-9568	Riley Moore Falls	0.7
Sumter NF - Pickens RD	(864) 638-9568	Earls Ford	0.3
Sumter NF - Pickens RD	(864) 638-9568	Long Mountain Tower	0.1

Sumter NF - Pickens RD	(864) 638-9568	King Creek	0.5
Sumter NF - Pickens RD	(864) 638-9568	Chattooga Picnic	0.5
Sumter NF - Pickens RD	(864) 638-9568	Lee Falls*	See Hike 10
Sumter NF - Pickens RD	(864) 638-9568	Moss Mill Creek	0.4
Sumter NF - Pickens RD	(864) 638-9568	Yellow Branch	0.4
Sumter NF - Pickens RD	(864) 638-9568	Chattooga*	See Hike 2
Sumter NF - Pickens RD	(864) 638-9568	Burrells Ford	0.7
Sumter NF - Pickens RD	(864) 638-9568	Station Cove*	See Hike 9
Sumter NF - Pickens RD	(864) 638-9568	Hwy 76 Portage	0.2
Sumter NF - Pickens RD	(864) 638-9568	Fork Mountain*	See Hike 3
Sumter NF - Pickens RD	(864) 638-9568	Opossum Creek	2.5
Sumter NF - Pickens RD	(864) 638-9568	Winding Stairs*	See Hike 6

Pickens County

Clemson University, Dept. of Forest Resources	(864) 656-4826	Indian Creek	0.9
Clemson University, Dept. of Forest Resources	(864) 656-4826	Treaty Oak	0.4
Eastatoe Creek Heritage Preserve	(803) 734-3893	Eastatoe Creek*	See Hike 14
Foothills Trail Conference	(864) 467-9537	Foothills NRT*	See Hikes 11, 15, 17
Keowee-Toxaway State Nat. Area	(846) 868-2605	Cherokee Interpretative	0.3
Keowee-Toxaway State Nat. Area	(846) 868-2605	Raven Rock Hiking*	See Hike 13
Keowee-Toxaway State Nat. Area	(846) 868-2605	Natural Bridge Nature*	See Hike 13
Sadlers Creek State Park	(864) 226-8950	Pine Grove	0.6
SC Botanical Garden System	(864) 656-3405	Botanical Garden	5.0
Table Rock State Park	(864) 878-9813	Pinnacle Ridge*	See Hike 16
Table Rock State Park	(864) 878-9813	Carrick Creek*	See Hike 16
Table Rock State Park	(864) 878-9813	Mill Creek Pass*	See Hike 16
Table Rock State Park	(864) 878-9813	Pinnacle Mountain*	See Hike 16
Table Rock State Park	(864) 878-9813	Table Rock NRT*	See Hike 16

Spartanburg County

Campobello-Gramling Elementary School	(864) 472-6495	Campobello-Gramling	0.8
Spartanburg City/County Parks & Rec. Dept.	(864) 596-3737	River Birch	0.6
Spartanburg City/County Parks & Rec. Dept.	(864) 596-3737	Cottonwood	1.5

| Spartanburg City/County Parks & Rec. Dept. | (864) 596-3737 | Duncan Park | 0.8 |

MIDLANDS
Abbeville County

Calhoun Falls State Park	(864) 447-8267	Cedar Bluff	1.8
Calhoun Falls State Park	(864) 447-8267	Blue Hole	1.0
Sumter NF - Long Cane RD	(803) 637-5396	Long Cane*	See Hike 27
Sumter NF - Long Cane RD	(803) 637-5396	Parson's Mountain*	See Hike 28

Aiken County

Aiken Chamber of Commerce	(803) 641-1111	Hitchcock Woods	20.0
Aiken County Department of Recreation	(803) 642-7559	Spann-Hammond Park	0.7
Aiken Rec. Dept.	(803) 641-7630	Hopeland Gardens	0.3
Aiken Rec. Dept.	(803) 641-7630	Virginia Acres	1.0
Aiken State Park	(803) 649-2857	Jungle Nature	3.0
Bishop Gravatt Center	(803) 648-1817	Sparkleberry	1.5
Redcliffe State Park	(803) 827-1473	Redcliffe	1.7

Anderson County

| COE - Lake Hartwell | (706) 376-4788 | Hartwell Lake Dam | 0.7 |

Bamberg County

| Rivers Bridge State Park | (803) 267-3675 | Lupine Nature | 0.5 |

Barnwell County

| Barnwell State Park | (803) 284-2212 | Barnwell Lake | 1.5 |
| Barnwell State Park | (803) 284-2212 | Discovery | 0.2 |

Cherokee County

| NPS - Cowpens NB | (864) 461-2828 | Interpretive | 1.1 |
| NPS - Kings Mountain NMP | (864) 936-7921 | Walking* | See Hike 33 |

Chester County

Chester County/City Park and Rec. Dept.	(803) 385-2530	Wylie Park	0.3
Chester State Park	(803) 385-2680	Caney Fork Falls	1.3
Landsford Canal State Historic Site	(803) 789-5800	Hilltop	0.2

Landsford Canal State Historic Site	(803) 789-5800	Canal Trail*	See Hike 35
Sumter NF - Enoree RD	(803) 276-4810	Woods Ferry Hiking	1.5

Chesterfield County

Cheraw State Park	(843) 921-1418	L. Juniper Boardwalk*	See Hike 41
Cheraw State Park	(843) 921-1418	Cheraw Nature*	See Hike 41
Cheraw State Park	(843) 921-1418	Turkey Oak*	See Hike 41
FWS - Carolina Sandhills NWR	(843) 335-8401	Tate's*	See Hike 40
FWS - Carolina Sandhills NWR	(843) 335-8401	Woodland Pond*	See Hike 40
SCFC - Sandhills State Forest	(843) 498-6478	Sugar Loaf Mountain	0.6

Edgefield County

Sumter NF - Long Cane RD	(803) 637-5396	Lick Fork Lake*	See Hike 30

Fairfield County

Fairfield County Recreation Commission	(803) 635-4725	Fortune Springs	0.3
Lake Wateree State Park	(803) 482-6401	Desportes Nature	0.7

Greenwood County

Lake Greenwood State Park	(864) 543-3535	Greenwood Lake Nature	0.8
Lake Greenwood State Park	(864) 543-3535	Lake View	3.0
NPS - Ninety Six NHS	(864) 543-4068	Ninety Six Nature	1.0
NPS - Ninety Six NHS	(864) 543-4068	Interpretative	0.5
NPS - Ninety Six NHS	(864) 543-4068	Ninety Six Historic	1.0
NPS - Ninety-Six NHS	(864) 543-4068	Gouedy	1.0

Kershaw County

Historic Camden Revolutionary War Site	(803) 432-9841	Historic Camden Nature	0.7
Indian Waters Council, BSA	(803) 765-9070	Pine Tree Hill	10.5

Lancaster County

Andrew Jackson State Park	(803) 285-3344	Andrew Jackson	1.1
Andrew Jackson State Park	(803) 285-3344	Lake	1.0

Laurens County

Laurens County Park	(803) 984-2621	Laurens County Park Nature	0.8
Whitten Camping and Nature Programs	(803) 833-2733	Whitten Exercise	3.0

Lee County

Lee State Park	(803) 428-3833	Artesian Nature	1.0
Lee State Park	(803) 428-3833	Sandhill Nature	0.6

Lexington County

Batesburg-Leesville High School	(803) 532-4423	Outdoor Learning Center	2.5
Lexington County Recreation Commission	(803) 791-1361	Granby Gardens Nature	0.8
Lexington County Recreation Commission	(803) 791-1361	Guignard Park	0.3
The South Carolina Nature Conservancy	(803) 254-9049	Peachtree Rock*	See Hike 31

McCormick County

Baker Creek State Park	(864) 443-2457	Wild Mint	0.8
Baker Creek State Park	(864) 443-2457	Baker Creek Walking	0.7
COE - Clarks Hill Lake	(864) 333-1100	Modoc Nature	2.2
COE - Clarks Hill Lake	(864) 333-1100	Clarks Hill	1.0
Hickory Knob State Park	(800) 491-1764	Beaver Run	1.0
Hickory Knob State Park	(800) 491-1764	Turkey Ridge	0.3
John de la Howe School	(864) 391-2131	John de la Howe School Interpretive	1.9
Sumter NF - Long Cane RD	(803) 637-5396	Turkey Creek*	See Hike 29

Newberry County

Dreher Island State Park	(803) 364-4152	Billy Dreher Nature	0.2
Sumter NF - Enoree RD	(803) 276-4810	Buncombe*	See Hike 32
Sumter NF - Enoree RD	(803) 276-4810	Molly's Rock Hiking	0.6

Orangeburg County

Orangeburg Recreation Department	(803) 534-6211	Webster Woods	0.5
Orangeburg Recreation Department	(803) 534-6211	Edisto Gardens	1.5
Santee State Park	(803) 854-2408	Sinkhole Pond Nature*	See Hike 37
Santee State Park	(803) 854-2408	Oakpinolly Nature*	See Hike 37
Santee State Park	(803) 854-2408	Limestone Nature*	See Hike 37

Richland County

Harbison State Forest	(803) 896-8890	Eagle*	See Hike 36

Harbison State Forest	(803) 896-8890	Midlands Mountain Multiple Use*	See Hike 36
Harbison State Forest	(803) 896-8890	Stewardship*	See Hike 36
Harbison State Forest	(803) 896-8890	Firebreak*	See Hike 36
NPS - Congaree Swamp NM	(803) 776-4396	Weston Lake Loop*	See Hike 38
NPS - Congaree Swamp NM	(803) 776-4396	Oakridge*	See Hike 38
NPS - Congaree Swamp NM	(803) 776-4396	Kingsnake*	See Hike 38
NPS - Congaree Swamp NM	(803) 776-4396	River*	See Hike 38
NPS - Congaree Swamp NM	(803) 776-4396	Bluff*	See Hike 38
Columbia Parks & Rec. Dept.	(803) 733-8331	Maxcy Gregg Park	0.3
Columbia Parks & Rec. Dept.	(803) 733-8331	Columbia Canal (paved)	5.0
Columbia Parks & Rec. Dept.	(803) 733-8331	Earlewood Park	0.5
Columbia Parks & Rec. Dept.	(803) 733-8331	Sidney Park	0.5
Columbia Parks & Rec. Dept.	(803) 733-8331	Congaree River	0.5
Riverbanks Zoo	(803) 779-8717	Woodlands Walk (paved)	0.2
Sesquicentennial State Park	(803) 788-2706	Sandhill Nature	1.9

Sumter County

Manchester State Forest	(803) 494-8177	Nature	1.0
Poinsett State Park	(803) 494-8177	Coquina Nature*	See Hike 39
Poinsett State Park	(803) 494-8177	Laurel Group*	See Hike 39
Poinsett State Park	(803) 494-8177	Hilltop*	See Hike 39

Union County

Musgrove Mill State Park	(864) 427-5966	Enoree River Nature	1.5
Sumter NF - Enoree RD	(803) 276-4810	Jews Harp Springs	0.8
Sumter NF - Enoree RD	(803) 276-4810	Brocks Creek	1.1
Sumter NF - Enoree RD	(803) 276-4810	Rose Hill	1.3
Union County Recreation Commission	(864) 427-1208	Foster Park	0.6

York County

Anne Springs Close Greenway	(803) 548-7252	Springfield*	See Hike 34
Anne Springs Close Greenway	(803) 548-7252	Lake Haigler Nature*	See Hike 34
Anne Springs Close Greenway	(803) 548-7252	Hiking*	See Hike 34
Bethelwoods	(803) 366-3722	Bethelwoods Nature	0.8
Bethelwoods	(803) 366-3722	Wagon Camp	0.8

Camp Thunderbird	(803) 831-2121	Camp Thunderbird Nature	0.6
Kings Mountain State Park	(803) 222-3209	Kings Mountain Hiking NRT*	See Hike 33
Museum of York County	(803) 366-4116	York County Nature	0.5
Rock Hill Parks Recreation and Tourism	(803) 329-5627	River Park	2.4

COASTAL PLAIN

Beaufort County

FWS - ACE Basin NWR	(843) 889-3084	Combahee Section*	See Hike 58
FWS - Pinckney Island NWR	(912) 652-4415	Pinckney Island*	See Hike 61
Hunting Island State Park	(843) 838-2011	Lighthouse Nature	0.3
Hunting Island State Park	(843) 838-2011	Island	7.0
Hunting Island State Park	(843) 838-2011	Marsh Boardwalk NRT	0.4
Sea Pines Forest Preserve	(843) 671-6486	Trail System*	See Hike 62

Berkeley County

Cypress Gardens	(843) 553-0515	Nature*	See Hike 50
Cypress Gardens	(843) 553-0515	Perimeter*	See Hike 50
Cypress Gardens	(843) 553-0515	North Nature*	See Hike 50
Francis Marion NF	(843) 336-3248	Huger Loop	2.0
Francis Marion NF	(843) 336-3248	Battery Warren	1.0
Naval Weapons Station	(843) 764-7601	Marrington Plantation*	See Hike 51
Old Santee Canal State Historic Site	(843) 899-5200	Old Santee Canal*	See Hike 49
Santee Cooper	(843) 761-4068	Lake Moultrie Passage (Palmetto Trail)*	See Hike 48

Charleston County

Charles Towne Landing State Park	(843) 852-4200	Animal Forest	0.8
Charles Towne Landing State Park	(843) 852-4200	Charles Towne Garden	2.4
Charleston Department of Parks	(843) 724-7321	West Ashley Greenway	7.5
Charleston Trident Convention Bureau	(843) 853-8000	Old Walled City	2.3
Francis Marion NF	(843) 928-3368	Sewee Shell Mound*	See Hike 45
Francis Marion NF	(843) 928-3368	I'on Swamp*	See Hike 46
Francis Marion NF	(843) 928-3368	Swamp Fox NRT*	See Hike 47
FWS - Cape Romain NWR	(843) 928-3368	Old Fort Loop*	See Hike 44

FWS - Cape Romain NWR	(843) 928-3368	Sheephead Ridge Loop*	See Hike 44
FWS - Cape Romain NWR	(843) 928-3368	Bull Island Wildlife NRT*	See Hike 44
Hampton Plantation State Park	(843) 546-9361	Nature	3.0
James Island County Park	(843) 795-7275	Walking	0.5
Magnolia Plantation and its Gardens	(843) 571-1266	Magnolia Gardens*	See Hike 52
Magnolia Plantation and its Gardens	(843) 571-1266	Magnolia Wildlife*	See Hike 52
Middleton Place	(843) 556-6020	Middleton Place	1.8
NPS - Fort Sumter NM	(843) 883-3123	Fort Moultrie	0.5
Palmetto Islands County Park	(843) 884-0832	Osprey	0.2
Palmetto Islands County Park	(843) 884-0832	Marsh	0.6
Palmetto Islands County Park	(843) 884-0832	Palmetto Nature Island	1.3
Santee Coastal Reserve	(843) 546-8665	Bike/Hike*	See Hike 43
Santee Coastal Reserve	(843) 546-8665	Marshland*	See Hike 43
Santee Coastal Reserve	(843) 546-8665	Woodland*	See Hike 43

Clarendon County

Clarendon County Recreation Department	(803) 473-3543	Pocotaligo Swamp	0.5
Santee NWR	(803) 478-2217	Wright's Bluff Nature	1.0
Woods Bay State Park	(843) 659-4445	Mill Pond Nature	0.9

Colleton County

Bear Island WMA	(843) 844-8957	Bear Island*	See Hike 56
Colleton State Park	(843) 538-8206	Cypress Swamp Nature	0.3
Donnelley Wildlife Management Area	(843) 844-8957	Boynton*	See Hike 57
Edisto Beach State Park	(843) 869-2156	Spanish Mount*	See Hike 54
Walterboro-Colleton County Rec. Comm.	(843) 549-2729	Colleton	2.6
Walterboro-Colleton County Rec. Commission	(803) 549-2729	South Pine Street	0.3
Westvaco	(843) 871-5000	Bluff	3.1
Westvaco	(843) 871-5000	Edisto Nature NRT*	See Hike 55

Darlington County

Kalmia Gardens of Coker College	(843) 383-8145	Kalmia Gardens	1.5
Darlington Recreation Dept.	(393) 393-3626	Williamson Park	1.4

Dillon County

Little Pee Dee State Park	(843) 774-8872	Beaver Pond Nature	1.3

Dorchester County

Francis Beidler Forest	(843) 462-2150	Four Holes Swamp*	See Hike 53
Givhans Ferry State Park	(843) 873-0692	River Bluff	1.5
Givhans Ferry State Park	(843) 873-0692	Canal Nature	3.6
Old Dorchester State Park	(843) 873-1740	Boosho Creek Nature	0.7

Florence County

City of Florence Recreation Dept.	(843) 665-3253	Jeffries Creek	0.8
City of Florence Recreation Dept.	(843) 665-3153	Lucas Park	0.6
City of Florence Recreation Dept.	(843) 665-3153	Timrod Park	1.0
Greater Florence Chamber of Commerce	(843) 665-0515	Beauty	12.0
Lynches River State Park	(843) 389-2785	Stagecoach	1.1

Georgetown County

Huntington Beach State Park	(843) 237-4440	Kerrigan Nature*	See Hike 42
Huntington Beach State Park	(843) 237-4440	Boardwalk*	See Hike 42
Huntington Beach State Park	(843) 237-4440	Sandpiper Pond Nature*	See Hike 42

Hampton County

Webb Wildlife Center	(803) 625-3569	Savannah River Swamp*	See Hike 59

Horry County

Myrtle Beach State Park	(843) 238-5325	Sculptured Oak Nature	1.0

Jasper County

FWS - Savannah NWR	(912) 652-4415	Walkable dikes*	See Hike 60
FWS - Savannah NWR	(912) 652-4415	Tupelo*	See Hike 60
Sergeant Jasper State Park	(843) 784-5130	Nature	0.5

Marlboro County

Camp Pee Dee (843) 479-3051		Canoe Lake Nature	1.6

ABBREVIATIONS USED IN THIS APPENDIX:

BSA: Boy Scouts of America
COE: Army Corps of Engineers
FWS: U.S. Fish and Wildlife Service
NB: National Battlefield
NF: National Forest
NHS: National Historic Site
NM: National Monument
NMP: National Military Park
NPS: National Park Service
NRT: National Recreation Trail
NWR: National Wildlife Refuge
PRC: Parks and Recreation Commission
RD: Ranger District
SCFC: S.C. Forestry Commission

Index

Page numbers in *italics* are maps.
Page numbers in **bold** are photos.

About the Authors

John Clark

John Clark lives in Columbia, South Carolina, where he is active in environmental affairs, race relations, and higher education. His professional background includes public policy, planning, public relations, college teaching, and writing. An extensive traveler, he has studied at the University of Paris, France, and the University of Addis Ababa, Ethiopia, and holds degrees from Davidson College and Syracuse University.

John Dantzler lives in Columbia, South Carolina. He has been a writer, editorialist, environmental policy analyst, property manager, rental truck manager, economist, forensic economist, industry analyst (automobile and forestry), humorist, fisheries policy analyst, naturalist, photographer, political consultant, public transportation analyst, energy analyst, conference rapporteur, dishwasher, grant writer, editor, and proofreader. He has traveled extensively in Europe, including Russia, and the United States. On the whole, and after much consideration, he likes his home state of South Carolina best.

John Dantzler

FALCON GUIDES ® are available for where-to-go hiking, mountain biking, rock climbing, walking, scenic driving, fishing, rockhounding, paddling, birding, wildlife viewing, and camping. We also have FalconGuides on essential outdoor skills and subjects and field identification. The following titles are currently available, but this list grows every year. For a free catalog with a complete list of titles, call The Globe Pequot Press toll-free at 1-800-243-0495.

HIKING GUIDES

Best Hikes Along the Continental Divide
Hiking Alaska
Hiking Arizona
Hiking Arizona's Cactus Country
Hiking the Beartooths
Hiking Big Bend National Park
Hiking the Bob Marshall Country
Hiking California
Hiking California's Desert Parks
Hiking Carlsbad Caverns
    and Guadalupe Mtns. National Parks
Hiking Colorado
Hiking Colorado, Vol. II
Hiking Colorado's Summits
Hiking Colorado's Weminuche Wilderness
Hiking the Columbia River Gorge
Hiking Florida
Hiking Georgia
Hiking Glacier & Waterton Lakes National Parks
Hiking Grand Canyon National Park
Hiking Grand Staircase-Escalante/Glen Canyon
Hiking Grand Teton National Park
Hiking Great Basin National Park
Hiking Hot Springs in the Pacific Northwest
Hiking Idaho
Hiking Indiana
Hiking Maine
Hiking Maryland and Delaware
Hiking Michigan
Hiking Minnesota
Hiking Montana
Hiking Mount Rainier National Park
Hiking Mount St. Helens
Hiking Nevada
Hiking New Hampshire
Hiking New Mexico

Hiking New Mexico's Gila Wilderness
Hiking New York
Hiking North Carolina
Hiking the North Cascades
Hiking Northern Arizona
Hiking Northern California
Hiking Olympic National Park
Hiking Oregon
Hiking Oregon's Eagle Cap Wilderness
Hiking Oregon's Mount Hood/Badger Creek
Hiking Oregon's Central Cascades
Hiking Pennsylvania
Hiking Ruins Seldom Seen
Hiking Shenandoah
Hiking the Sierra Nevada
Hiking South Carolina
Hiking South Dakota's Black Hills Country
Hiking Southern New England
Hiking Tennessee
Hiking Texas
Hiking Utah
Hiking Utah's Summits
Hiking Vermont
Hiking Virginia
Hiking Washington
Hiking Wisconsin
Hiking Wyoming
Hiking Wyoming's Cloud Peak Wilderness
Hiking Wyoming's Teton and Washakie Wilderness
Hiking Wyoming's Wind River Range
Hiking Yellowstone National Park
Hiking Yosemite National Park
Hiking Zion & Bryce Canyon National Parks
Wild Country Companion
Wild Montana
Wild Utah
Wild Virginia

■ *To order any of these books, check with your local bookseller*
*or call The Globe Pequot Press® at **1-800-243-0495**.*
Visit us on the world wide web at:
www.FalconGuide.com

FALCON®

FALCONGUIDES ®Leading the Way™

BEST EASY DAY HIKES SERIES
Beartooths
Boulder
Canyonlands & Arches
Cape Cod
Colorado Springs
Denver
Glacier & Wateron Lakes
Grand Staircase-Escalante and
   the Glen Canyon Region
Grand Canyon
Grand Teton
Lake Tahoe
Mount Rainier
Mount St. Helens
North Cascades
Northern Sierra
Olympics
Orange County
Phoenix
Salt Lake City
San Diego
Santa Fe
Shenandoah
Yellowstone
Yosemite

12 SHORT HIKES SERIES
Colorado
Aspen
Boulder
Denver Foothills Central
Denver Foothills North
Denver Foothills South
Rocky Mountain National Park-Estes Park
Rocky Mountain National Park-Grand Lake
Steamboat Springs
Summit County
Vail
California
San Diego Coast
San Diego Mountains
San Francisco Bay Area-Coastal
San Francisco Bay Area-East Bay
San Francisco Bay Area-North Bay
San Francisco Bay Area-South Bay
Washington
Mount Rainier National Park-Paradise
Mount Rainier National Park-Sunrise

■ *To order any of these books, check with your local bookseller*
*or call The Globe Pequot Press® at **1-800-243-0495**.*
Visit us on the world wide web at:
www.FalconGuide.com

FALCON®

FALCONGUIDES® Leading the Way™

FIELD GUIDES

Bitterroot: Montana State Flower
Canyon Country Wildflowers
Central Rocky Mountains
    Wildflowers
Chihuahuan Desert Wildflowers
Great Lakes Berry Book
New England Berry Book
Ozark Wildflowers
Pacific Northwest Berry Book
Plants of Arizona
Rare Plants of Colorado
Rocky Mountain Berry Book
Scats & Tracks of the Pacific
    Coast States
Scats & Tracks of the
    Rocky Mountains
Sierra Nevada Wildflowers
Southern Rocky Mountain
    Wildflowers
Tallgrass Prairie Wildflowers
Western Trees
Wildflowers of Southwestern
    Utah

FISHING GUIDES

Fishing Alaska
Fishing the Beartooths
Fishing Florida
Fishing Georgia
Fishing Glacier National Park
Fishing Maine
Fishing Montana
Fishing Wyoming
Fishing Yellowstone
    National Park
Trout Unlimited's Guide to
    America's 100 Best Trout
    Streams
America's Best Bass Fishing

BIRDING GUIDES

Birding Georgia
Birding Illinois
Birding Minnesota
Birding Montana
Birding Northern California
Birding Texas
Birding Utah

MORE GUIDEBOOKS

Backcountry Horseman's
    Guide to Washington
Camping Arizona
Camping California's
    National Forests
Camping Colorado
Camping Oregon
Exploring Canyonlands &
    Arches National Parks
Exploring Hawaii's Parklands
Exploring Mount Helena
Exploring Southern California
    Beaches
Family Fun in Montana
Family Fun in Yellowstone
Hiking Hot Springs of the Pacific
    Northwest
Recreation Guide to WA
    National Forests
Touring Arizona Hot Springs
Touring California & Nevada
    Hot Springs
Touring Colorado Hot Springs
Touring Montana & Wyoming
    Hot Springs
Trail Riding Western Montana
Wilderness Directory
Wild Montana
Wild Utah
Wild Virginia

ROCKHOUNDING GUIDES

Rockhounding Arizona
Rockhounding California
Rockhounding Colorado
Rockhounding Montana
Rockhounding Nevada
Rockhound's Guide to New
    Mexico
Rockhounding Texas
Rockhounding Utah
Rockhounding Wyoming

HOW-TO GUIDES

Avalanche Aware
Backpacking Tips
Bear Aware
Desert Hiking Tips
Hiking with Dogs
Hiking with Kids
Leave No Trace
Mountain Lion Alert
Reading Weather
Route Finding
Using GPS
Wild Country Companion
Wilderness First Aid
Wilderness Survival

WALKING

Walking Colorado Springs
Walking Denver
Walking Portland
Walking Seattle
Walking St. Louis
Walking San Francisco
Walking Virginia Beach

■ *To order any of these books, check with your local bookseller
or call The Globe Pequot Press® at **1-800-243-0495**.
Visit us on the world wide web at:*
www.FalconGuide.com

FALCON®

FALCONGUIDES ® Leading the Way™

WILDLIFE VIEWING GUIDES
Alaska Wildlife Viewing Guide
Arizona Wildlife Viewing Guide
California Wildlife Viewing Guide
Colorado Wildlife Viewing Guide
Florida Wildlife Viewing Guide
Indiana Wildlife Vewing Guide
Iowa Wildlife Viewing Guide
Kentucky Wildlife Viewing Guide
Massachusetts Wildlife Viewing Guide
Montana Wildlife Viewing Guide
Nebraska Wildlife Viewing Guide
Nevada Wildlife Viewing Guide
New Hampshire Wildlife Viewing Guide
New Jersey Wildlife Viewing Guide
New Mexico Wildlife Viewing Guide
New York Wildlife Viewing Guide
North Carolina Wildlife Viewing Guide
North Dakota Wildlife Viewing Guide
Ohio Wildlife Viewing Guide
Oregon Wildlife Viewing Guide
Puerto Rico and the Virgin Islands WVG
Tennessee Wildlife Viewing Guide
Texas Wildlife Viewing Guide
Utah Wildlife Viewing Guide
Vermont Wildlife Viewing Guide
Virginia Wildlife Viewing Guide
Washington Wildlife Viewing Guide
West Virginia Wildlife Viewing Guide
Wisconsin Wildlife Viewing Guide

HISTORIC TRAIL GUIDES
Traveling California's Gold Rush Country
Traveling the Lewis & Clark Trail
Traveling the Oregon Trail
Traveler's Guide to the Pony Express Trail

SCENIC DRIVING GUIDES
Scenic Driving Alaska and the Yukon
Scenic Driving Arizona
Scenic Driving the Beartooth Highway
Scenic Driving British Columbia
Scenic Driving California
Scenic Driving Colorado
Scenic Driving Florida
Scenic Driving Georgia
Scenic Driving Hawaii
Scenic Driving Idaho
Scenic Driving Indiana
Scenic Driving Kentucky
Scenic Driving Michigan
Scenic Driving Minnesota
Scenic Driving Montana
Scenic Driving New England
Scenic Driving New Mexico
Scenic Driving North Carolina
Scenic Driving Oregon
Scenic Driving the Ozarks including the
     Ouchita Mountains
Scenic Driving Pennsylvania
Scenic Driving Texas
Scenic Driving Utah
Scenic Driving Virginia
Scenic Driving Washington
Scenic Driving Wisconsin
Scenic Driving Wyoming
Scenic Driving Yellowstone & Grand Teton
     National Parks
Scenic Byways East & South
Scenic Byways Far West
Scenic Byways Rocky Mountains

- *To order any of these books, check with your local bookseller
or call The Globe Pequot Press® at **1-800-243-0495**.
Visit us on the world wide web at:*
www.FalconGuide.com

FALCON®

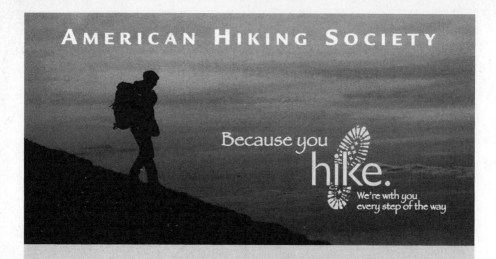